AND THAT'S THE GOSPEL TRUTH

Jack McArdle ss.cc

And that's
the Gospel truth

REFLECTIONS ON THE SUNDAY GOSPELS

Year A

the columba press

First published in 2001 by
the columba press
55a Spruce Avenue, Stillorgan Industrial Park,
Blackrock, Co Dublin

Cover by Bill Bolger
Cover photograph by Marie McDonald
Origination by The Columba Press
Printed in Ireland by Colour Books Ltd, Dublin

ISBN 185607 342 4

Contents

Introduction 7

First Sunday of Advent 9

Second Sunday of Advent 12

Third Sunday of Advent 16

Fourth Sunday of Advent 20

Christmas Day 24

The Holy Family 28

Second Sunday of Christmas 33

Baptism of the Lord 37

First Sunday of Lent 41

Second Sunday of Lent 46

Third Sunday of Lent 51

Fourth Sunday of Lent 55

Fifth Sunday of Lent 59

Passion (Palm) Sunday 65

Easter Sunday 71

Second Sunday of Easter 75

Third Sunday of Easter 80

Fourth Sunday of Easter 85

Fifth Sunday of Easter 89

Sixth Sunday of Easter 93

Ascension 98

Seventh Sunday of Easter 102

Pentecost Sunday 107

Trinity Sunday 111

Corpus Christi 115

Second Sunday of the Year 120

Third Sunday of the Year 124

Fourth Sunday of the Year 129

Fifth Sunday of the Year   133
Sixth Sunday of the Year   137
Seventh Sunday of the Year   141
Eighth Sunday of the Year   145
Ninth Sunday of the Year   149
Tenth Sunday of the Year   154
Eleventh Sunday of the Year   157
Twelfth Sunday of the Year   161
Thirteenth Sunday of the Year   165
Fourteenth Sunday of the Year   169
Fifteenth Sunday of the Year   173
Sixteenth Sunday of the Year   177
Seventeenth Sunday of the Year   182
Eighteenth Sunday of the Year   186
Nineteenth Sunday of the Year   191
Twentieth Sunday of the Year   195
Twenty-First Sunday of the Year   200
Twenty-Second Sunday of the Year   204
Twenty-Third Sunday of the Year   208
Twenty-Fourth Sunday of the Year   212
Twenty-Fifth Sunday of the Year   216
Twenty-Sixth Sunday of the Year   220
Twenty-Seventh Sunday of the Year   224
Twenty-Eighth Sunday of the Year   228
Twenty-Ninth Sunday of the Year   232
Thirtieth Sunday of the Year   237
Thirty-First Sunday of the Year   241
Thirty-Second Sunday of the Year   245
Thirty-Third Sunday of the Year   249
Feast of Christ the King   253

INTRODUCTION

The four gospels are spread over a three-year period, so that we are presented with every part of all four over those years. This is Year A, which begins on the First Sunday of Advent, and will be back in circulation three years later.

In presenting these reflections, I have a hope in my heart, and a prayer on my lips. I know many people who are reflective and contemplative by nature, and the word of the Lord is a personal word for them. They would like to know what the Sunday Readings are beforehand, so they can prepare their hearts to welcome that word. They also continue to ponder that word throughout the following week. They are too mature in their Christian responsibility to settle for sitting back, and leaving it all to the preacher. The Church that is being reborn today is one in which each of us must share equal responsibility. We are no longer like the F. A. Cup Final in Wembley, where nearly one hundred thousand spectators, badly in need of exercise, are sitting down very comfortably, criticising twenty-two pressurised human beings, badly in need of a rest! In today's church, we are all invited to get down out of the stands.

This book is not written for homilists, even if a few of them have a peep or two! It is written for the ordinary punter in the pew. It is written for the small groups in parishes who meet during the week to reflect on the readings for the following Sunday. It is written for the house-bound. Indeed, it is written for anyone who needs material for reflection, and who benefits from being presented with material that has some structure and order to it. There is no reason why someone should not pick up this book, and open it at any chapter, irrespective of what time of year it is.

The lay-out and structure of what is presented is purely arbitrary, and need not be adhered to in any way. It is presented with one intention, and that is, with a genuine desire to be most helpful. To know that it helps someone will give me great joy. My decision to confine myself to the gospel of each Sunday was made in the context of my own work-load, bearing in mind the limits of time available to both writer and reader.

This is one of a set of three books, one for each year A,B, and C.

FIRST SUNDAY OF ADVENT

Gospel: Matthew 24:37-44

Central Theme

If what happened that first Christmas night were to literally happen again, year after year, there still would be people who would find some reason for putting off getting ready to meet him until next year. Jesus never comes at the right time! Some things never change! Just as, on that first Christmas morning, when the Messiah came, there were many hearts and homes closed against him, so will it continue to be *per omnia secula seculorum* (forever and ever). And one of those times will be his Final Coming; time will be no more; and the last train will have left the station. All diets start on Monday! Today is the day you were always going to do all those things you kept putting off till tomorrow! There is nothing more powerful than an idea whose time has come.

Parable

John finally made it to the movies! There was a movie made about him, and it was called 'I'll quit tomorrow'. He was a chronic alcoholic, and he spent his life convincing himself, and everyone else, that he was going to quit tomorrow. The opening scene of the movie is quite dramatic. The coffin is being lowered into the grave, while his wife and four young children are huddled together, by the graveside. For John, tomorrow had come, and, yes, he had quit drinking …

Teaching

Some things never change, but one thing has changed. Bethlehem is no longer outside Jerusalem! It is in your heart, and it is there that the manger must be prepared for this Christmas. Because of our brokenness, and the human condition, we have nothing better to offer, nor does God choose to be born anywhere else than where Salvation is most needed.

At the time of creation God offered a covenant of infinite, endless love. When we rejected that, he sent his Son Jesus to offer us a covenant of infinite, endless mercy and forgiveness. If we reject that, he will send Jesus, once again, to proclaim a time of infinite and final justice. God doesn't send me anywhere

9

when I die. He eternalises the choices and the decisions that I make now. It certainly won't be God's fault if I am not infinitely happy for all eternity.

We all know people who live with a worldly mind-set. They are continually checking the latest news from the Stock Exchange, the trends in world marketing, or the changes in international currency. For us, lesser fish, we watch out for sales, for bargains, for special deals. We arrive at the surgery with our latest symptoms, and we call the emergency services at the slightest hint of danger. As a rule, we are normal, sensible people, who don't take chances, and we live with a fair degree of enlightened common sense. *What Jesus is talking about in today's gospel is something very, very serious ...*

Response
It is vital for us to appreciate the wonderful gift of *Time*. God is totally a God of *now* ('I am who am'). The only *yes* in my whole life in which he is interested is my *yes* of *now*. Today is a very unique and special gift, and not everyone received that gift. Because it is a gift, could that be why we call it 'the present'?! Written on the gift are the words 'batteries included'. With each day comes the daily bread for living that day.

Did you ever reflect on the possibility that you might be walking around half-asleep? The Advent liturgies call on us to 'Arise from your slumber'. Quite a lot of me could be dormant, and, if I died this moment, and God asked me 'Did you enjoy my creation?', would I have to admit that I never really took much notice of it. Oh, I travelled to other countries to admire the scenery, but I may not have bothered too much about my own back garden. This very day is entirely unique. It has never happened before, and it will never return. The same is true of this Christmas. I can approach this Christmas as if it were the only such once-off occasion in my whole life, and that would make all the difference.

Mary said *yes* at the annunciation, and so Christmas followed. Christmas is God saying *yes* to us, as he comes to rescue us, to set us free from our own bondage, and to bring us safely home for all eternity. My own personal *yes* could be the only piece of the formula of salvation still not in place ...

Practical
Take at least one minute out today, go down into your heart,

open the door, and say your own personal *yes* to Jesus for this Christmas. You don't have to understand it … just do it!

As the holly, the decorations, the jingle bells, and all the down-town razzmatazz builds up, just continue to keep in touch with your heart, where you want the manger to be. As you buy Christmas gifts, or convey good wishes this Christmas, just make sure that all of that is coming from your heart, so that your gift is really a gift, and your good wishes are really a blessing.

Let your heart continually pray the simple one-word prayer of *yes*. Do this, and leave the rest to God. This will be your most blessed, and your most sincere Christmas ; it could be the beginning of the alertness that Jesus asks for in today's gospel. When he comes will he find you ready …? The road to hell is paved with good intentions. When all is said and done, there's much more said than done …

Story

There is a famous and beautiful picture of Jesus knocking on a door. When this picture was first shown to the public, the artist's attention was drawn to a serious flaw. There was no handle on the door! The artist explained that this was very deliberate, because it represented the reality. The door is the door of the human heart, and there is no handle on the outside. Jesus cannot enter unless I open the door and invite him in. 'I stand at the door and knock. If anyone opens the door, I will come in and we will share a meal as friends.' If I open the door and let Jesus in, then I can be sure that, later on, I will hear another knock. If I ask 'What is it now?', he will answer 'I want back out again'! Back out again through my words and actions, etc.

SECOND SUNDAY OF ADVENT

Gospel: Matthew 3:1-12

Central Theme

Preparing for the coming of the Lord. John the Baptist, back then, was a figure of the role of the church today. With all of the many dimensions of our preparations for Christmas, we, as Christians, must give priority to the preparation of our hearts, of our inner beings. (Jesus didn't come to be locked in a tabernacle. He came to make his home in the human heart.) As with last Sunday, there is a sense of urgency about the call to prepare the way. Not everything in our lives is important, just because it appears urgent. I can be so busy with the urgent that I overlook the important. The call of today's gospel is both urgent and important. Preparation for an event and the actual event are not exactly the same thing. John predicts an extraordinary outpouring of blessing from 'the one who is coming after me'. Our preparation for Christmas is but the beginning of blessings and of gifts that will continue for eternity.

Parable

One of my earliest memories, growing up in the country, was the coming of electricity. This was awaited with great excitement. With each day, the postman kept us up-to-date on 'where they are now', as the poles continued to be erected. Finally, the great day arrived. We had electricity! Gone was the old wireless, with its wet and dry battery; gone was the tilley lamp in the kitchen, and the hurricane lamp in the farmyard. With all the excitement, it was some days before I noticed something really strange, something that really baffled me. An elderly couple living nearby had not applied for the electricity, and nothing there had changed. I just couldn't understand this, because I failed to grasp the simple fact that they were free to make that decision if they chose to do so. The wires passed by, within a few yards of their front door; yet, they decided to remain as they were, with their tilley lamp and their hurricane lamp, and in a house that had nothing of the brightness or the facilities for common comforts that all their neighbours now enjoyed. It has taken me years to understand and to apply the message behind that simple incident …

Teaching

God does not give me anything, but he offers me everything. He offers me peace, but I'm completely free to live in misery, and die of ulcers, if I so choose. He is constantly reminding me, offering me, calling me, inviting me … This Christmas is yet another opportunity to listen to his message, and to respond afresh. I cannot live today on a *yes* of yesterday. When I was a child I knelt in front of the crib in the local church, with a sense of awe. The whole thing seemed so real back then. What has changed? 'Jesus Christ is the same yesterday, today, and always.' I have changed, of course, which is what is supposed to happen, as my life unfolds. That sense of awe of my childhood should now be much more widespread. It should encompass life itself, the sacrament of the present moment, and my own personal vocation to accept the message of Christmas, and integrate it into my daily living. The inner child of yester-year is still there, and the ability to experience a sense of awe is always possible to recapture.

Life is difficult, and it is very fragile. One heart attack, and it's all over. Life is what happens when you're making other plans. If you want to hear God laugh, just tell him your plans! Here's another Christmas, where it can be 'here we go again', or it can be something very beautiful, very special, and very life-giving. It is an opportunity to be recycled. It is like going through another cycle in the washing-machine of the Lord, and, for some people, it could be their 'final rinse'!

Response

Don't just drift into Christmas, and don't allow it become a time of year which most people wish was over and done with. Take some definite time out, not a great deal, to reflect on what Christmas is all about, and what, if anything, it means to you. I remember hearing an elderly lady recall a habit her father had. He went to Confession once a month. On the day before Confession, he walked the farm in silence, and he spent the whole day in some sort of quiet inner prayer. Even the mother whispered to the children, 'Don't bother your daddy today. He's going to Confession tomorrow.' It would be so easy and so simple for the cynic to comment on such a practice, but I really don't think it is something upon which any of us is qualified to comment. If that's what the man thought he should do, then, he was perfectly entitled and justified in doing it.

Prepare a pathway for the Lord's coming. Make a straight road for him. Can you honestly recognise things in your life, in your behaviour, in your relationships, that can be obstacles to this time of love, of reconciliation, of freedom from bondage? What do you find within yourself that spoils or limits the gift that you are, now that we are approaching that time of year when gift-giving becomes part of our living?

Why wait till you die to face the judgement of God? Today, this very day, you can come to the Lord with the wheat and the chaff, with all that you are, and allow him separate the chaff, and dispose of it in the furnace of his love. Because of the extra-ordinary nature of the love expressed by God in the whole story of Christmas, it would be a special and grace-inspired response if I tried to meet that love with an open and honest heart. If he is a Saviour coming in search of sinners, then 'Here I am, Lord ...'

Practical
God could have chosen to love us from a distance. However, he decided to join us on our human journey. There are stations and bus stops on that journey, and Jesus can come aboard in my life at any point of the journey, but only if I stop and ask him. On the other hand, I can be on a journey, through compulsion, addiction, or self-will run riot, and it is bound to end in destruction. Like a rapid-rail, or an Underground, I can decide to get off at any one of the stations. Jesus will be waiting for me on the platform ...

When I was baptised, someone else said *yes* on my behalf. Confirmation wasn't much better, as I was marched up to the altar. Sooner or later, and much sooner rather than much later, I myself must say my own personal *yes*. The first time I was car-ried into a church I wasn't consulted, and the next time I'll be carried into a church, I'm not going to be consulted either. Somewhere in between those two events, I must make a personal, sincere, and conscious decision about my Christian vocation. Years ago, a 'vocation' was something that a priest or a nun had! That is not true anymore. The greatest calling, or vocation, that can be given a human being is the call to be a follower of Jesus.

Jesus is the reason for the Season. Strip back all the tinsel and wrapping, and discover the *real gift* of Christmas. Your own per-sonal, and mostly private, input into this Christmas, is what will make all the difference in the world. No matter what gifts or cards you receive from others, the greatest gift of all is one you can choose to give yourself ...

Story

Togo was a young African boy, who was always asking questions. He had a great thirst for knowledge, and was prepared to go to any lengths to get that knowledge. One question that intrigued him more than any other was 'What language does God speak?' Nobody could answer his question, so he set off in search of the answer. He travelled from country to country, but still failed to find the answer. Finally, one cold, snowy, wintery night he arrived at what was no better than a makeshift hut, outside Jerusalem, in a place called Bethlehem. He looked, and was just about to ask his question, when a young woman beckoned him to enter. As he entered he saw a young couple, with a newborn baby wrapped up in some clothing, and lying on the straw of a manger in the corner. The young woman spoke. 'Welcome, Togo. We have been expecting you.' Togo was amazed, but the young woman continued, 'You have been asking what language God speaks. Come over and sit by the manger for a while, to reflect, and to listen. God speaks the language of love, of gentleness, and of belonging. He speaks the language of everybody who is poor, who is homeless, who is weak, who is powerless. It is only in speaking their language that he can let them know why he came, and what he wants to offer them. His language is so simple that the intellectual and the worldly-wise will dismiss it as meaningless. It is a language that only children, and those with the heart of a child, can understand.' Yes, indeed, Togo had, at last, found the answer to his question.

THIRD SUNDAY OF ADVENT

Gospel: Matthew 11:2-11

Central Theme

Long before Jesus came, the prophet Isaiah spelt out the signs that would distinguish him as the Messiah. 'When he comes, he will open the eyes of the blind and unstop the ears of the deaf. The lame will leap like a deer, and those who cannot speak will shout and sing.' When the disciples of John the Baptist asked Jesus if he really were the Messiah, Jesus simply asked them to look around and see for themselves. The words of the prophet were being fulfilled right there before their eyes. Jesus then went on to give John the highest possible commendation, because John had fulfilled his own mission with total fidelity, and was now in jail for his courage and his commitment. John had prepared the way for Jesus, and, in his own words, he then got out of the way. 'I must decrease so that he can increase.'

Parable

The early followers of Jesus came on the scene in the context of a time when they must have sounded like visitors from outer space. Everything they did and said was completely against the norms of life at that time. The Jews were totally bound up in the total commitment to law, and the law, in all its details, took precedence over everything else. The early Christians spoke of, and practised a law of love, where love took precedence. The Romans were into power, conquest, and the spreading of their Empire, while the early Christians spoke of poverty, of sharing, and of surrender. They spoke of power in weakness, of victory through forgiveness, and of a kingdom that ran contrary to every accepted definition of the day. Amidst all the puzzlement, there was one thing about them that drew equal acknowledgement from all who watched them. 'See how these Christians love one another.' Their actions spoke louder than their words. Like Jesus with the disciples of John, they gave witness in their own lives to the very message that they preached. Giving witness is the only authentic way to preach or to spread the gospel. What I am is my message, not what I say. If I enter your house and tell you I have measles, when I actually have chickenpox, which are you likely to catch?

* He's a role model for us all and to-day we celebrate the birth of this wonderful, wonderful man, J the B.

Teaching

Isaiah had foretold the signs. Jesus pointed to the signs as proof of who he was. Before leaving his apostles, he commissioned them to go forth, and spread the good news among all the nations. 'And these are the signs that shall accompany those who believe in me : The blind will see, the lame will walk, and the poor will have good news preached to them'.

Let go, and let God. Like John, I begin to get out of the way, once I stop trying to play God. Only God can do God-things. I am powerless over persons, places, and things. Only God can change the human heart, including, of course, my own heart. Because of original sin, (and the freewill which God gave his people) God's creation was totally messed up, so Jesus came to set things right again. Once Jesus appears on the scene, it is time for us mere mortals to get out of the way, and let him do what is needed. Like John the Baptist, we can prepare the way, and make straight the paths, as we unwrap the deceits, the sins, and the sickness that he has come to remove.

'I assure you, of all who have ever lived, none is greater than John the Baptist.' The greatness of the Baptist came from his humility, and his willingness to yield to someone greater than himself. Many of the people believed him to be the Messiah, but he strongly denied it, and would not allow anyone afford him the rightful place reserved for the One who would follow him, the One for whom he was preparing the way. There is a striking similarity between Mary and John the Baptist. They kept Jesus and his message at the centre of all that they did, and, in a way, they were like signposts pointing to Jesus.

Response

Look again at the people whom the world calls great. Many of them may be great, by any standards, but some may appear to have feet of clay, when compared to the standard of greatness proposed by Jesus. It takes true greatness to be able to forgive, to admit that I'm wrong, to turn to another and ask for help. It takes true greatness to minister with great love to those who, because of a mental disability, are unable to say 'thanks'. These angels of charity are the greatest people on earth.

How great Thou art, how great Thou art. If you were to write your own obituary notice, what are the things in your life that could deserve the term great, in that their value is eternal, and will continue long after your departure from this earth?

Look again at the little people in your life, those who carry out
the day-to-day humdrum services that keep life going all
around you. Can you find any greatness among them? Begin
with those closest to you, the ones you are more inclined to take
for granted. It was Jesus who said that the prophet is never accepted in his own home.

Practical

Like an alcoholic trying to attain and maintain sobriety without
the help of a Higher Power, can you identify some one thing in
your life that can be changed or improved, only if you are willing to get out of the way, and let God be God? God is, as it were,
on standby, waiting and willing to move in, and do for you
something that you have been unsuccessfully struggling with
for years.

Jesus was lavish in his praise for John. He was grateful for
what John had done. Find someone in your life who has merited
your gratitude, and who deserves your praise, and follow the
example of Jesus ... I sometimes joke that if you want to hear
something nice about a person, you will have to wait for the
funeral! Why not send someone the flowers when she can still
smell them? They're of little use to her on the lid of her coffin!

As you go away from church today, could you tell someone
else, in a few simple words, something important that you heard
here this morning? If you can think of what it is, and remember
it, maybe you'll get a chance to share that with someone today.

Story

An old missioner in Africa had reached the end of his days, and
he was recalled to Ireland, to retire in a purpose-built retirement
home. He had been an extraordinary man of God, and of
common-sense goodness. He became totally involved with the
people. He helped them with their crops, with their animals,
and in building their make-shift houses. His life was his greatest
sermon and, when he did preach, he did so in their language,
and he spoke about things that were part of their everyday lives
and experiences.

He was being replaced by a newly ordained priest, fresh
from a brilliant academic preparation in Rome, and someone
who was going places in the institutional Church. The old man
was asked to remain on for a while to act as interpreter; and, as
the young man was so intelligent, this would be for a very limited

period of time. The first Sunday, the young man got up to speak. His opening sentence was 'God is infinite in his nature, and transcendental in his essence.' He paused for a moment to allow for a translation. The old man was seen to have a look of puzzlement on his face, as he yanked up the twine holding up his trousers, scratched his head, thought for a while, and then spoke: 'He said that he's awful glad to be with you'!

By their fruits you will know them ... These are the signs that will accompany those who speak in my name ...

Preachers like that young man, [print], *rarely influence people. They can't see past their eyes to Christ.*

Those like the old man, [print], those like John the Baptist, never fail.

FOURTH SUNDAY OF ADVENT

Gospel: Matthew 1:18-25

Central Theme

Today's gospel sets the scene for the birth of Jesus. Mary was to be married to Joseph. In the meantime, the angel had appeared to Mary, she had said her *yes*, and Jesus was already conceived within her womb. Mary was wrapped in mystery, in something she humbly accepted as being from God, and something she herself couldn't possibly understand. Her role, the role of the humble servant, was to obey, and leave it to God to take care of the details. One of those details was how Joseph would react when he heard what had happened. He was a good man, and he was deeply troubled when he discovered that Mary was pregnant. He decided on an honourable course of action, when God stepped in, as Mary expected and, through the medium of a dream, all Joseph's troubles and fears were resolved. He, too, was humble, and his role was to obey and accept the directions given him by God.

Parable

I spent many years teaching in schools. One of those subjects was swimming, on two afternoons a week. The whole thrust of the exercise was to get the pupils to trust me enough to follow exactly all the instructions I gave. The earlier ones were simple, such as jumping in at the shallow end, holding the bar, kicking their feet, etc. Inevitably, after many visits to the pool, the big test always arrived. The pupil was now at the deep end, clinging to that bar for dear life! Letting go of the bar, and following my instructions, was a very real test of their trust in me, and their faith in themselves. The sheer delight on the face, when someone made it to the other side of the pool, was ample reward for all efforts invested. The reality, of course, was that any one of them could have let go of that bar, and swum the width of the pool the very day they came there. However, they were not ready yet. They still did not have enough faith either in themselves or in me. I was always deeply aware of the many many bars they would have to let go of during their lifetime, as each major decision came up. (Please excuse the pun, but many of them may have found it difficult, if not impossible, to let go of their local bar! I have met a few!)

Teaching

It is really very difficult for us to know our place before God. I know I speak of the impossible here, but imagine how you would feel if you could actually see yourself placed against the background of an infinite omnipotent God. Even the atom would look like a mountain by comparison with your own sense of nothingness. Humility is truth; that means, accepting things exactly as they are. Pride is frightfully destructive, and its expressions are obnoxious: arrogance, haughtiness, aloofness, disdain, sarcasm, etc., etc. My own father had a habit of correcting us by saying, 'You don't seem to know your place.' I'm sure he was right, but I now ask my heavenly Father, through the action of his Spirit, to ensure that I always know my place.

Mary and Joseph didn't actually do anything. They said their *yes*, and left the doing to God. Obedience comes from the Latin word *obedientia*, which, literally means, to hold one's ear against. It was a matter of listening, when one really wanted to know what to do, or which road to take. It was always considered as part of the role of the prophets.

Whenever I think of single mothers, I recall that Mary would have a special place for them in her heart, because she came within a whisker of being one herself. The penalty for that, in her day, was to be stoned to death; so we have come some way from there, thank God. For her, of course, it was a very stark option between trusting the Lord, and facing the consequences, if her trust was misplaced.

Response

If all of this was too much for Mary to understand, what chance have you or me? In my younger days, it was customary to say a prayer which began with the words 'Jesus, Mary, and Joseph, I give you my heart and my soul.' That would be a lovely prayer to repeat, as we move towards the celebration of Christmas.

Speaking of prayers, what is prayer for you? Is it you talking to God, or God talking to you? 'Speak, Lord, your servant is listening', or 'Listen, Lord, your servant is speaking'? If you don't listen, you'll never know what God wants you to do! If you ask him, be prepared to listen, and you will certainly receive the answer. The organ that God gave me with which to pray is my heart, not my tongue. If my heart is not praying, then my tongue is wasting its time. On several occasions, we are told that 'Mary held all these things, and pondered them in her heart.' That was where she heard the answers.

Dreams were always accepted as one way through which God spoke to people. The Old Testament is full of examples of such. Without wishing to turn this into a dream workshop, let me put this thesis to you: When you are asleep, when your ego is off guard, your inner child has a chance to let its presence be known and that, in essence, is what a dream is. All the fears, frustrations, and struggles of that inner child are acted out in the dream. Sometimes the inner child wakens you up, which is what we call a nightmare, and it usually has to do with running away from something. There can often be things in our lives from which we are running away, or from which we should run away.

Practical

Joseph, we are told, was a just man. 'Just' means being fair, treating people properly. One of the best comments I ever heard at a funeral was that 'He was a wonderful human being'. Justice has lost its edge in today's world. People shouldn't have to fight for their rights. You have rights, even if others prevent you exercising them. How do you weigh on the scales of justice, when you look at your relationships?

Joseph was prepared to go to any lengths to protect Mary from embarrassment. We can be quite destructive in our careless use of words, in starting the rumour, in fuelling the gossip. Can you find one such example from your own life?

Did you hear about the priest who dreamt he was preaching a sermon, and he woke up, and he was? Even if you fell asleep during this reflection, did you hear anything that you can take into your day, and put it in practice? What does today's gospel say to you today? I'm sure that most of us will probably have at least one meal today and, perhaps, several snacks. The word of God here today is the nourishment, or the food for our souls, for our inner beings. 'Not on bread alone does man/woman live', says Jesus, 'but on every word that comes from the mouth of God.'

Story

The young monk was on his own in the chapel, and he was pouring out his heart to the Lord. He was having some doubts about his vocation. He was, by nature, somewhat insecure, and he was always looking for certainties, or for proof for everything. He kept repeating the same prayer, again and again.

'Lord, if I only knew that I would persevere. If I only knew that I would persevere.' Finally, the Lord spoke to him, and said, 'And if you knew for certain that you would persevere, what then would you do? How, then would you live your life? Go and do that now, and begin living your life that way now and, in doing that, you will persevere.'

In the mind, it is only mental assent; in the heart it is faith; and when it gets down into the feet, it becomes faith in action. And that is the kind of faith the Lord is waiting for, and it is in that faith that the presence and power of the Lord is seen, and experienced …

CHRISTMAS DAY

Gospel: Luke 2:1-14

Central Theme
Words are often the weakest method of communication. However, we have to use words, and today's gospel is an attempt, in simple language, to describe what happened on that extraordinary day, thousands of years ago. It speaks of Jesus being born, and of the second meeting of heaven and earth, on that same night, when the angels appeared to the shepherds. This was the beginning of a process that is still on-going, as I speak. It is an old story that is ever new.

Parable
I don't know a great deal about gardening or horticulture, so I'm just passing on to you something that I heard from a person who works in this field (if you'll excuse the pun!). If you took a branch from an oak tree, and grafted in on to an apple tree, it would never produce apples. It is a different species of tree, with different genes. If you took a branch from a crab tree, and grafted it on to an apple tree, you would be coming nearer to the ideal, even though this branch would never produce apples either. It is, of course, of a similar species and genes, but there remains one last obstacle. The branch of the crab tree is full of its own sap, so the sap from the apple tree cannot enter into it. Firstly, it is necessary to stick the branch of the crab tree in the ground, and leave it there until it is completely drained of all of its own sap and, to all intents and purposes, looks as if it is actually dead. It is then grafted on to the apple tree, it draws new life from the tree, and within a year, it is producing apples. If Jesus did not take on my nature, I could never be grafted on to him. Our species and genes would be different, and I could never possibly become a branch of the vine that he is …

Teaching
'Jesus is the same yesterday, today, and always.' With God there is no such thing as time. All of time is totally present to him right now. God's work among us is always in process, it never comes to an end. In God's eyes, Christmas is an everyday event, that involves Jesus knocking on the door of my heart, seeking admission. The God-dimension never changes, the offer is always

there, the good news is delivered with greater consistency than the morning newspaper. What happens after that is totally dependent on whether I accept the offer, open the door, and make my heart available as a manger.

One very important point: The shepherds were given the message by angels, which is fairly good authority, and yet they said, 'Let us go to Bethlehem and see for ourselves this wonderful thing which the Lord has made known to us.' The life of the Christian is a journey from revelation to faith. It involves coming to find out for myself the truth and the reality of what I had been told by my parents, teachers, or preachers in church. I have to cross that bridge ... The gospel is in between two phrases. At the beginning, we are invited to 'Come and see', and, at the end, we are instructed to 'Go and tell'.

The Jesus of Bethlehem is the same today as he was last year, as he was that first Christmas night. What can have greatly changed are the conditions within my heart. It could happen, for example, that today is the first day he has really felt at home in my heart, because it might be the first occasion in which he is genuinely welcomed, and made at home. If I can get this right, then, of course, this will certainly be the greatest Christmas in my life.

Response
When you think of a washing machine, you are conscious of all the cycles through which the wash must go. If you were told now that you were on the final rinse, and that this was your last Christmas on earth, what difference would it make to your celebration of this day?

Have you got a clear idea in your mind exactly what is meant, and what is entailed, in going to Bethlehem to see for yourself this news which the Lord has told you? Bethlehem, for you, is not a place on a map, it is a space within your heart. It is not possible for a human being to fall on his knees, cry out to God, and not be heard. Maybe you haven't been broken enough yet? Maybe you have not yet arrived at any conviction about your powerlessness, and your inability to manage your life. There is little point in speaking about a Saviour to someone who is not convinced that he is a sinner. We own nothing. Everything we have, including life itself, can be snatched from us in an instant.

This is a time of gift-giving, and that is just wonderful. All of the gift-giving, however, is based on the fact that God gave us his greatest gift of all, his Son Jesus. St Paul reminds us, 'Having given us Christ Jesus, will the Father not surely give us every-thing else?' All is gift, from creation to salvation, redemption, and eternal life. 'In this is love, not that we love God, but that God first loved us.' The whole idea of Christmas, of love, of gift, of life began with God, comes from God, and belongs to God. Therefore, without God at the centre, the celebration of Christmas is a mockery and a total charade.

Practical
For some people Christmas is not a happy time. It is a time of loneliness, a time when a departed one is most keenly missed, when one spends this day far away from family and home, or when, because of alcohol, it becomes a day of violence and abuse. Do I have it within my power today to ensure that those around me find happiness, at least in so far as I can contribute to that?

With all the thanks expressed today for gifts received, make sure you take a few seconds out, now and then, during the day, to say 'Thank you, Father, for sending Jesus.' 'Thank you, Jesus, for coming to speak our language, and to walk the journey with us.' Our greatest thanks, of course, is not expressed in words, but in an inner disposition of gratitude, that is, in itself, real prayer. It is not possible to be grateful and unhappy at the same time …

The coming of Jesus on earth, or into our hearts and homes, is but the beginning of a journey. His coming is more than a one-day-wonder. It is the beginning of a journey, the beginning of a story, that ends with the words 'And they all lived happily ever after'. This journey is lived, one day at a time, with each new day requiring its own *yes*. Life is a journey towards something, which is its completion. Jesus came to lead us on that journey. 'They who follow me will not walk in darkness, but will have the light of life.' Like the Wise Men following the star, we are given a way in which to walk, and the gospel is a map for the journey. Jesus himself is our Moses, as well as our manna. 'Man/woman will live for evermore, because of Christmas Day.'

Story
The young couple were newly married, blissfully happy, but very very poor. It was during the Depression in the late 1920s. It was impossible to find work, and social security was almost

non-existent. There was one special possession that each had, which gave great joy to each, and to both. She had an absolutely beautiful head of hair, that drew attention wherever she went. He had a gold pocket watch, which was very precious, because it was a family heirloom from the days of plenty. Part of their love for each other was his joy and delight as he looked at her beautiful hair, and she was forever admiring his gold watch.

It was Christmas Eve. He had gone out in search of a few hours work, and she was at home. Each, unknown to the other, was totally preoccupied with the same single thought, i.e. how on earth can I possibly get some little gift to give the other for Christmas? As she thought about it, she had a sudden reckless impulse, so, out she goes, down town, into a hairdressing salon, has all her hair cut off. She was paid for the hair for use as material for a wig; not much money, but just enough to buy a chain for her husband's watch. She was both happy and afraid, as she returned home – happy to have something to give him, and afraid that, when he saw her cropped hair, he would be annoyed. Her heart missed a beat, mostly from fear, as she heard her husband coming in downstairs, and climbing towards their apartment. She faced away from him as he entered, but finally, she had to turn around. His face was aghast, so she ran towards him with her gift, explaining why she did it, and showing him what she had bought for him. He appeared to wilt with weakness, as, without a word, he reached in his pocket, and handed her a gift. Not a word was spoken, as she opened her gift, to discover that he had bought two beautiful ivory clips for her hair ... and he had sold his watch to be able to do so.

Love is the only gift that is worthy of Christmas ...

FIRST SUNDAY AFTER CHRISTMAS (HOLY FAMILY)

Gospel: Matthew 2:13-15, 19-23

Central Theme
Today's gospel tells us about Mary and Joseph bringing Jesus to Egypt, to avoid the evil plans of Herod, and of their return from there, when that danger had passed. It is a very simple story, but a very significant one, and one from which we can learn a great deal about God's overall plan of salvation for all of us.

Parable
We are all too familiar, unfortunately, with the reality of refugees in today's world. On two continents, in recent years, we have seen the ravaged faces of young and old, of mothers and babies, all fleeing before the destructive onslaught of the bully and the tyrant. With all their riches, and all their power, such tyrants are miserably poor, and tragically weak. The greatest evil is that it always seems that it is the innocent who are the victims of greed, aggression, and violence. Not much has changed in this world since the time of Jesus. He himself would be the first to say that, when we look at any one of those innocents on our television screens, we are looking at him.

Teaching
The journey to and from Egypt has a very powerful significance. For the Hebrews, Egypt was a place of slavery and returning from there was the redemption of God, who lead them into the Promised Land. Moses had been a foreshadowing of Jesus, who has come to us in our slavery, to redeem us, and to lead us safely home. His journey into Egypt was a symbol of his joining us in our exile. In becoming like us, he was joining us in our humanity, and was prepared to accompany us on our journey into freedom.

Twice in today's gospel, we are told that what Jesus did was to fulfil a prophecy that had been made about him. In other words, there was a deliberate purpose in the act. He had come to do the Father's will, and to carry out everything that was ordained for him to do. If he was to undo the evil of the original disobedience, then he had to become obedient unto death, even death on a cross. He lived in the sure knowledge that what happened to him was the Father's will. This is not predestination, or being programmed in such a way that one loses one's free will. Far from it. What happened to Jesus is what Jesus wanted to happen. He gave himself into the Father's hands, with a deliberate offer of 'Not my will, but yours, be done.' His prayer to the Father was total trust, abandonment, and obedience.

Sometimes we hear the expression about being 'anchored' in life, implying that one's security comes from within, and I am not tossed around by the storms that surround me. This is farfetched, even as I say it, because Jesus was a helpless infant at the time of today's gospel. However, throughout all of his adult life, 'my meat is to do the will of him who sent me.' Both he and his life were the fulfilment of a promise, the completion of a plan. If the Old Testament was radio, the New Testament was television. His had come to fulfil the promises of the prophets, and to complete the work of creation, by making it possible for sin to be forgiven, for slavery to be turned into freedom, and for death to become eternal life.

Response
Very few of us, if any, have experienced the trauma of being a refugee, or of being homeless. Our security is important to us, and we need to have a sense of being in control. I personally have been deeply impressed, and indeed in awe, at colleagues who left home and headed off into a completely unknown and uncharted mission field. This was pure gospel to me. They took Jesus at his word, went where they felt he wanted them, and trusted him totally to provide, to bless and to fulfil his promises. In today's gospel, Jesus is a helpless child, but, in their own way, each of those of whom I speak were also powerless. It is in such powerlessness that God's power works most effectively.

Jesus was brought to Egypt as a result of a dream Joseph had, and, again, following another such dream, he was brought back to Nazareth. The Joseph of the Old Testament was mocked by his brothers as being a dreamer. Many of us interpret that to mean that a dreamer is someone who sits around with a head full of crazy and impossible ideas, but who never does anything to make those dreams come true. It is important for us to remember that some of the greatest human beings this world has ever seen have been dreamers, have been people with dreams. We all remember Martin Luther King's famous speech, which includes those immortal words 'I have a dream ...' Unlike those nocturnal dreams that we all have when we sleep, the real dreamer is the one who is most awake and alert. Joseph was fully open to any word from God, and he was willing and ready to carry out that word. 'Happy are they who dream dreams, and are prepared to take the steps to make those dreams come true.'

Humility is a difficult concept to grasp, and this can be caused by the fact that its meaning is so simple. It is nothing more than the plain and simple truth. It is a gift that enables me see myself as I really am and, being fully conscious of my human weakness, I can easily see how dependent I am on God, and why I should live every day with a constant awareness of that dependence. Mary and Joseph were humble people. When she visited Elizabeth, Mary spoke of how God had regarded her lowliness, and how he had done wonderful things for her because of her own powerlessness to do any of that herself. She magnified God, which is like looking at something through a strong magnifying glass. The bigger your God, the smaller your problems. Despite the human hardships, Mary was quite willing to leave everything, and head off into a foreign country, if that is what God wanted her to do. Sin is pride, which is my way of insisting that I do things my way; that my way is best. Jesus refers to the Holy Spirit as the Spirit of Truth. The Spirit had come upon Mary at the annunciation, and she would continue to be led by that Spirit throughout her life.

Practical

I said earlier than when I look into the face of one of those refugee children, I am looking into the face of Jesus. Racism and bigotry is the worst form of blindness, and there is no nation on earth that can pretend to be free of that. Racism and Christianity certainly don't go together. 'Whatever you do to the least of these, my brothers and sisters, that's what you do to me.' I myself may not have had to experience the trauma of being a refugee or of being homeless, but I can find out a lot about myself when I reflect on how I see, and how I relate to those who are in such a predicament. I don't necessarily have to personally meet one such person to discover what my inner attitudes are.

The first time I was carried into a church, I wasn't consulted, and the next time I'm carried into a church I won't be consulted either. To attempt to run the show in the meantime is insanity. I own nothing. Everything I have is on loan. One heart attack and it's all over. Humility is the gift of seeing and accepting things as they really are. Saying *yes* to God can be a constant and continual form of prayer. I don't ever have to worry what I'm saying *yes* to, because God will always make that perfectly clear, as time goes by. He doesn't treat us like robots, nor does he ever want to avail of our services without our goodwill, and willing co-operation. In Twelve-Step recovery programmes for alcoholics, narcotics, etc., Step Three says 'We made a decision to turn our will and our lives over to the care of God …' What the person is really saying is, 'You should have seen me and my life when I was in charge!' You could do nothing better than take a few moments out today to reflect on the whole idea of turning things over to God. When you die you're going to have to let go of everything, anyhow, so why not begin with little things now?

I spoke earlier of the significance of Jesus going into Egypt, the land of slavery for the Jews, and his subsequent return from there. Slavery is a word I could do well to dwell on. I could be quite enslaved and not know it. The alcoholic is the last one on the block to believe that he is an alcoholic. If Jesus is to be my Redeemer, then I must be willing to get in touch with those areas in my life which are in need of redemption, in need of being restored to healthy and happy living. There is no doubt at all in my mind that the Spirit will certainly reveal all of this to me if I am willing to find out. As you listen to me now, or as you read this, remember that there are two characteristics of the Word of God, i.e. it is always challenging, but it is never discouraging. I hope that you will be challenged by today's gospel, and that you will be prepared to accept it as a pointer for you today, rather than as something that happened thousands of years ago.

Story

I remember a simple incident in which I was involved many years ago. It was very early in the morning, and I was travelling to give a Retreat in a place quite a distance from home. I passed through many small towns and villages on the way. As I was leaving one town I encountered a young man thumbing a lift. I stopped to give him a lift, and discovered that he was going to a town only a few miles short of my own destination. I went through the usual litany of questions. 'Are you going to work … etc.' He told me what was happening. There was a centre for alcoholics in the town where I met him, and it is well known the length and breadth of the country. The previous evening, under pressure from family and friends he had decided to check himself in. He attended the opening session on the previous night and, as soon as the doors were unlocked the following morning he made good his escape. I'll never forget his comment, and the sense of shock in his voice as he spoke it. 'Do you know what they wanted me to do in there? They wanted me to change my whole life!' That was too much, and he got out of there before anything happened! I've often thought of him since, and have wondered what happened to him. If he was not prepared to change his whole life he is probably dead by now. The road that was pointed out to him seemed impossible to travel. Without knowing it, he took the most difficult road of all and, as I said, it may well have cost him his life.

SECOND SUNDAY AFTER CHRISTMAS

Gospel: John 1:1-18

Central Theme

This gospel is pure poetry. It is as if John opened his mouth, and let the Spirit of God within him pour out the sparks of the furnace within his heart. It is hard to grasp the profound nature of what he writes, compared to the letters he wrote at the end of his life, which can be summarised in one sentence: 'Little children, let us love one another, because God loves us.' This is written with the total conviction of who Jesus is, why he came, and what happens if we are open to his message. At the end of his gospel, John will have to admit that, if he wrote down all the things Jesus did and said, the whole world couldn't contain all the books. John is known as the beloved disciple, and it is obvious that his heart is overflowing with love, gratitude, and joy, because of the Jesus he is about to write about in the following pages of his gospel.

The heart of the message is that Jesus came to his own, the Jews, but they did not accept him. The message is now offered to all of us and, for those of us who do accept it, Jesus will allow us full membership within the family of God. This privilege is pure gift, and has nothing to do with merit, birthright, or achievement.

Parable

When I was a kid we had a popular song for all singalongs called 'All my granny has left you is her old armchair'. It was about the jeers and sneers of family members directed against the one who was left an old armchair, while they shared her house and property. The part of the song that always gave me great joy was when the one who received the chair discovered that all of granny's savings were carefully concealed within the chair and that he turned out to be the lucky one; something that wiped the sneers off the faces of the others, and filled them with a jealous rage.

A poor way to illustrate today's gospel, but I'm sure you get the idea. In John's day, for example, Jesus had left them nothing tangible beyond the memory of a man who had died as a public criminal and, I'm sure, in the eyes of John's family, he was seen to be really foolish to have followed such a one, and he deserved nothing but disdain.

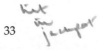

33

Teaching
I like the following statement: 'For those who do not understand, no words are possible, and for those who do understand, no words are necessary.' That is part of John's problem in today's gospel. While he witnessed Jesus healing the blind, he himself had come to see much clearer. All of the miracles Jesus worked for him were within him. Jesus was, indeed, the light that had come into the world and John, as one of his followers, had been handed the torch to carry that light to others. John the Baptist was not the light, nor is John the Evangelist claiming that he is the light. The role of one was to prepare the way, the role of the other was to proclaim the message, and guide others to the Way, which is Jesus.

From the very beginning, Jesus was not accepted. John would later write in one of his letters, 'You are children of God. Only those who are of God will listen to his voice. The proof that the word is from God is that the world will not listen to it.' The Word became flesh ... Word can mean many things. It can be a word in a dictionary: it can mean a message as in 'Did you get any word from John yet?'; it can mean a promise as in 'I give you my word on that'. Jesus is the Word of God, he is God's message, God's statement, God's promise. Jesus wants decisions, not discussions. 'You are either for me or against me,' he said. One of the ways of not getting around to doing something is to talk about it long enough. Debates and discussions can turn the flesh back into word again, and what is a reality becomes a thesis or a theory, something involving mental assent, which has nothing whatever to do with faith.

The Law was given through Moses and, by the time Jesus came along, the people were totally hamstrung by the love of law. This law was studied and taught by the scribes, imposed by the Pharisees, and scrupulously obeyed by the people. Jesus came to replace this love of law with the law of love. John is really excited about that, as we see in the last paragraph of today's gospel. Many years later, as an old man in exile on the island of Pathmos, he had simplified the gospel message to one simple truth: 'Little children, let us love one another, because God loves us.' (Do you remember hearing words like that from Mother Teresa?)

Response
There are none so deaf as those who don't want to hear. You

could be sitting there wondering what I'm going to say, while I'm up here wondering what you're going to hear, and we can all forget that only God can speak God's word, and only those who want to hear will actually hear that message.

There are two parts to the history of salvation: What Jesus did, and whether we accept that or not. He came to his own, but they weren't interested. For you, for me, for any or all of us gathered here today, however, it is our moment of decision. The only *yes* God is interested in is my *yes* of now. I cannot live today on a *yes* that was said on my behalf at my baptism. For those who did receive him he gave the right to become children of God. All they had to do was to trust him to save them. That is the offer that is made to us today. God doesn't give me anything; he offers me everything.

In the beginning was the Word ... John also knows only too well that, at the end, the Word will still be there. Jesus is the Alpha and the Omega, the beginning and the end. In other words, no matter whether people accept or reject his word, no matter what way the world chooses to behave, no matter how bad things might appear to be, at the end of time Jesus will be Lord; the kingdom of this world and the kingdom of Satan will have come to an end, and there will only be the kingdom of God, which Jesus came to establish. (It is significant that the last Sunday of the church calendar is the Feast of Christ the King.) It's like knowing the result of the race before you go into the bookies. You can have no excuse for not being on a winner. God won't send you anywhere when you die. Rather will he eternalise the decisions and directions you take now.

Practical

Give some serious thought today to the *yes* of your baptism, to ensure that you personally have taken full responsibility for it, and that you are a member of the Christian family by deliberate choice, and not by some coincidence or accident of birth.

If the Word becomes flesh, if Jesus takes on our human nature, then, surely, he has taken on your human nature. This should lead to some serious reflection along the following lines: If Jesus has taken on my human condition, then I am faced with a serious situation. He can take over and effect only that which I allow, and the limits to what he can do in and through me, are set by me. The implications of such a possibility are frightening. There is nothing automatic about God. He will not enter where he is not welcome. And he needs my goodwill as the foundation for all his work in me. Did you hear about the man whose beard went on fire, and he prayed it would start raining? He himself wasn't prepared to do anything …

Story
There was a dark cave deep down in the earth, and it had never seen light. One day the sun invited it to come up to visit it. The cave was amazed at the light, and it invited the sun to come down to visit it, because the sun had never seen darkness. The following day the sun came down into the cave, looked around, and asked, 'Where's the darkness?'

When the sun entered, there was no darkness anymore, just as when Jesus, the Light of Life entered this world …

THE BAPTISM OF THE LORD

Gospel: Matthew 3:13-17

Central Theme
Today marks the beginning of the mission of Jesus. On a human level it may seem strange that he had not done anything of great significance over the previous thirty years. I will share some thoughts on that point later on in this reflection. This day was D-day for him. It is very clearly implied that he had come to the Jordan in obedience to a word from the Father. His explanation to John is very inadequate, but John was enough of a prophet to obey without always understanding. The action of John, and the purpose of Jesus coming there was clearly confirmed by both the Father and the Spirit.

Parable
I have had the privilege of leading a pilgrimage to the Holy Land on several occasions. One of the highlights of the trip was the ceremony of total immersion in the river Jordan, when each person renewed the promises of baptism. It was a very moving time, and it was easy to imagine the Spirit descending, and the Father confirming each of us as his son or daughter. Many of those who travelled with us over the years still speak of that moment with great emotion, and with special remembrance.

Teaching
In Matthew's account, today's gospel is prefaced by John the Baptist proclaiming the coming of the Messiah, and it is followed by Jesus encountering Satan in the desert. There is a definite pattern to all of this. The Spirit has shown John who Jesus was and, once the Spirit had come upon Jesus, Satan is waiting his chance to test that Spirit. One of the greatest gifts we receive from what Jesus achieved is that, with the Spirit within, we can face up to any evil spirit we meet on the road of life. John the evangelist writes in one of his letters , 'Little children, there is a power within you that is greater than any evil power you may meet on the road of life.'

John the Baptist had that wonderful gift of humility. He knew his place before his God. When some people asked him if he were the Messiah, he very emphatically denied any such claim. When Jesus came to him to be baptised, he was shocked, and he had no doubt that it was Jesus who should be baptising him. However, without understanding, once Jesus said that this was how he wanted things to be, John had the necessary humility to obey, and to bow to a higher authority. Original sin continues to show itself in endless forms, each of which is but another attempt to play God, to do things my way. John the Baptist was an extraordinary humble man. No wonder Jesus said, at a later date, 'There has not been born of woman a greater prophet than John the Baptist.'

The baptism of Jesus is an extraordinary moment in our story of salvation. Not only did Jesus join us in our sinfulness, but the Father and the Spirit are seen and heard to be there with him. The language of the gospel may appear so simple, when we are told that 'the heavens were opened', but considering the banishment incurred through original sin, it is indeed a powerful statement. Later on, when Jesus will have completed his journey on Calvary, we are told that 'the veil of the Temple was rent in two'. For the first time, we were free to enter into the Holy of Holies. Today's gospel is the beginning of a journey which, through our own baptism, each of us is asked to travel.

Response

The church calendar is marked with very special and specific holy days, such as Christmas, Easter, or Pentecost. It is only when I begin to reflect on what really happened, and I begin to get into the heart of the matter, that I begin to see the importance of today, when we celebrate the baptism of the Lord. It is a truly significant feastday, and a cause for celebration. It is very evident that our own baptism marks the beginning of our own personal Christian journey. In a way it marks our common birthday.

I said earlier that there is an obvious pattern in the unfolding of the journey of Jesus. He told us that, if we follow him, we will not walk in darkness, but will have the light of life. There is nothing automatic about being a Christian. It involves personal decisions, decisions that need to be constantly renewed. When a baby is born, that fact is registered in the records of the state, and a certificate is available to show the date and the place of birth, together with the name of one or both parents. If the baby is put up for adoption, the natural mother is allowed several months to retain the option of changing her mind about her decision. If her decision is unchanged, she signs the adoption papers, and the baby becomes a member of a new family, with different parents, and a different surname. The adopting parents go through a very thorough scrutiny to ensure their suitability, before the baby is entrusted to their care. Baptism is our ceremony of adoption. It doesn't make us children of God, because that is already a fact through our creation. Just as the natural mother normally does not abandon her baby, but ensures it is given security and a sense of belonging, so we are registered as members of the Christian community, and are given our place within the Body of Christ, which we call church. As I said, the natural mother is given plenty of time before she finally decides that this is what she wants to do. In our case, however, we are the ones who are given the time, and we are the ones who must decide for ourselves if we really do want to belong to this family, which we call Christian, or followers of Christ. Sooner or later, it is up to me to sign my own certificate …

Practical
It is very important that each of us should have a sense of purpose and pattern to our Christian living. When I set out on a journey it is necessary to have a definite idea of where I intend going, and the destination at the end of the journey. Signposts point the way; they do not compel me to travel that way. Have you ever come across a signpost that has been deliberately turned in the wrong direction by someone with a perverted sense of humour? As a Christian, I have very clear and definite signposts, and I always have the option of following them or not. Sometimes, because of road-works, I encounter a detour. When I follow the detour, my whole attention is given to every sign, until I get back on the road on which I wish to travel. In following my Christian vocation it is vital that I maintain a constant reflection on where I am going, why I am going in that direction, and that I have a definite pattern to my journey.

Many of us carry some form of personal identification, membership cards, or work-place name tags. Get a copy of your baptism certificate, which can easily be obtained from the church in which you were baptised. Put it in your wallet or in your handbag, and carry it on your person. Let it be a constant reminder, and let it evoke a whole new *yes* every time you see it.

You can renew your baptismal vows any day you wish. This could easily be part of your prayer life, from time to time. The words or formula don't matter. Some simple statement like the following would be quite sufficient : Lord Jesus, Saviour, I want to belong to you, to be part of the family of God, and to live according to the rules of your kingdom. I renew the commitment of my baptism, and I ask for the grace to live out my Christian life.

Story

A friend of mine vouches for the truth of the following incident. He was travelling down the country one day. His journey brought him along some by-roads, where the signposts were few and far between. After a while, he was unsure if he was on the right road, so he decided to ask the first person he saw. Eventually he came across a farmer driving his cows home for milking. He stopped the car, and asked him if he was on the right road to Somewhere, just to give the place a name. The farmer told him that he certainly was on the right road. My friend expressed his thanks, and was about to move forward when the farmer added, in a very nonchalant way, 'You're on the right road, but you're going in the wrong direction!'

FIRST SUNDAY OF LENT

Gospel: Matthew 4:1-11

Central Theme

Today's gospel is very significant. Jesus has just been baptised in the Jordan, the Spirit has come upon him, he is being led by the Spirit, and now he comes face to face with Satan. They are like boxers, entering the ring from either direction. In the Book of Revelation, the last book of the Bible, there is an account there of the battle in heaven between Michael the Archangel and Lucifer. Lucifer was defeated, and was cast down to earth. Notice the word earth, which is repeated four times in that one account. Since that time, Lucifer is known as Satan, which literally means the enemy. Jesus has come to reclaim for God what is God's. He has come right into the kingdom of Satan, which is on this earth, and he is going to redeem all those held captive my Satan. The word redeem was used to describe what happened when a slave was bought from his owner, and given his freedom.

Satan tests Jesus in the three areas of living where most of us fail and fall. Satan wanted to find out whether Jesus was really the Messiah, the Son of God. If he were a mere human, he would fall at any one of the hurdles Satan had thrown in his way. The first hurdle had to do with human appetites, which is very close to the bone. Our appetites are part of who we are, and they will always be there. Jesus pointed to something even more import-ant than bread, and he quoted scripture to prove it, so Satan didn't succeed there. Next Satan tested him in the area of re-sponsibility – again, an area where all of us fail. We can fail to take proper responsibility for our health, for our relationships, for our proper use of the gift of life, and all of these can break down, and something good is destroyed. Once again, Jesus re-sponds that we must take responsibility for our actions, and not act independently of God's expectations of us. Satan tried one last throw of the dice, using the big one, pride. This is what had caused Satan's own downfall, and the Fall in the Garden. Power, wealth, glory, control, etc., are always very tempting to the human spirit. However, we all know there is a price to be paid. It involves compromise, corruption, or loss of moral values. The price Satan demanded was extreme. That Jesus should be asked to adore Satan was the end of the line for Satan, and he was fully exposed to the power, the authority, and the divinity of Jesus, and was dismissed with the words 'Get out of here, Satan.' The battle was over, and heaven celebrated the victory of Jesus.

Parable
In one of Aesop's fables there's a story about an argument between the wind and the sun as to which of them was the stronger. The wind was very proud of his strength. It could uproot whole buildings, and level the strongest tree. In its eyes, the sun had warmth and nothing else. To settle the argument, they agreed to test their respective strengths against a man who was wearing an overcoat. It was agreed that whichever of them compelled the man to take off his overcoat, that one was the stronger.

The wind began the test. It blew and blew, even to gale force, but the only reaction from the man was to wrap his coat tighter around him. The sun took over. It didn't actually do anything. It just shone in the sky, and let the heat reach the man. Within minutes, the man removed his overcoat.

Teaching
When Jesus returned from the desert, he headed for the temple, where he began his public ministry. If we are to walk with him in Christian ministry, then we, too, have to overcome in ourselves those things that get in the way of Christian living. We live in a world where half the people are dying of hunger, while the other half is on a diet, trying to lose weight. The Irish people have the reputation of being generous, and yet the total annual contribution, from public and private sources, to the hungry people of the world, is less than what is spent in the pubs in twelve nights. There can be a big difference between what we want and what we need.

God gives me nothing for myself. He doesn't give me my gift of speech to go around talking to myself! Life itself is a gift, and we all possess many gifts and talents. We will have to account to God for how we have spent those gifts, and we have to take responsibility for what we do with them. God gives me what it takes to live the worthwhile life, to do the good, and to provide the service, but he will not force me in any direction against my will. If I have the will, he will supply the power. He will do the good through me, but I must supply the hands, the feet, the voice, and the heart.

There are many false gods in this world, and each has many

committed followers. The false gods are wealth, pleasure, power, control, and unbridled selfishness. There is only one true God, and following him is the only path that leads to happiness in this life and in the next. Satan is very clever, and if we are not on our guard, he can lead us into ways of living that lead to death and destruction. Jesus overcame Satan, and he hands that power to those who follow him. 'I have given you full authority over the evil one. Nothing shall harm you. Your names are registered as citizens of heaven', he tells us. St John says, 'There is a power within you that is greater than any evil power you will meet on the road of life.'

Response

The Hebrews marked their doors with the blood of the lamb, so that the angel of death passed them by, and could not harm them. At our baptism we were marked on the forehead with the oil of anointing, to signify that we are God's children, and that Satan has no authority over us. There is nothing automatic or magic in this. If someone comes up with a medicine that cures cancer, nothing happens until the sick person uses the medicine, and follows the directions on the bottle. Jesus asked us to follow him. It was never intended that we go backwards, or stand still on the Christian journey.

Because of the rapid growth in communications, and the real influence being exerted by television, advertising, and general affluence, it is becoming increasingly difficult to preserve a Christian ethos in our homes and families. The custom of having a house blessed, or of displaying some Christian symbol, such as a crucifix, is something that has been revered down the years, and no one of us can tell just what blessings resulted, or what disasters were averted by such a practice. The mothers of a previous generation never allowed their children out the door without throwing a sprinkling of holy water after them. In today's world, such a custom might be scoffed at; but it would be a great pity to discard the wisdom of hundreds of years just because I consider myself more intelligent than my grandparents. It is possible to know the price of everything and the value of nothing. St Paul speaks about what he calls the foolishness of this world …

Jesus said that you are either for me or against me. One advantage Satan has is that he has two groups on his side: He has those who are deliberately involved in evil-doing, and he has those who are doing nothing. All that is needed for evil people to succeed is that good people should do nothing. There are three groups of people in any society. There is a small group who cause things to happen. There is a larger group who watch things happening. And there's the vast majority who haven't a clue what's happening. The very fact that you are here this morning, or that you are reading this, is a very good indicator that you are not among those who do nothing. Scripture speaks the following words about the lukewarm: I wish that you were hot or cold, but because you are lukewarm, I will vomit you out of my mouth ... In today's language, that means you make me sick.

Jesus was led by the Spirit into the desert. After his encounter with Satan, we are told that he was led by the Spirit down into the Temple. At any single moment of my life there is always some spirit speaking to me. Sometimes it's the human spirit, at other times it's the Spirit of God, and at others it's the evil spirit. It is important to be able to discern these spirits. By their fruits you will know them, says Jesus. There is an inbuilt barometer within the human heart that responds to good and evil. It's called conscience. Most of that word is made up of the word *science*, which comes from the Latin *scio*, meaning I know. When I was a child I had a dog that looked guilty whenever he did something wrong! Any of you parents can look at a child and know rightly that he has been up to something he shouldn't. It requires great honesty and moral courage to live according to my conscience. When I use the word conscience, I am speaking of a good conscience, rather than a conscience that is perverse, blunted, or scrupulous. To thine own self be true, and then thou can't be false to anyone else, says Shakespeare.

Practical

Take a few moments out, sometime today, and reflect on your life in the light of today's gospel. How are you dealing with the temptations with which Satan tested Jesus?

Do you carry any religious object on your person? It is only by doing this that you will come to experience the blessings that come from it.

Do you know what it means to be led by the Spirit? Develop the practice of a short prayer to the Holy Spirit before all decisions and undertakings. This can be your protection against going down the wrong road in an undertaking, in a relationship, or in a decision. St Paul tells us that we should learn to live and to walk in the Spirit. This is something that I work on, that I practise, that I make part of everything I do and say.

Story
A stretch-limo pulled up in front of a retirement home one day, and a young man, full of his own importance, stepped out of it, and began walking towards the entrance. It was a beautiful sunny day, and many of the old folks were sitting out front, complete with straw hats and sunglasses. The visitor was a famous pop-star, and he was used to commotion and excitement wherever he went. On this occasion, however, nobody seemed to notice him, or to pay any heed to him. Full of his own importance, he stood in front of one old lady, and asked, 'Do you know who I am?' She didn't even lift her head, as she replied, 'No, but if you go in to the girl at the Reception, she should be able to tell you!'

In today's gospel, Jesus puts Satan in his place …

SECOND SUNDAY OF LENT

Gospel: Matthew 17:1-9

Central Theme
Today's gospel is where the veil was lifted slightly, and the apostles got a little glimpse into the real nature of Jesus. Of course, he was human and, up till now, their only experience of him was within that human framework. However, he was also divine, and something of that was seen in this situation. Peter, James and John were close friends of Jesus, and they were the ones who seem to have accompanied him on several occasions. On a human level, they could claim to know him well, to know how he thought, and to be familiar with his actions. The miracles were strong signs, of course, but then, even if only God could effect a miracle, he has been doing that through saints and prophets since the beginning of time. Today was different. There was something unearthly, something other-worldly about it. The natural human reaction in the presence of such is to be afraid, so the apostles were terrified and covered their faces. The face of Jesus became like a mirror, reflecting back the glory of the Father. The appearance of Moses, as the Lawgiver, and Elijah, as the Prophet, were very significant figures, because Jesus had come to announce that his mission was to fulfil the law and the prophets.

Parable
I have had the privilege of being at many a bedside when someone died. Many of them were ordinary unpretentious people, who never drew much attention during their lifetime. I have been deeply edified by many of them, as they approached death with a quiet dignity, and a serene confidence. There was a faith present that had been unnoticed during their lifetime, and they were seen at their very best at that moment. This was the acid test of their whole lives and, at this moment, they became transfigured into people who were at peace with themselves, and at one with God.

In today's gospel, the apostles had a glimpse of who Jesus really was.

Teaching
Because I am a human being, it is much easier for me to relate to

Jesus as a human being, who was also God. The extraordinary is found in the ordinary. In today's gospel, Jesus is raised above ground level, as it were. The next time that will actually happen will be on Calvary. No matter how much of his glory is revealed along the way, his ultimate purpose is to die so that we might live. Redemption does not mean lifting us out of our human condition, nor does holiness mean becoming so heavenly as to be no earthly good. Redemption is something that is effected deep down within us, where the real me dwells, where I am most truly myself. It is there that the bondage and the slavery is found, and it is from there that our freedom begins. The further down into my humanity I am prepared to go, where I am willing to name, claim, and tame my demons, the more I reflect the face of Jesus, the more glorified I become.

When the vision was over, when Moses and Elijah had gone, when the brilliance was dimmed, the apostles opened their eyes, (and these words are powerfully significant) they saw no one but only Jesus. It was back to reality, to business as usual. Peter had wanted to build some sort of permanent dwelling on the mountain, but Jesus knew that they had to come down off the mountain and face reality, and that is why he even referred to the fact that he was going to die. Martin Luther King referred to his vision of civil rights for his people, with the words, 'I've been to the mountain …' As he spoke he was back among his people again, and was soon to be killed. It is good to go to the mountain on occasions, in prayer, and get a wider view of life; but it is more important to return to earth, and face the realities of that life.

There are many instances in the gospels where we are told that Jesus went aside, he went up the mountain, he went away to be alone. These were times of prayer, in which he listened to his Father, and that is why he can tell us that I never say anything unless the Father tells me to. Our reality is limited to the horizons of our vision. There is no such thing as a fixed horizon, however, because the higher my point of vision, the further off the horizon. Faith is living with acceptance within my own horizons, and knowing that there are infinite possibilities and realities beyond that. It is living with the certainty of a Higher Power, because my path of life is strewn with obstacles that, on my own, I cannot cross. To face Calvary, Jesus sought and received the assurances of the Father. This was the Father's will, and the Father would see him through. That is why, instead of referring directly to his death, he told the apostles to reveal what they had seen only after he had risen from the dead. That is the kind of faith that comes from going to the mountain in prayer.

Response
I said earlier that it is more important for me to recognise the humanity of Jesus, and leave it to him to reveal his divinity. In other words, as a person, probably the highest compliment that could be paid to you is to describe you as a decent and whole-some human being. That is the foundation of everything God calls you to, because his grace builds on that, and never replaces it.

Going aside with the Lord would be a very good description of prayer. I can do this in the midst of the madding crowd. I can enter my heart and be with him whenever I choose. If I were to lay out the gospel story before you now, I could highlight those times when Jesus brought his apostles to one side. Those were special moments. It was at one such time that he explained the parables; it was at another that he taught them to pray, and gave them a prayer to say; it was at such a time that they saw him glo-rified, and on a later occasion they would witness his agony. These were moments of profound formation for them, and they came to know him better, and to understand his message better, as a result of those private moments.

The Bible tells us that when Moses came down the mountain after his meeting with God, that his face shone so brightly that people were unable to look at him. He was reflecting the glory of his encounter, and his face was reflecting the light within him. That is part of the role of a Christian. If I believe that I am saved, then I have a serious obligation to look saved. A cynical philoso-pher said one time, 'You Christians make me sick. You speak of having a Redeemer, but not very many of you look redeemed.' Christianity is about attracting, not promoting. Who and what I am is my message. If I enter your house and tell you I have chickenpox, when, in fact, I have measles, which do you think you'll catch? What I have, or what I say I have?

Practical
There is such a thing as a prayer place, and many people are very aware of that in their lives. For some, it's a bedroom; for others it's a favourite armchair; or for another it's a particular walk by the shore, or through the fields. It's a place were I can

get away from it all, and I have time to reflect. A life without reflection is not worth living. Reflection, meditation, prayer, etc., it matters little which word we use, because basically they are all different dimensions of the same thing. A friend of mine will return from a walk, with his eyes lit up, and a sense of excitement in his face. He has just watched a seagull gliding gently in the sky, turning this way, and then the other way, without moving a wing. He has heard an evening chorus, as he wandered through the trees, or he stood motionless to watch a robin. Such a person is really alive and, for such a one, prayer is a joy. 'I see his blood upon the rose, and in the stars the glory of his eyes; his body gleams amid eternal snows, his tears fall from the skies.'

The ideal of Christianity is to see Christ in everyone, and to be Christ to everyone. Not that easy! In fact, I often wonder how the Father can see Christ in some of them! However, have you ever heard the phrase, 'Oh, he's really nice when you get to know him'. In other words, it is only when you begin to be Christ to the other than you will begin to see Christ in that person. There would be little merit in it if you could see Christ in the other person first. Surely, there's at least one person in your life that you should have another look at …

Holiness is not what happens on the mountain. It's what happens when I am down into the reality and the humdrum of everyday existence. I can think of the mountain, of course, at such times, and I will get courage from the thought. When Jesus came down from the mountain, it was to head for Jerusalem, and face death. Our daily humdrum contains a thousand ways of dying; of all the many dyings we have to do in our loving of others; dying to our pride, our opinions, our biases, our intolerance, our impatience, etc. When is the last time you ever died for another? That was the last time you really loved someone, and greater love than this no one has that someone should die for another.

Story
The old monk had spent a great deal of his life with the Lord, either in contemplation, reflection, community prayers, or during his ordinary work detail. He always had a secret hope, and he never knew from where exactly it had come. He had a secret hope of actually seeing some visible sign of the reality of the Lord's presence in his life. Although he hesitated to use the word, he secretly longed for some sort of vision. One day he was

in the chapel praying, when, suddenly, he looked up, and there he saw Jesus in full physical, visible form. Jesus smiled at him, and the monk was so dumbfounded that he just stared, and smiled back. He was in the midst of the most beautiful experience of his life when suddenly the door-bell rang. It was the time of day when the homeless and the hungry came to the monastery for something to eat. Today was his turn to take care of them. Despite his excitement, he got up quietly, and went out to take care of the old man at the door. When the job was done, he rushed back into the chapel and, yes, Jesus was still there, waiting for him. He fell on his knees and thanked Jesus for waiting for him. Jesus smiled, and said, 'If you had not gone out to take care of that poor hungry man, I would not have remained on till you returned.'

Jesus was just as present at the door as he was in the chapel.

THIRD SUNDAY OF LENT

Gospel: John 4:5-48

Central Theme
Today's gospel contains many powerful insights into the mind of Jesus. It is almost impossible for us to imagine how radical this encounter with the woman really was. It went completely against everything that a religious Jew would have held sacred. His conversation with her and with his disciples showed clearly how Jesus thought about certain issues. The final part of the gospel, where he heals the official's son, would appear to be totally unconnected, except for the final line, where he says. 'Must I do miraculous signs and wonders before you people believe in me?'

Parable
In today's world it is quite common for parents to be worried about the next generation. Change is coming so fast, and all our traditional values are being challenged. The children are not going to church, they are living with a partner, or they have children while not being married. All of this seems to fly in the face of everything the parents were brought up to believe in. While I understand their confusion and their concern, I often speak to them about the situation in which one mother found herself. Her name was Mary, and her son was Jesus. Mary was reared in the very best and purest Jewish traditions. Her background and upbringing would have been very religious and very traditional. Just imagine, on a human level, the problems she might have had with her son! He appeared to deliberately kick against every single religious tradition that was sacred to her. He completely ignored the law on many issues. He touched the untouchables, he spoke to prostitutes and to Samaritans, and he hung around with the riff-raff of society. This wasn't rebellion for the sake of rebellion. It is worth reflecting on exactly why this was so, and what it tells us about Jesus.

Teaching
The most obvious point in today's gospel is the respect and the personal dignity that Jesus afforded a woman who would have been scorned by society. He spoke to her as a human being and, while he challenged her, he did so with respect. It is generally

accepted that she came to the well at midday because everybody else stayed indoors during the hottest part of the day. She had to avoid the scorn and disdain of her neighbours. Jesus knew that there was an emptiness within her that she had tried to fill in so many ways. He spoke to her of the life that he offered, of the Spirit that rises up like a fountain from within the heart of his followers. He offered her something that she really needed, and, by the end of the story, it seems that his words had got through to her.

Her attitude was typical of most people who are involved in any kind of compulsive or addictive behaviour. She was in total denial, and her arguments were coming from her head. Jesus, however, very gently confronted her with the truth. It was for people like her that he had come, and when his disciples urged him to have something to eat, he spoke of his real hunger. His desire to seek out and to find the lost sheep was his driving force, because that is why the Father sent him.

There is a very interesting and important point at the end of his encounter with the woman. She ran off to get her friends. They came to meet Jesus, and to listen to him. In what might be considered as rather 'catty', they then told the woman that they believed, not because she had told them, but because they had met him and listened to him themselves. I could apply that concept right here now. I would pray that you might believe, not because I am telling you, but because you have met Jesus, you have listened to him, and you have come to know him yourselves.

Response

The word incarnation might put us off, but the reality of it is very simple. God could have loved us from a distance, but he decided not to. He decided to come to where we're at, and to meet us as we are. 'I did not come to condemn the world … Neither do I condemn you,' says Jesus. In today's gospel we have a very good example of Jesus meeting someone and accepting someone exactly as she was. He was totally aware of how she was, and of the situations within her life. He sat down and chatted with her, listened to her, and gently challenged her. He wanted to free her from bondage, and to restore her dignity and self-respect.

Many of us have friends and associates who may not be as we would wish them to be. I know, on a human level, it can be difficult, but the Christian law of love must extend to all, without exception. Supposing you have a son or daughter not going to church, or involved in an irregular relationship. If you were to die right now, there is only one question you would have to answer about that person. 'Did you still love that person, as a parent is expected to love a child, or was your love lessened because your child did not live up to your standards for her?'

Jesus speaks of the harvest that is ready and waiting to be reaped. In other parts of the gospel he speaks of gathering the crop into his barns. This is his driving urge. He does not want any one of us to be lost. There is an Irish poem called 'Ag Críost an síol', and, in summary, it says that the seed is from God, the crop is for God, and may we all end up in his barns; the fish are God's, the sea is God's, and may we all end up in his nets. The only thing that could frustrate his plans and hopes for me is that I should choose to do my own thing, to go my own way.

Practical
Put yourself in the place of the woman at the well for a moment. Jesus looks at you, and he knows you through and through. How comfortable would you feel in his presence? Would you be able to fully open out the canvas of your life to his gaze, without fear of condemnation? If you get a few spare moments today, maybe you might try that. It is important to be fully open to him, and it is also important to accept his total acceptance.

I suppose it's fair to say that there are traces of bigotry, racism, biases, and self-righteousness within all of us. On a human level, it would be impossible to be any other way. It is only through the presence and the work of the Spirit within us that we can hope to be freed enough to begin to love others as Jesus loves us. I have just mentioned the importance of accepting his acceptance of us. The ideal, then, would be to begin extending that same acceptance to others.

What can I do personally about the vast harvest that Jesus speaks of? As a Christian, I must be concerned, it is my business, and I just cannot leave it to others. I begin, of course, with myself. Like the friends of the woman, I too come to meet him, to listen to him, and to believe him myself. Christianity is more about attracting than promoting. Your most effective sermon is your life. The greatest witness a recovering alcoholic can give is to walk sober down the main street of his home town. You write a new page of the gospels each day, by the things that you do, and the words that you say. People will read what you write, whether faithful or true. What is the gospel according to you?

Story

My mind goes back to many years ago when I was doing a CPE programme in a girls' prison near Philadelphia. I am thinking of a girl whom we will now call Tina. Tina was leaning against a wall, with the usual chewing gum, and quite a flow of aggressive, abusive, and not very nice language at the other girls in the vicinity. They were tough inner-city kids, and Tina was typical. I asked her how she came to end up in prison, and her answer was instant and totally nonchalant, 'I threw my baby out a third-storey window.' When I asked her why she did that, she simply replied, 'Because he wouldn't stop crying.' She showed no remorse whatever and, if I didn't know better, I might have accepted her as totally amoral, without a shred of human feeling. The following day Tina came swaggering down the corridor, chewing gum in the mouth, and the usual flow of language, as she passed some of the other girls. She walked into my office, and used a flick of her heel to slam the door shut behind her. Suddenly, there was a dramatic change. The other girls couldn't see her now. She was in a safe place. The bubble gum came out of the mouth, was thrown into the basket, and she sank into an armchair and began to sob her heart out. She was lonely, afraid, guilty, and very very confused. She had been out of her mind on drugs when she snapped, and threw the baby out the window. Here she was now, a frightened, worried, and very guilty and remorseful person. This was the real Tina, the person she dared not let the other girls see. They had their own pecking order and, for survival, it was necessary to keep up the tough exterior. I often think of Tina when I think of Jesus meeting the woman in today's gospel, for example. Repentance is a word that can loosely be translated as 'Will the real you please stand up?' Jesus sees the inner child in all of us, and he asks us to let that inner child come to him, because the kingdom of heaven belongs to those who have the heart of a child, and who acknowledge God as a very loving Father.

FOURTH SUNDAY OF LENT

Gospel: John 9:1-41

Central Theme

Like last Sunday, today's gospel is both lengthy and full of wonderful insights into the mind and mission of Jesus. It has to do with blindness of many kinds, not least being the deliberate blindness of the Pharisees, and of those who actually witnessed the miracle. One sentence of Jesus gets to the core of today's gospel. 'I have come to give sight to the blind, and to show those who think they can see that they are blind.'

Parable

With the growth of information today, there are vast changes occurring in all areas, effecting economics, politics, ecology, education, religion, social life, and genetics. This can spawn its own problems, but it must create constant problems for those who try to resist change. 'This is the way it was done, and that is the way it should continue to be done.' One example is in the area of medicine, and medical and remedial care. The whole scene is changing, and the growth in alternate forms of medicine is phenomenal. There are new words coming at us all the time. My generation knew nothing about reflexology, aromatherapy, psycho-synthesis, or acupuncture. Speak of Enneagram or Myers-Briggs, and you run the risk of being accused of some New Age involvement. Jesus came to make all things new, and when he enters a person's life, that person is changed utterly and forever. The religious leaders of his day were typical of fundamentalists down through the ages. Nothing must interfere with tradition, and it was necessary to live within the narrow confines of a very confining legal system. To live is to change, and to become perfect is to have changed often (Cardinal Newman).

Teaching

The word 'handicapped' is no longer acceptable, and should be replaced by 'a person with a disability', whether that be mental or physical. There was a time in the past when those with disabilities were considered useless, and unable to play a role in normal everyday life. They stood at the street corner, with a cap in hand, collecting what coins the passers-by gave them. You'll

notice quite often in the gospel, for example, that a blind man is
often also referred as being a beggar. I think we owe it to those
with disabilities to be sensitive in the language we use, even if it
was never intended to be offensive in the first place.

I really don't know why Jesus went through the ritual of the
spittle, the mud, and the water, in order to heal the man. He
healed other blind people with a touch, or simply a word. It
might well have been a test of faith. He sent the ten lepers on
their way, and they were healed as they journeyed along. He
sent the centurion home and, before he reached home he got
word that his servant was healed. I often think that this is how
Jesus heals many of us. We ask for his healing, and nothing
seems to happen immediately. The problem can be that we may
not have the faith to accept the simple fact that, when we asked
for his healing, we should go on our way, and expect to notice
the healing taking place as time goes by. If an alcoholic keeps
going to AA meetings he will get sobriety. He must, however,
keep showing up, and not give up until the miracle happens.

Jesus said, 'By their fruits you will know them. A healthy tree
produces healthy fruit, and an unhealthy tree produces unhealthy fruit.' That's what I meant earlier when I spoke about
alternate medicines. It matters little what the method is as long
as the person gets well, and the proper ethics and moral standards are involved. As the story unfolds today, you will notice
that the man's eyes were really opened, and that includes the
eyes of his soul. I think of Jesus healing the total person, or not at
all. I couldn't imagine him healing someone, and then to have
that person going away filled with resentment against another.
Such a person was not really healed at all. The man in today's
gospel was totally healed, and he ended up on his knees, worshipping Jesus.

Response
One good guideline for getting into the spirit of the gospels is to
remember that the gospel is now, and I am every person in it. If I
think of it as history, as something that happened all those years
ago, then I will totally fail to feel part of it. We all suffer from
blindness of many kinds. We witness this every day, when we
read of racial violence, of ethnic cleansing, of racial prejudice. It
is easier to notice this in others. We can see the speck in another's
eye, and fail to see the beam in our own. There are none so blind
as those who don't want to see.

I think it is very necessary to personalise my prayers for healing. What I mean by this is that I can say many prayers by rote, I can rattle off novenas, and pray to all the saints in heaven, and I may not actually be coming into the presence of Jesus, or making any personal contact with him. That is why it is important to hear these stories in the gospels. Come before Jesus, look him straight in the eye, tell him what your problem is, and ask him, please, to heal you. Tell him that you believe as best you can, and ask him to increase your faith. When you experience his healing, your faith will increase enormously.

If I am every person in the gospel, then there must be a Pharisee lurking inside me somewhere! This is a more serious form of blindness than physical blindness and, for the person concerned, it is almost impossible to notice. For example, to refer to the alcoholic again, part of the problem of being an alcoholic is that alcoholism is the only disease known to man or woman where part of the disease is that it denies its own existence. Hopefully, John will eventually come to see, to believe, and to accept that he is an alcoholic; something that everyone else knew about him for years. We all have our blind spots, and it is very right that Jesus should refer to the Spirit as the Spirit of Truth, who will lead us into all truth, and the truth will set us free. From the very beginning, when Adam blamed Eve, and Eve blamed the devil, we have all inherited the tendency to live in denial of those things we just don't want to see.

Practical

A very practical and simple prayer is 'Lord, that I may see'. It is a short prayer, but when it comes from the depths of my heart, it is a powerful prayer. Remember the other blind beggar named Bartimeus? He was told that Jesus was passing by, and he was determined to get his attention. Those around him tried to silence him, but he shouted all the louder. And he also was cured. To another man Jesus asked the very pointed question, 'Do you want to be healed?'

Tolerance is the ability to accept someone who is different, and not to be harsh in my judgements of things I don't fully understand. Prejudice comes from the idea of pre-judging, of passing judgement before all the facts are known. There is an old Indian prayer which says, 'Lord, please help me not to judge my brother until I have walked a few miles in his moccasins.' I am not at all suggesting that any of this is easy. Christianity is about taking up my cross every day. It is about dying to myself, to my opinions, to my pride, and to my self-righteousness. It involves a willingness to unscrew the top of another's head, and try to see things from that person's point of view. I don't have to agree with the other, or to accept something that I clearly see to be wrong. Resisting judgements and condemnation does not mean that I suspend my ability to form and express an opinion.

There is a saying that goes something like this: The greatest good you can do for another is not to share your riches with him, but to reveal his riches to himself. It is good to confirm others, and make them feel worthwhile. Many people have grown up with very poor self-images, and they just cannot see the good in themselves. This is another form of blindness, and it is a blindness in others that any one of us can heal. The most certain proof that the Spirit of God lives in you is your willingness and ability to confirm other people. You cannot confer confirmation on another if you yourself have not had a Pentecost.

Story
There was a man in a psychiatric hospital one time, and one of his problems was that he was convinced he was dead. The psychiatrist tried every trick in the book, but nothing could change his mind. Finally, as he thought, he got a brilliant breakthrough. He got the man to agree that a corpse is lifeless, and therefore, not having any blood, it cannot bleed. Having got a clear acceptance of that simple fact, the psychiatrist proceeded to drive home the point. He got a pin, took the man's finger, and gave him a good enough prod to draw blood. He squeezed the finger until the blood was clearly evident, and he then proclaimed, 'Now can you see? That's blood. You are bleeding.' The man looked at the blood in apparent disbelief, and then he turned to the psychiatrist with a look of amazement, and said, 'Well, what do you know! Corpses do bleed.'

FIFTH SUNDAY OF LENT

Gospel: John 11:1-45

Central Theme

Have you noticed that gospels these Sundays are very long? (Next Sunday's gospel is the Passion narrative, which is the longest gospel in the liturgical calendar.) Once again, today, we have a story that contains very central issues of the message and mission of Jesus. It is about love, about friendship, about life, and about death. There are some beautiful human touches like, for example, when Jesus wept for his friend Lazarus, or when their encounter reveals a very warm relationship between himself and Martha and Mary.

Parable

Some years ago a book appeared, called *Life After Life*, which was closely followed by another book on the same subject. They dealt with what were called 'near-death' experiences. To all intents and purposes, a person may be seen and be presumed to be dead and, then, through electric shock, or some such means of resuscitation, the heart is got pumping again and the person recovers. During that time, between the apparent death and the re-commencement of heart activity, the person had experienced what I have called the 'near-death' experience. Many of these experiences had a great deal in common. They experienced themselves outside the body, looking down at the body. They were conscious of being drawn towards a tunnel of very bright light and, for those who travelled along that tunnel for any length, they could see pre-deceased relatives of theirs coming to meet them. One thing they all seemed to share in common was that, when the heart got going, and they had to return to the life they had known, they were disappointed and some of them were clearly annoyed. In general, it could be said that they lost all fear of death through the process, and were willing to face it again when the time came.

Teaching

Lazarus had gone through that experience, except he had gone all the way. In fact, he was dead for four days. I am in no position to make a comment, but I can only presume that, on his return, he had no memory of his experience. Don't forget, Lazarus was brought back to life. Unlike Jesus, at a later stage, Lazarus still had to travel down that same road. In a way, you could say that Jesus didn't do him any great favour. I can understand the strong response of Jesus when he met the widow of Naim going to bury her only son. It is normal for a child to bury a parent, but it is never easy for a parent to have to bury a child. Lazarus, Martha, and Mary were special friends of Jesus; so much so that Jesus wept at Lazarus' graveside. They were tears of love, not tears of despair. Grief is the price you pay for love. If you never want to cry at a funeral, then don't ever love anyone. That would be a very high price to pay to avoid something that is essentially part of life itself.

There is obviously a plan and purpose in all this. After all, Jesus had plenty of warning, but he seems to have deliberately held out going straight to Bethany. Even when he knew that Lazarus was dead, he said 'Lazarus is dead. And for your sake, I am glad that I was not there, because this will give you another opportunity to believe in me. Come, let's go see him.' It is hard to imagine that Jesus let Lazarus die just to strengthen his disciples' belief in him by raising Lazarus to life again! I don't pretend to know why it happened as it did, but I can hazard one possibility. Jesus was with people in a particular place and, because they took up his full attention, he wasn't about to run off and leave them just because Lazarus was sick. Lazarus was his friend, but these people were also very important to him, because God has no favourites. Having let nature take its course, and discovering that Lazarus was dead, he went to be with his friends Martha and Mary in their hour of grief. Seeing their grief, and experiencing his own sense of loss, he raised Lazarus from the dead. He did this because he had the power to do this. It would effect good in the lives of many people, apart from Lazarus himself. It would strengthen the faith of his apostles and especially would it have a direct foreshadowing significance in the fact that he himself was soon to die. Through Lazarus, Jesus was preparing his apostles was what was to come. When he spoke of his own death, he always added that he would rise again.

The core message of today's gospel is in the words Jesus addressed to Martha. 'I am the resurrection and the life. Those who believe in me, even though they die like everyone else, will live again. They are given eternal life for believing in me, and will never perish. Do you believe this, Martha?' Martha's answer was direct, and to the point. 'Yes, Lord', she told him. 'I have always believed that you are the Messiah, the Son of God, who has come into the world from God.' Do you believe this? This is the question each of us must answer. Everyone of us has to deal with death as part of life, both for ourselves and for those around us. After the consecration of the Mass, we often use the words, 'Dying you destroyed our death, rising you restored our life ... Lord, by your cross and resurrection you have set us free ...' Today we have to face up to what those words really mean, ask ourselves if we believe what we say.

Response
Jesus came to remove the weeds from the good wheat. He came to remove those things in human nature that were not part of the Father's creation. Sin, sickness, and death are not part of God's creation. When the farmer, in another story in the gospel, was asked where the weeds had come from, he replied that an enemy had done this. (The word Satan means enemy.) When the workers volunteered to pull up the weeds, the farmer said that he would take care of them himself because, in attempting to pull up the weeds, they would damage the wheat in the process. Today's gospel clearly points and highlights the fact of the control that Jesus had over death. On many occasions, he had shown his power and authority, when he ordered Satan to depart, either from him or out of the souls and the lives of others. God is the origin and the giver of all life, and only God can manage, control, and restore life, as he chooses. For you and me, life is not manageable. One heart attack and it's all over. Life is a very precious gift, entrusted to each of us by God. That is why it is the duty of the Christian to respect and protect life, at all levels, at all ages, and at all stages. God is most certainly pro-life.

There are a few occasions in the gospels when we are told that Jesus wept. I'm sure we all accept that Jesus was a really genuine, authentic, and sincere person. If he wept, it was surely because of some deep emotion, stirred up by love, hurt, or sadness. We might find it easier to accept the fact that Jesus could raise the dead than to believe he could weep like any one of us. It can be so easy for us to forget the fact that, in taking on our humanity, he experienced everything of what it is to be human. I don't believe I can have any meaningful personal relationship with Jesus until I am ready and willing to accept him as walking beside me in life, and sharing with me in all of the struggles, the tensions, and the other aspects of human living. It can be difficult to imagine that Jesus is interested, and would love to be involved in even the smallest undertaking of my life. He came so that he could be a totally down-to-earth God, but I can easily slip into the mentality of keeping him at a distance, and see myself as working to get to where he is. Just imagine a circle with Jesus in the middle, and I am at the edge of the circle. I want to get to him, but between where he is and where I am, I can see many obstacles, sins, weaknesses, etc. If I could only just get rid of those, I would arrive at the centre, bloodied but unbowed, and then, perhaps, Jesus could pin a medal on me and say, 'Well done!' That, of course, is absolute heresy. The whole purpose of Jesus coming was that I could actually begin with him, just as I am, whether that means going straight to the centre of the circle, or allowing him join me on the edge. It is only with him, and alongside him that any change for the better can happen in my life.

There is a lot of material for reflection, for teaching, and for prayer in today's gospel, but I will mention just one more. Jesus raised Lazarus from the dead, but Lazarus would have died again within a very short while, because he was bandaged from head to toe, and he would have smothered. Jesus turned to those around him and asked them to complete his work, 'Unwrap him and let him go.' This is a very good example of how Jesus involves us directly in his work. We all know people who need to be freed from bondage of one kind or another. They need affirmation, confirmation, encouragement, and a sense of their own worth before they can begin to experience freedom again. In my dealing with others, I can lift them up or put them down. I can be Jesus' touch-person in their lives and, while it is he alone who can give them new life, I can help complete his work, and greatly enable their freedom.

Practical
In my life up till now have I taken time out to reflect on the reality of death, on the finality of my own death? I don't mean this as a morbid exercise. I mean it as a very practical and realistic approach to life itself, which inevitably includes death. I have a very strong feeling that when I face up to my fear about dying, I will overcome many of my fears about living. I don't have any doubt about life after death, nor do I question that, or concern myself too much about it. I am, however, quite concerned about

life before death. Everybody dies, but not everybody lives. Some people settle for existing and, when they do die, you might require a doctor's certificate for assurance, because there was never much life there at any time! You could write on the tombstone, 'Died at forty, buried at eighty!'

Give some thought to the fact that Jesus wept. They were tears of love, not tears of despair. Later on he himself would struggle with his own death. The birth pains at the beginning of life are repeated at the end, when we are born into that third and final stage of life. The first birth is often followed by post-natal depression, while that second birth is followed by bereavement. The cord is cut one last time. It can be difficult to say goodbye, and some people hate goodbyes. When I die, and catch up with those who have gone before me, I won't have to say goodbye again. Jesus wept, because even for a brief while he was separated from a very dear friend. A good friend is one of the most precious gifts of life. Think of Jesus as a good friend, as a very very good friend. He himself uses the words as he speaks to us, 'You are my friends ...'

I feel certain that every one of us here could think of someone whom we could help on the way to personal freedom. I am thinking of very simple ways, like a word of encouragement, an hour of our time, a remembrance of a birthday or an anniversary. They are people who may not be ready to ask for, or accept help. I can watch someone destroy himself with alcohol, and I can do absolutely nothing until that person is ready and willing to face up to reality. The most I can do for others is to heal sometimes, to help often, and to care always. I honestly believe that when I am ready and willing to help, that the Lord will send people in my path. 'The greatest among you are those who serve', Jesus said. If you want to be great in the kingdom of God, then become a basin of water and towel person, as Jesus showed when he washed the feet of his disciples.

Story
The Greek writer Plutarch tells the following story about Alexander the Great. One day Alexander came upon Diogenes the ancient philosopher, and he was examining some bones. He had two sets of human bones in two separate boxes. When Alexander asked him what he was doing, he said he was reflecting on some of the more important lessons of life. 'For example', said Diogenes, 'the two sets of bones here are those of your

father, and of one of his slaves. I have examined them now for
some time, and I honestly must confess that I cannot find any
difference between them.'

John Quincy Adams, at 80 years of age, was shuffling along
outside his house one day, when a neighbour greeted him with
the question, 'And how is Mr John Quincy Adams this morning?' The old man replied, 'John Quincy Adams himself is very
well, thank you. But the home he lives in is sadly dilapidated. It
is tottering on its foundations. The walls are badly shaken, the
roof is worn. The building trembles, and shivers with every
wind, and I'm afraid John Quincy Adams will soon have to
move out of it, move on, and change residence and address. But
he himself is very well.'

PASSION SUNDAY

Gospel: Matthew 26:14-27:66

Central Theme
This is Matthew's account of the Passion. More than any of the others, it highlights the betrayal of Judas, the denial of Peter, the fact that the others ran away and, finally, that Judas hanged himself. It does, of course, cover the story from the Last Supper to the death and burial of Jesus, but the contrast between the resoluteness of Jesus, and the weakly cowardice of his followers is most evident.

Parable
I was reading an article recently by a confrère of my own in which he was recalling his days in the novitiate. The Novice Master was very strict and, on occasions, could be quite severe. Manual labour was a big thing back in those days. The one thing that stuck out in my confrère's mind was the fact that, no matter how difficult or distasteful the work, the Novice Master always took a full share in the task. This made a big impression on his novices. He never asked them to do anything that he himself was not prepared to do. My friend declared that his own personal love of the Congregation, and his own sense of mission in union with others, was born through that unspoken, but clear statement from his Novice Master.

Teaching
It is significant that our gospel today begins with the disciples' query to Jesus about where he wished to celebrate the Passover. This was to be a much more realistic Passover than they had expected. It is obvious that Jesus himself knew what was coming. To risk being simplistic, one could say that Jesus seems to be more upset and hurt that one of his friends should betray him, and another should deny him, than that he himself should face death. His death had already been determined by his enemies. It is said that only my friends can really hurt me, because I expect more from them. Jesus knew that he was surrounded by enemies on every side. They had hounded him, had listened to his every word to find something to use against him, and were determined for some time past that they had to get rid of him. Everything he did and said seemed to come from a person who

worked outside of the rules and constraints that it was their duty to impose and uphold. His disciples, however, should surely have come to know the heart and the mind of Jesus by now, and that they should turn their backs on him was something that he felt very deeply. At the moment of his arrest we are told that 'at this point all the disciples deserted him and fled'.

Throughout his lonely vigil in Gethsemane he did all within his power to obtain or retain the presence and support of his disciples. His spirit was deeply crushed and he felt totally alone. With all his soul he cried out to the Father. 'If it's possible, let this chalice pass from me. But not my will, but yours be done.' Part of him would welcome an escape route, but that could never be, and he could never accept it, if it was not the Father's will. Original sin was one of disobedience, and redemption would come through the path of obedience, even on to death. The Father's will was the one constant in his life. Earlier, he had told his apostles that his very meat, what kept him alive, was to do the will of him who sent him. Remembering what I said just now about the apostles deserting him, it is significant that the only words Matthew gives us from Jesus on the cross is the cry, 'My God, my God, why have you forsaken me?'

It is not surprising to read that, at the moment of his death, there were signs and movements in the earth and sky. The veil of the Temple was rent in two, from top to bottom. This was what separated the people from the Holy of Holies, where God was considered to dwell. The obvious message now was that we all had access to the full presence of God. The graves of the dead were uprooted, and the dead arose and appeared to many. In other words, nothing would or could ever be the same again. The barriers had been breached between this world, the world of God, and the world of the dead. The Red Sea had opened up once again, and it was possible to cross dry-shod from one stage of life to the next. Earlier, when Jesus had gone down into the river Jordan, taking on all our sins, we are told that 'the heavens were opened', the Father's voice was heard, and the Spirit was seen to descend upon Jesus. The journey of redemption begun in the Jordan was now completed. It is ironic that the Pharisees took special precautions to protect the tomb. Jesus was now safely beyond their grasp, the battle was over, the victory was won, and they would very properly find themselves guarding an empty tomb a few days later.

Response

If I accept that the gospel is now, and that I am every person in it, then I must look at the role of Peter, Judas, and the other disciples in an uncritical and objective way. It is interesting to note that Judas, of his own accord, went to the leaders and offered to betray Jesus. He wasn't approached nor was he bullied or blackmailed. There was something in him that should stir up fear in the best of us. It is so easy to confuse wealth with riches. I could be a very rich person and not possess a penny. On the other hand, I could possess enormous amounts of wealth, and be pitifully poor. Wealth and money have a way of turning on their owners, and taking over control of them. The most precious possessions I have in life is life itself, my health, and my relationships. I could be extraordinarily rich in all of this. The tragedy then would be if I failed to appreciate that fact. Judas has lent his name to acts of wrong-doing that are especially evil. I might not do something like that myself, but I certainly must look within my heart, and discover the germinating seeds of such behaviour. It may show itself in the simplest ways, where I put myself and what is mine before the welfare of another. I can know the price of everything and the value of nothing, and fidelity to friends and to the responsibilities of relationships may not be among my more important priorities.

Peter comes out of the story much better than Judas. We may be afraid to admit our greed, but we cannot be condemned for our fears. There is something very likeable about Peter and, in our hearts, many of us might identify with him. He had a brash self-confidence, and a veneer of bravado that covered up the coward and the very weak human being within. In his heart, however, he was essentially a good man, and Jesus seemed to have been very fond of Peter, and to have chosen him among his small group of personal friends. Peter obviously appreciated Jesus for the extraordinary gift that he was. I couldn't imagine Peter taking money in exchange for Jesus. The thing that saved Peter was that he was totally convinced of Jesus' love for him. When he first met Jesus, we are told that 'Jesus looked at Peter ...' Now when he denied him, we are told in another Passion narrative, that 'Jesus turned and looked at Peter ...' Peter saw that the look had not changed in the slightest, and he went out and cried bitterly. In one way his sin was similar to that of Judas. Each had turned his back on Jesus, one for money, and the other to save his own skin. The response to the failure of each, however, was

entirely different. Judas saw himself as being outside the possibility of God's love and forgiveness. He didn't have much in the
areas of faith, hope, or charity. Peter, on the other hand, knew
that everything was still OK. He had the love, he had the faith,
and he obviously had the hope. It is very significant that Peter
should write in one of his letters, 'Always have an explanation
to give those who ask you the reason for the hope that you have.'

Throughout all of today's Passion narrative, Jesus himself
shows a very earthy humanity. He reveals every emotion in the
book, from disappointment to hurt, from grief to terror, from
courage to total surrender. On the one hand he would submit
himself totally to what was to happen, while reminding his
apostles, 'Don't you realise that I could ask my Father for thousands of angels to protect us, and he would send them instantly?
But if I do, how would the scriptures be fulfilled that describe
what must happen now?' Throughout the rest of the narrative
Jesus speaks twice. He felt compelled to answer one question,
because it was couched in words that he would take seriously, 'I
demand in the name of the living God that you tell us whether
you are the Messiah, the Son of God.' I imagine that if the question had not been asked in the name of his Father that he might
have chosen to ignore it. The other words he spoke were words
of prayer, taken from one of the Psalms, 'My God, my God, why
have you forsaken me?' It certainly was a prayer, and not a cry
of despair. On very special occasions there can come a cry of
prayer from deep within our souls. It is not possible to cry out to
God like this and not be heard. There is an awesome sense of
loneliness in this particular Passion narrative. At no stage is
Jesus alone, but throughout most of it he is completely on his
own. The soldiers even took and divided among themselves the
very clothes he had worn. He was stripped of everything, and he
let go of everything, even life itself. And he did all of that for you
and for me.

Practical
The Wednesday of Holy Week used be called Spy Wednesday. It
was a way of highlighting the role played by Judas. It could and
should be a time for all of us to look within our own hearts and,
with Judas in mind, to see what we discover there. This is a good
time for reconciliation, for renewal of commitments, and for
strengthening of hope. The only real sin a Christian can commit
is to lose hope. There is nothing impossible with God and, in my

darkest hour, it is a very special gift of God to hold on to the hope that all is well, and all will be well, and all manner of things will be well.

'By this shall all people know that you are my disciples, if you have love, one for another', says Jesus. Whenever I fail to show love, I am denying Jesus, in so far as I am not giving any evidence that I am one of his disciples. The core of Christian living is its witness value. It must be seen, it must be evidenced, it must be witnessed. 'See how these Christians love one another' was the comment of those who first encountered the early Christians. Moral cowardice is the most frequent and the worst form of cowardice. 'Fear doth make cowards of us all,' says Shakespeare. To keep silent in the face of injustice and evil is moral cowardice of the most serious kind. This is certainly to deny Jesus. There are many moral and ethical issues today that are completely against the teaching of Jesus. Legislation permitting some of these makes its way into our national Constitution, because people who profess to be Christian are afraid to stand up and be counted, or they just don't bother themselves to get involved. All that is needed for evil people to succeed is that good people should do nothing.

I have already referred to the sense of loneliness that comes across in today's gospel. This is what happens in a person's life when there is no sense of accompaniment; where there is no sense of anyone travelling alongside, sharing the journey. Living as a Christian today is my chance to experience the accompaniment of Jesus along every step of the journey of life. In one way, his journey is over, and he does not need me to accompany him. On the other hand, he has chosen to travel the same journey all over again, in, through, and with each one of us. While he is accompanying me, I too can accompany him, and that is what we call prayer. Prayer is giving God time and space in my life. It is being with him, and for him, even if all others are too busy to spare the time. It is working on my relationship with him, and for any relationship to grow and develop, there must be time and space. The traditional prayer of the Stations of the Cross can become a real time for deep and personal reflection. It may be of such a nature that I might drop into a church and spend a few minutes at just one of the stations. It can be a way of identification, and of personal involvement in the journey of salvation that Jesus undertook for me.

Story

There is a certain understanding in the Russian Orthodox Church that is typified by the following scenario. It is the day of the General Judgement. The people are making their way into heaven. Jesus is standing outside the gate, welcoming them. Then he is seen to look off into the distance, and to search the horizons with his gaze. Someone asked him why he was doing that, and he said that he was waiting for Judas ...

There is another story about Judgement Day. All the 'good people' are gathered outside the gate, waiting to march in in triumph. They looked around and see many of their friends there, members of sodalities, and other church groups to which they had belonged. They were delighted to arrive here together, and were impatient for the great entrance. Suddenly, there was a huge cheer in the distance. When they asked what that was, they were told that Jesus had forgiven 'the others'! This infuriated them. How could he do such a thing for such a collection of scumbags? They themselves had worked hard to arrive at this moment, and now all the others are going in as well. Suddenly, there was the loud blast of a horn. When they asked what that was, they were told that that was the Judgement. The problem was that they were still outside the gate! Apparently, no one had told them that Jesus had died for everyone ...

EASTER SUNDAY

Gospel: John 20:1-9

Central Theme
This account has Mary Magdalene finding the empty tomb and running to the apostles for help. It is the only account where the apostles are directly involved, and where neither Jesus himself nor the angels were there to give instructions. It is interesting to note that John was one of those who took part in the events of today's gospel, and that this is his own personal account of that experience.

Parable
I remember well one of the reactions I had when I saw the Grand Canyon or Niagara Falls for the first time. My whole spirit was absorbing the awesomeness of it all. I had a camera, and I used it to the best of my ability. I tried to capture the vision, the emotions, the experience, and the wonder of it all. I later came to realise the futility of such attempts when I came home and tried to explain to someone else what my experience had been. The one over-riding thought I had was that it would be necessary for the other person to go out there and see what I saw, before there was any hope of real understanding or appreciation taking place. For those who don't understand, no words are possible, and for those who do understand, no words are necessary. I think of that when I read John's account of the resurrection. It is purely factual. It tells the facts as they unfolded, because there was no point in attempting to capture what was really happening within all of them on that great Easter morn.

Teaching
Jesus had told his apostles very definitely on more than one occasion that he would have to die, but that he would rise again, and return to them. From other examples of their behaviour, we have no reason to believe that they actually believed him, or that they understood exactly what he was talking about. They had seen him work wonders, they had seen him exercise authority over demons, and they considered him invincible, and it is unlikely that he would allow anyone take such control over him that they would put him to death. One of the biggest barriers Jesus encountered then, and today, is that not everybody takes

him too seriously. 'The sin of this world is unbelief in me ...
When the Son of Man comes will he find any faith on this earth?'

It is very fitting, then, that two of the leaders among his apostles should personally visit the tomb, and find out the fact of resurrection for themselves. There are no angels to tell them. They
see what they see, and they remember what Jesus had said. In
the words of today's gospel, 'he saw, and he believed, for, until
then they hadn't realised that the scriptures said that he would
rise from the dead'. Part of their responsibility for the rest of their
lives would be to witness to the fact of his resurrection.

The resurrection of Jesus is at the heart of the Christian message. Death is called, in scripture, 'the final enemy', and it completes the final and eternal victory of Jesus. It is in that victory
that our hope lies. 'By your cross and resurrection you have set
us free ... Dying, you destroyed our death, rising you restored
our life ...' The only thing we are sure of is that every single one
of us is going to have to take that final leap of faith that we call
death. When Jesus bowed his head on Calvary he trusted the
Father to catch him, as it were. He returned, and spent forty
days with his apostles to impress on them that he had overcome
death, and there was no longer any gamble or uncertainty in it
for them. We already share in resurrection, as we await our own
entry into the fullness of that new and eternal life.

Response

To fully appreciate resurrection I have to get in touch with my
own brokenness. I have to reach down within my being, and un-
cover all the fears, the demons, the sin. It is only then that I will
genuinely seek and welcome hope and good news of victory. In
other words, there is little point in speaking about a Saviour to
someone who is not convinced that he is a sinner. A tomb or
grave normally betokens death, decay, and disintegration. The
tomb of Easter morning is something very different. Just as Jesus
wants the manger of Bethlehem to be within my heart, so does
he want that tomb of resurrection and new life to be down within
my brokenness.

When I consider that the gospel is now, and I am every person in the gospel, then I must put myself within the story of this
morning's gospel. The apostles were told the news of resurrection by Mary Magdalene. They responded immediately by running to the tomb to see for themselves. I'm not exactly sure when
I first heard about the resurrection of Jesus. All I know is that it

was many years later when I personally came to see and experience this for myself. This discovery came in moments of darkness and of brokenness, when I cried out for help. It is not possible for a human being to fall on his knees, cry out to God, and not be heard. We all have our moments when we cry out 'My God, my God, why have you forsaken me?'

On Easter morning, we are told that the stone was rolled away from the mouth of the tomb. This can be quite significant, when I think of my heart as the tomb of resurrection. Can I identify something akin to a stone that is holding me back from enjoying the fullness of life? This could be anything from an addiction, a compulsion, a resentment, or some hidden and dark secret that I have never shared with anyone. Quite often I'm as sick as my secrets. Resentments can be real bondage. If I have a resentment against you, it is as if I am drinking poison, and I am expecting you to die!

Practical

If you want Easter to be a living experience for you, you have to go down into your heart. Look for the areas of darkness and of death. Where is it that you need new life, that you need to be raised up, that you need the stone to be rolled away? Give some thought to that today.

Are you a person filled with hope, or are you a doomsday prophet? Because of the resurrection of Jesus, the only real sin I can commit, as a Christian, is not to have hope. This applies to myself, to the church, to the world.

Think of those family members who have gone ahead to the third and final stage of life. With your regret at their passing, how much does hope play a part in your remembrance of them? Do you really believe that they have not actually gone away, but they have simply gone ahead? Do your consider your death as an opportunity to catch up with them, and to be in a situation where you won't have to say goodbye again?

For several weeks before Easter we prepared during a time we call Lent. For the next fifty days we prepare for Pentecost. Just as the stone was rolled away from the tomb, and Jesus came out into new and resurrected life, so the doors of the Upper Room will be flung open, and the apostles will come bounding out into a whole new life-experience, the experience of living and walking in the power of God's Spirit. This, in effect, is the most significant result of everything that Jesus had accomplished. We all have a personal stake in Pentecost, and that will figure largely in our liturgies over the coming weeks.

Story
The little girl was out for a walk with her grandad. They took a short-cut through a cemetery. As they were walking along, the little girl was fascinated by all the crosses, statues, monuments, and floral wreaths on either side, so, like any such child, she had many questions to ask. 'What are those things?' she asked her grandad, pointing at the graves and tomb stones. The grandad was caught unawares. How do you explain the facts of death, let alone the facts of life, to a four-year old? Anyhow, he had a go. 'These were people who lived in those houses down there, and one day Holy God came and took them away to live with him, in his house, with all his angels.' The little girl thought about that for a while and, as most parents know, when you answer one question, you are sure to get another one. 'And did they go off to live in Holy God's house?' she asked. 'Yes, they did', said the grandad, hoping that was the end of the matter. Suddenly, the little eyes lit up, and she turned to her grandad with a smile of understanding, and, with complete conviction in her voice, as she said, 'I bet you, grandad, when they went off to live with God and all his angels in his house, that this is where they left their clothes.' And she was right … that's what the angel said on the morning of the resurrection … if you're looking for Jesus, he's not here … but come on in and see where he left his clothes.

SECOND SUNDAY OF EASTER

Gospel: John 20-19-31

Central Theme
Today's gospel is about two of the many appearances of Jesus to his disciples after his resurrection. Today's account is special, because he appears to the larger group, from which Thomas is missing, and then he appears when Thomas is present, because Thomas didn't believe the story the others told him. Here we have Jesus looking for very definite belief and conviction about the fact and truth of his resurrection.

Parable
Recently, a sister of mine underwent very serious and critical surgery. The doctors were not at all encouraging, and we all had plenty of reason for concern. There were many prayers, and much calling for the prayers of others. In using that event as the basis for a parable, I do not, of course, adhere strictly to the events as they actually occurred. Her time in the surgery seemed to be forever. We had run out of things to talk about as we waited in a nearby lounge. Finally, the surgeon emerged from the theatre, called my brother-in-law to one side, and, for a few moments, they were in deep conversation together. The tension was palpable. Finally, my brother-in-law turned to us and, with a smile as broad as the Atlantic, he gave us the thumbs-up sign. The response was electrifying. The reason I make a connection between this and today's gospel is because of what happened during the next few days. The phones were busy. I am part of a large far-flung family, and everyone wanted to learn the truth first-hand. Again and again the very same people phoned just to make sure! I answered many of the calls. My brother-in-law was in bigger demand and, of course, a few days later, my sister herself was able to receive phone calls. The final haul was when some of my family actually travelled to Dublin to see for themselves. Some of them, like Thomas, even asked to see the wounds!

Teaching
Faith and knowledge must not be confused. I can know something in my head, and not really believe it down in my heart. I know that Jesus is God, but Satan knows that also. It is how I respond to that knowledge that can lead to faith. Faith, in a way,

is in my feet, and it enables me to step out with confidence in my decisions and in my words. It comes from experiential knowledge, rather than academic knowledge, or something I learned from a textbook. Thomas was told the good news of resurrection, but he was not prepared to believe until he had experienced that fact for himself.

It is difficult for the human mind to know anything of God. Our terms of reference are so limited and so conditioned, and Thomas Aquinas tells us that when we speak about God, there is only one thing we can be sure of, i.e. that we're wrong! God is so much more than anything we could say or think about him. God, however, does not wish to be clouded in mystery. The coming of Jesus on earth, with his action-packed life and his very public death was a very down-to-earth statement from God. If Thomas wants to touch the wounds of Jesus, then Jesus will make that possible, and invite him to do so. A very real invitation of the gospel is 'Come and see for yourself.' I believe that if I really and genuinely want to know the risen Lord that he will meet that wish and, through the action of his Spirit within my heart, I will come to know him in a deep and personal way.

Thomas believed because he had seen. Jesus said that the real test is to believe without having seen. The atheist would believe if I could provide all the proofs. That would not be faith. Faith is a response to love. If I am convinced of God's love for me, either as a Father, or as Jesus my Saviour, then I will accept his promises, and trust him to keep his end of the offer. The word 'covenant' is used a lot in scripture. A covenant is not the same as a contract. I go into a shop, give the money, and walk out with a newspaper under my arm. That is a contract and, once the conditions are met, there ceases to be any responsibility. A covenant, on the other hand, is something that cannot be broken, and that does not end, even if one side is unfaithful to it. John and Mary remain husband and wife, even if they are living apart. As things stand with the church today, that covenant still remains, even if they get a civil divorce. Jesus announced 'a new and eternal covenant', and he is very definite and insistent that heaven and earth will pass away before his promises or covenant will fail. All he asks is that we believe him. 'The sin of this world is unbelief in me'.

Response
I don't think it too strong to say that to be a Christian is to be

someone who knows the risen Lord. It is experiential knowledge, rather than academic learning. Resurrection must touch
on all those areas of dead-wood within my own spirit, and call
all of my being into the fullness of life. 'I came that you should
have life, and have it to the full.' I don't think I will ever properly
come to any sort of personal involvement in the gospel until I
make it all present tense, and until I personally enter into every
event and aspect of it. If my heart can be the manger for
Christmas, it can be the tomb for Easter, and the Upper Room
for Pentecost.

On the morning of the ascension, the apostles were looking
up into the heavens, when angels appeared to them, and asked
them why they were looking up there. Jesus had told them
where they would find him from now on. He is to be found in
the marginalised, the outcast, the broken, and the suffering.
These are the wounds in the Body of Christ today. If you ever
come across the Body of Christ without the wounds, then you
can be sure it's a phoney. 'Whatever you do to the least of these,
that is what you do for me.' I can reach out and touch the
wounds of Jesus any day I choose.

Quite often, the wounds in the body are within my own spirit.
Even if I am involved in healing, I too can be a wounded healer.
I don't honestly think that I can reach out to you in a sincere and
genuine Christian way, if I bypass the hurts and brokenness
within my own spirit. Does it make any sense to you if I say the
following: Before I go to Confession I should be ready to look
myself straight in the eye in a mirror, and give myself absolution
first? Otherwise I am asking God to do something for me that I
am not prepared to do for myself. Even after going to Confession
some people can remained riddled with guilt. I believe that my
effectiveness as an instrument for reconciliation in the lives of
others is directly connected to whatever reconciliation I am able
to effect within my own heart.

Practical
There is an ad for bread which claims that it is 'Today's bread
today'. It would be a good idea if I took today's gospel for today,
and not something that I might do something about some other
time. The Lord comes to make his home in you as you approach
the altar for communion. How can you touch his wounds? How
can you experience his resurrected nature, and the fullness of
life that he offers? The simplest way, I would suggest, is that I

ask for that. After all, I must ask myself why does he come to me in the first place? Surely it must be to effect his salvation, redemption, and resurrection within me. Your prayer would be a very deeply personal one, that may or may not require words. It certainly would be wrong of me to suggest what words you should use. The Lord looks at the heart, rather than listening to the words.

If the gospel begins with the invitation to 'Come and see', then it surely ends with the words 'Go and tell'. As a Christian, who has come and seen for myself, I have a responsibility to go and tell. There is a very important proviso included in this, however. You have no responsibility for whether the other person accepts or rejects what you have to say. The apostles told Thomas what they had experienced, but he was totally free to believe that or not. Jesus told his disciples that if people refused to believe them they were to shake the dust of that town from their shoes, and go ahead to the next town. Jesus alone is the Saviour. I am not asked to save anybody's soul. All I'm asked is to tell others that they are saved, or to point the Way of salvation to them. Like John the Baptist, I point to Jesus, and say, 'There is the Lamb of God ... follow him.'

There is a little postscript to today's gospel to which I have not referred. John tells us that his selection of events is just a sample of the many many other events in the life of Jesus. He presents these to us in the hope that they might lead us to believe in him, and thus to receive the abundant life that flows from such faith. The events in the life of Jesus are continuing right here, right now, as I speak. When the final chapter is written, how will our role in the events be seen?

Story
The village had its own wise old man, to whom people came for advice on everything. His wisdom and knowledge was greatly respected by all. A young man from the village was given the opportunity to go away to college. He obtained several degrees and, in his heart, he considered himself to be so much more intelligent and informed than the old man. One day he decided to show that he was so much cleverer, and he decided to embarrass the old man by setting up a situation where he would be proven wrong. He caught a little bird, which he held firmly concealed in his hand. He would ask the old man if the bird were alive or dead. If the man said the bird was dead, he would release his

grip and allow the bird to fly away. If he said the bird was alive he would squeeze it so tight that it would immediately die. He approached the old man, showed him the beak of the tiny bird sticking out from his fist, and asked him, 'Old man, tell me: is this bird dead or alive?' The old man looked at him, and very calmly replied: 'The answer to that question, my son, depends totally on you.'

As you look within your heart, is Jesus dead or alive?

THIRD SUNDAY OF EASTER

Gospel: Luke 24:13-35

Central Theme
Today's gospel is like a gospel within a gospel. The story has so much of what is central to the whole message that it is often used at great length to highlight the core teachings about Jesus and his mission. It is so rich in meaning that it is not possible to deal with it adequately within the confines of a single homily.

Parable
The example I am going to use limps a little, but it does contain a lot of what today's gospel is about. Hurling is one of Ireland's national sports. Offaly was one of the teams that were considered favourites to win the All-Ireland championship. They were beaten at the semi-final stage. Both team and supporters made their way back home bitterly disappointed. What they did not know was that they were actually going to win the All-Ireland final, and become the national champions! What was a dismal failure was dramatically turned around by the most unusual of circumstances. It seems the referee had made a mistake in calculating the time, and had brought the game to an end with four minutes of play remaining. The decision was made by the sporting authorities that the only solution was to order that the entire game be replayed. This time Offaly *did* win, and went on to win the final. Like the disciples on their way to Emmaus, the victory was already theirs, even if they didn't know that, or were prepared to believe and to accept that possibility.

Teaching
There is a very clear contrast here between how we see things and how God may look at the very same situation. Failure or impossibility are words that are not in the language of God. For these disciples it was all over. For the previous few years they were on to a good thing. Life had been exciting, and they were in the middle of it all. It is unfair to blame them, but they just didn't grasp a great deal of what Jesus had said. Nothing happened that Jesus had not already warned them would happen. We can empathise with them, because most of us find ourselves in turmoil or in difficulties, because we forgot or we failed to take seriously the promises of the Lord. He promised that he would

be there for us, that he would never abandon us in the storm, that he would walk every step of the road with us, and that he would bring us safely through the desert and the Red Sea of death into the Promised Land of the Father.

It is more than interesting that Jesus used scripture as his way of enlightening them. Scripture is the word of God. It contains the promises of the Lord, and it reveals the heart of God. The words of scripture are not at all like the words in our daily newspaper. The word of God is empowered as by an electric current, and it is inspired and shot through with the Spirit of God. With God's word comes the power to respond to that word, and to carry it out. Because of various factors, the study of scripture was not greatly emphasised or appreciated within Roman Catholic circles. It was seen as more of a Protestant thing, and it was something that ordinary lay persons could not be trusted with interpreting properly. That trend, thankfully, is now reversed, and this is a very important part of the whole process of church renewal.

It is very significant that they recognised Jesus in the breaking of bread. Breaking of bread among friends was a living symbol of friendship and belonging. What was special about the way Jesus broke the bread is something at which I can only hazard a guess. It must have been the whole atmosphere of self-giving that he invested in the act that revealed to them who he really was. There was a level of sincerity, of giving, of sharing, of sacredness that must have been unique to Jesus, and it must have been something they had experienced on previous occasions. This unique something touched their deepest hungers, and the nourishment provided was no longer just a physical thing. It was food that required them to open their hearts as well as their mouths to receive.

Response
Life is a journey that is made up of many journeys. It is a wonderful gift of God's Spirit to have the sense of being accompanied on the journey, of being led by the Spirit, of having a sense of direction in life. All of this is only possible through my own personal *yes,* and my willingness to be open to the accompanying presence of the Lord. 'You'll never walk alone when you walk with God' is a very important truth as well as just the words of a song.

The only real sin for the Christian is not to have hope.

Because of Jesus we already have the victory. We are a risen people, a people of power, a people to whom Jesus has entrusted full authority over all the power of the evil one. Once again, all of this makes no difference whatever, unless I personally take possession of what Jesus offers me and makes possible for me. Again and again and again I am called on to repeat my own personal *yes*. The only *yes* in my whole life the Lord is interested in is my *yes* of now. There is another hymn which is called 'Open my eyes, Lord, I want to see Jesus', and in it is the prayer that I might be able to touch him, and to give myself to him. Today's gospel is for today, and it is today that I need to become aware of his presence with me on the journey of life.

To what extent do I experience my presence at eucharist as being a genuine breaking of bread? As you know, familiarity can breathe contempt or, at best, can bring about a sense of routine where there is no great personal involvement, and where the actions and words can become lifeless and nothing more than superficial routine. (There is a story told about a bishop who dreamt he was preaching a sermon, and he woke up to discover that he was!) Like the disciples in today's gospel, the journey should bring me closer to revelation and to the experiential knowledge of the Lord. Life is a mystery to be lived rather than a problem to be solved. It is in the travelling of the journey that the revelation takes place. Life is a journey towards completion. We are a pilgrim people and, in the words of Paul, 'We have not here a lasting city, but we wait for one that is to come.'

Practical
Today's gospel is something that should be read and reflected on again and again. If there are enough Mass leaflets, you should hold on to the one you have, and bring it home with you. You can read it as often as you wish, but it will come alive for you only when you put yourself into the story; when you identify those areas of failure and discouragement in your life; when you face up to those areas and times of loneliness that you experience. There is a hole in the heart of each human being, and different people try different ways to fill that emptiness. Some try drugs, others try money, while others try to fill the emptiness by living it up. One of life's most costly lessons is to learn that these ways just don't work.

Supposing you were asked, by someone who knows nothing about Jesus or his message, what exactly the resurrection of

Jesus means to you in your own life, and on a personal basis. What would your answer be? It would be a great blessing to be able to give a ready and convincing reply to such a question. Peter writes that we 'should always have an explanation to give those who ask us the reason for the hope that we have.' Both in life, and in facing up to the reality of death, I can give witness to Christian hope. I know a person who will not read a newspaper or listen to a news bulletin before midday, because the news is usually bad news, and he doesn't want to begin his day by taking on board all the bad news from around the world. I'm not advising or advocating that anybody should do this, because it is precisely in the midst of all this that the Christian is expected to give witness to hope, to good news, and to victory.

What would it mean to you if I challenged you to take full and personal responsibility for what happens within you as you come here to Mass? How do you think you would do that? Where would you begin? In what way do you think your eyes could be opened, and that you would personally recognise the presence of the Lord? Jesus is a very personal God. He asks very personal questions. 'Who do you say that I am? Will you also go away? Do you love me more than these?' I cannot continue to presume that Jesus is present somewhere within the community if I myself do not personally experience that presence. Mary and Joseph made that mistake one time. They presumed that Jesus was somewhere in the crowd, and they were home before they realised that he had remained back in Jerusalem. It's so easy for any of us to take things for granted, but, when it comes to Jesus and his message, that possibility must be faced up to with sincerity, and with a sense of personal mission and commitment.

Story
There were two young boys who differed from each other in that one of them was a pessimist, and the other was an optimist. One of them was forever conscious of the things he did not have, and all the ways in which things might go wrong, while the other went to play every game of football, totally convinced that today his team was going to win. By way of experiment, they were put into separate rooms for an hour. The pessimist was put into a room that was filled with toys, and the optimist was put in a room that was filled with manure from the farmyard. When the hour was up they both were checked on. The pessimist was sitting on the floor in the midst of all the toys, and he was crying.

When asked why he was crying he replied that there was no drum. When the door of the other room was opened, the optimist was totally unconscious of being watched, because he was so busy. He had a small shovel and he was busily shovelling the manure to the other corner of the room. When asked why he was doing this he replied with total confidence, 'With all this manure, I'm convinced that there must be a pony here somewhere!'

FOURTH SUNDAY OF EASTER

Gospel: John 10:1-10

Central Theme
Today's gospel is a very simple explanation of what it means to have a personal relationship with the Lord, and to know him on a personal basis.

Parable
I had the privilege of accompanying pilgrimage groups to the Holy Land on several occasions. I have many memories, of course, and many of the gospel incidents and stories have never been the same, now that I can visualise the location and understand the references. One of the more obvious ones has to do with sheep and shepherds. We can easily forget that when Jesus spoke about sheep and shepherds, he was speaking to people who knew exactly what he meant, and who had everyday evidence of the truth he presented. I cannot pretend to understand the process that is part of what goes on within the mind of an animal. We often speak of horses and dogs as being very intelligent, and that is obviously so. We think of sheep as animals who are always following. If one sheep goes through a gap, all the others will follow. Being a shepherd in Jesus' time was a full-time commitment. The shepherd knew every single one of his sheep individually. There could be several flocks mixed together, but when one shepherd called out a word, his sheep, and only his, responded to the call, and followed him. A shepherd always led his sheep. Wherever he went, they followed. In it interesting to know that the goat-herd always had to drive the goats because, by nature, they were not followers. Jesus refers to the final judgement as a time when he will separate the sheep from the goats.

Teaching
Jesus came 'to do and to teach'. In other words, he did something, and then he taught his followers to do the same. He was a brilliant teacher, in that he brought his listeners from things they knew to things they may not have known. They were all familiar with shepherds and sheep. These were within sight as he spoke. He speaks of the sinner as a sheep that has lost its way, and he

declares his commitment as a shepherd as someone who is willing to die to protect the sheep entrusted to him.

We are all familiar with the extraordinary relationship that
can develop between a person and an animal. Watching sheep-
dog trials always fascinates me. The intelligence of the dog is
uncanny. The shepherd directs his instruction to both dog and
sheep. He must have a very real relationship of trust with both.
The trial is basically one of communication. The shepherd gives
the word, the dog picks up that word, and the sheep are guided
according to that word. The relationship is truly unique, even if
the shepherd and dog have never met these particular sheep before. There is a hierarchy established. The shepherd controls the
dog, and the dog controls the sheep. The dog is but an extension
of the shepherd, and it is the shepherd's will that predominates.

Part of being a shepherd is to accept that responsibility for
the life of the sheep is part of the job. In Jesus' day, it was not unknown for a shepherd to be killed by robbers or by wild animals
that tried to steal or to kill his sheep. The commitment of the
shepherd to his sheep was not unlike the commitment of a sol-
dier defending his country from invasion. He may have to pay
the supreme sacrifice in carrying out his duty.

Response

Jesus speaks of the true sheep. Like any other animal, a sheep
can become sick and, in such a condition, may be willing and
ready to follow anybody. The true sheep, however, is one who
has a sense of commitment, who follows with a sense of loyalty.
Jesus tells us that we are either for him or against him. Nobody
else can make that decision for me. Someone else spoke on my
behalf at baptism but, sooner or later, I have to make up my own
mind, make my own decision, and follow that decision. I never
think of God actually sending us anywhere when we die. Rather
will he eternalise whatever direction I choose to travel now. If I
choose to follow him now, and accept him as my Good Shepherd
then, of course, I will end up in his flock for all eternity.

Even within my own limited experience of farm life, I have
known children who had specific names for calves, lambs, or
kittens. When a new pup arrives in a house, the first thing that's
done is to give it a name. Jesus tells us that he calls his own
sheep by name, and each follows him. This call is what we mean
when we use the word 'vocation'. Unfortunately, for far too
long, this word was the preserve of priests and religious but,

thankfully, each one of us is becoming more and more aware of our own personal call or vocation. The greatest vocation possible for a human being is the call to be a follower of Jesus. How I choose to follow that call is of secondary importance, whether in the single, married, clerical, or religious life. My baptism is much more important than my ordination.

Jesus tells us that he came that we should have life and have it more abundantly. Another translation puts it, 'My purpose is to give life in all its fullness.' When Jesus speaks of the fullness of life, he is speaking about now. This is not something that is going to follow after death. I myself am more concerned about life before death, than life after death. The question is not 'Is there life after death?', but 'Is there much life before death?' Everybody dies, but not everybody lives. Some people settle for existing, and when they eventually die, you have to get a doctor to certify it, because there was never much life there in the first place! You could write on their tomb-stones 'Died at forty; buried at eighty'. To follow Jesus is to find salvation, to find green pastures, to experience the fullness of life.

Practical

It is hard to imagine Jesus being more practical that when he spoke about himself being a shepherd, and they being his sheep. The very concept of what that meant was in their bones, it was an everyday experience for them. He is speaking about a relationship here, and all of life is about relationships. We sometimes become confused by words like 'devotion', for example, devotion to Our Blessed Lady. Unless we replace that word with the word 'relationship', and proceed to develop a personal relationship with her, we will never get anywhere near making her a real part of our lives, or a key element in our salvation.

The quality of a person's life is not measured by the length of it but by the depth of it. Some people, who are young in years are quite old in their spirit and mentality. On the other hand, there are others, who have many years under their belts, but they are the life and soul of the party. It stands to reason that if a person is filled with the Spirit of God, such a person in 'on fire', as it were, and that fire is contagious. At one stage, Jesus refers to his disciples as his sheep and, at a later stage, he appoints them to be shepherds who, in turn, are to take care of his other sheep. To assume this responsibility, is to take on the life and mission of Jesus himself.

The world today is full of ways, means, paths, and methods, all guaranteeing to lead you to life and happiness. Many of these are quite effective and most helpful, and I do not, in any way, wish to rubbish them or belittle them. What I am saying, however, is that, as a Christian, I do have full access to the fullness of life, to the source of all healing, to Life itself. 'Jesus is the same yesterday, today, and always.' I can never become immune to his love, or to his healing. Part of the role of the shepherd was to seek and find the lost one, as well as take particular care of the sick one. To this day, it is normal to see a shepherd walking along, being followed by a few hundred sheep and, on his shoulders, he is carrying one which is lame, unwell, or unable to keep up with the movement of the others.

Story
Abraham Lincoln pointed to a sheep one time, and asked someone close by: 'Supposing that sheep's tail was a leg, how many legs would it have?' 'Five legs', came the instant reply. 'No, no', replied Lincoln, 'pretending that its tail is a leg doesn't make it a leg, so the sheep would still only have four legs!'

Is today's gospel fact or fantasy for you? Is it nothing more than just a nice idea, a pretty concept, or is Jesus really who and what he is, when he tells us that he is the Good Shepherd, and we – you and I – are actually members of his flock, who follow him, and for whom he takes total responsibility?

FIFTH SUNDAY OF EASTER

Gospel: John 14:1-12

Central Theme
We had wandered far away from the garden, and Jesus has come to bring us back. There is only one Way to get back to the Father, and Jesus is that Way.

Parable
I remember hearing a priest describe an experience he had in London some years ago. The whole city was fog-bound. He came out of a convent where he had celebrated eucharist, only to discover that he literally couldn't see his hand in the fog. The community house in which he lived was less than a mile away, but there was no way he could even attempt to walk down the road. Footpaths, lamp-posts, parked cars, etc., were all enveloped and invisible in the fog. He had decided to return to the convent when he heard footsteps approach from his left. He stood still, and listened. Suddenly, out of the fog came a man, walking briskly and confidently. He spoke to the man, who stopped and bade him goodnight and made to continue on his way. It was a few seconds before it dawned on the priest that the man was blind and was totally oblivious of the fog. The priest explained his predicament, and the man said, 'Oh, I know that place well. Here, take my arm, and I'll bring you there.' And that was how the priest got home. He knew the way alright, but he couldn't find it!

Teaching
Most of my generation grew up on promises. We were always making promises to God, renewing baptismal promises, making lenten and New Year promises, etc. It would, indeed, be a real conversion if we were to turn that around, and begin to give top priority to the promises that Jesus makes to us. Today's gospel contains a wonderful promise. He is going to prepare a place for us and then, one day, he will come to bring us with him so that, where he is, we also will be.

Jesus has two things to say about his promises that are very important. Firstly, he says that heaven and earth will pass away before his promises pass away. Secondly, he says that the sin of this world is unbelief in him; in other words, the problem is that people do not believe his promises. Elizabeth said to Mary, 'All these things happened to you because you believed that the promises of the Lord would be fulfilled.'

I should be very clear in my mind what my image of God is. Is he still the old man away up in the sky, with the long white beard, who is watching my every move, who is demanding that I meet his expectations of perfection, who is going to get me sooner or later; and, having spent my life trying to keep him happy, I'm still terrified to meet him when I die? Jesus puts the whole thing very simply. 'I never say anything unless the Father tells me to. If you hear me, you hear the Father, if you see me, you see the Father, if you do what I say, you are obeying the Father. The Father loves you as much as he loves me.' I'm afraid that Philip in today's gospel represents a lot of us. Sometimes the message can be so simple that we fail to see it. Genius is the ability to discern the obvious.

Response

Today's gospel certainly calls for a response. 'Don't be troubled. You trust God. Now trust in me.' That's a very simple and direct appeal. Faith and trust are both a response to love. I have to believe that the other person cares about me and my welfare before I can trust that person. That's really what Jesus is asking for in today's gospel. His whole life, and especially his death, was one great act of love.

Faith, of course, is a gift, and I don't believe that Jesus would ask me to believe in him or to trust him, without offering me the gift to be able to do so. This, primarily, is the work of the Spirit. The Holy Spirit completes the work that Jesus began. The first part of the programme of salvation is what Jesus did. The second and final part is the response that the Holy Spirit makes possible within our hearts. This response is what we call faith. It is in our hearts and, hopefully, it can also make its way down into our feet, when we have to step out in faith so often in life.

It would be funny if it weren't sad, when Jesus, in calling for faith, says, in effect, if everything else fails, then 'believe because of what you have seen me do'. He goes on to say that if we did that we, too, could do what he did, and even greater things. That is surely a major promise, and it is hardly much of an exaggeration to say that it is among the promises that may be least believed and acted on. Several times in the gospels, Jesus speaks of giving us power and authority. The truth of the matter, of course, is that he *offers* us everything, rather than *gives* us anything.

Practical
Over the years I have owned or used many kinds of cars. Some used diesel, some unleaded, and others leaded petrol. When it comes to understanding and responding to the promises of Jesus, the only Power that works is the Holy Spirit. It is the Spirit that translates for me what Jesus wants me to know. Words, in themselves, can be the weakest form of communication. At a graveside, for example, a hug or an arm around a shoulder can say much more than many words. If you and I join together now, for example, and ask the Holy Spirit to inspire us, and to reveal the core message of today's gospel, then, we can be sure, that will happen.

It can help us if we think of prayer as being more a question of listening than speaking. Prayer is not so much us speaking to God who does not hear, as God speaking to us who do not listen. There is a vast difference between, 'Speak, Lord, your servant is listening', and 'Listen, Lord, your servant is speaking.' It is almost as if Jesus is annoyed with Philip for not listening. No matter how many times, or in how many ways, Jesus gave the message, Philip still hadn't grasped it. I'm sure we can all identify with Philip. I suggest, however, that we have to do more than that. We have to learn to be still, to listen, and to be with Jesus for periods of time. What I really mean is that we have to pray. I hesitate to define what I mean by this, because it can be a very personal thing. I can have a heart that prays all the time while, in actual fact, I may not be saying many prayers. There is a great difference between praying and saying prayers. I could teach a parrot to say a prayer, but I could never teach a parrot to pray.

Jesus compares faith to a grain of mustard seed. For those of us not familiar with the significance of that, it is as tiny as a single grain of sand. I remember collecting a few grains of mustard seed one time (in the Garden of Gethsemane), and I had to use a strip of cellotape to ensure that they didn't slip from the pages of my Bible. On the other hand, I looked around at the actual mustard trees around me, and it was awesome to think that each of them began from something so tiny. The very fact that you are listening to me now (or the fact that you are reading these words) is a very clear indicator that that grain of faith is within you. When a healthy baby is born, he/she already has everything it takes to walk, talk, swim, etc., but it is going to take years of daily practice before those skills are acquired. Faith must be exercised, or it will never grow. It is a great tragedy when we come across a baby that hasn't grown or developed, and who still, after several years, is living in the body and with the mind of someone a few months old.

Story
There is a story told of a tombstone in the cemetery, which bore the inscription: 'Remember, stranger, as you pass by, as you are now, so once was I. As I am now, so you shall be; so prepare yourself to follow me.' To which some wit with a piece of chalk added the words, 'To follow you I'm quite content. But how do I know which way you went?' Jesus calls himself *The Way*, rather than just one of the ways. The early Christians were known as followers of *The Way*. It is central to the Christian message that, because of Jesus, I have a very clear and definite direction in my life. Jesus is more than a signpost. A signpost points to a place, but it doesn't oblige you to travel down that road. A 'stop' sign doesn't lean out and stop you. Sometimes, with some form of perverted humour, we come across a signpost down the country that has been deliberately turned around, to send someone in the wrong direction. Those of us brought up in the country were very familiar with well-worn paths through forests, or across fields. The instinct of the migrant bird that can make its way, with certainty, to some definite spot several thousand miles away, is something that is completely beyond my comprehension. Thank God, as a Christian, I have a very clear and definite Way and Path to follow, and I know that if I follow that Way, it will bring me home.

SIXTH SUNDAY OF EASTER

Gospel: John 14:15-21

Central Theme
Today's gospel is a very good example of Jesus looking me
straight in the eye, as he holds both my hands, and in very simple and straight language, makes some wonderful promises to
me.

Parable
I have many memories of boarding school. One of the less happy
ones was when we went to the gym. I believe now that I was
nervous by nature, and I dreaded the exercises that involved
vaulting over the 'horse', as we called it. The teacher would
stand by to catch you if you got it wrong. Which was all very
well, except for one problem. He had a habit of constantly giving
instructions to all and sundry, and when I was in the process of
vaulting, he was quite capable of turning to answer a question
from someone, and was just not there when you got it wrong,
and came crashing down on the other side. The fact was that I
just did not trust him to be there for me, and this was a source of
constant anxiety for me. He would get annoyed at my hesitancy
to run forward, while I was watching his every move, in the
hope that I had his attention. I had absolutely no sense of having
a 'safety net' at the other side, and I was paralysed with fear. I
often recall those times when I reflect on the need people have to
have someone to trust, to have someone on whom they can rely,
of someone who will be there for them when needed. This particular dimension of my relationship with Jesus is very very
important to me.

Teaching
I spoke on Sunday last about how my generation grew up on
promises. The problem was that it was we who were making the
promises. It was part of every New Year, lent, parish mission, retreat, etc. There was no end to the list of promises I made to God
over my lifetime! I made promises in thunder-storms, or when a
plane was being tossed about, as it passed through turbulence. I
must confess that my track record in keeping the promises was
not too good, because I always seemed to be making many of the
very same promises I had made before! Call it maturity, common

sense, or simply quiet desperation, but, in recent years, I have stopped making promises. I have now turned my attention to the promises Jesus makes to me, and that has had a profound effect on my life.

In today's gospel, Jesus promises to send the Spirit, and he also promises that he will never abandon us, or desert us in the storm. 'Heaven and earth will pass away before my word passes away.' Elizabeth said to Mary, 'All these things happened to you, because you believed that the promises of the Lord would be fulfilled.' Later on, as the apostles waited with Mary in the Upper Room, I can easily imagine she could have had a real problem getting them to stay there. It would not have been easy to get Peter to sit around for nine days, while there was nothing happening. The Spirit, of course, did come, because Jesus had promised that he would send the Spirit. It is possible that Mary was the only person in that room who was certain that the Spirit would come.

Original sin was one of disobedience. Therefore, the whole purpose of Jesus' mission was to do the will of the Father in heaven. He considered obedience as a very real way of loving. In today's gospel he goes so far as to say that if we love him, we will obey him. His instructions are very clear and uniquely simple. He speaks of forgiving others, of not condemning, of having compassion, and of trying to love others as he loves us. He gives us a very simple and clear programme for living, and part of his promises is that this programme will work. All we have to do is to trust him, and to obey him.

Response
Most of us were reared to achieve something. Good results in school were praised, medals won in dancing or singing competitions were displayed with pride. All of this is only right. It can, however, present certain and definite problems when transferred over into the spiritual field. Only God can do a God-thing. Jesus promises the Spirit, but it is only that same Spirit that can enable us to be open to that truth, and to avail of that offer. In other words, God makes the offer and he supplies the grace to be able to accept and avail of the offer. Even when Jesus asks us to obey him, he knows that, of ourselves, we don't have what it takes to do that. There is some sort of basic rebelliousness within us that often expresses itself as self-will run riot. What I am saying here, quite simply, is that the whole thing, from beginning to end, is total and absolute free gift.

If I am to accept, believe, and act on the promises of the Lord, it is evident, then, that I should know what those promises are. The same applies to the whole question of obedience. If I am to obey him, I should be in no doubt about what he wants me to do, or how he wants me to live. I don't agree that this is simply a question of being taught, or of education *per se*. I suggest it has much more to do with my own openness and willingness to obey. I personally believe that the Spirit will be more than willing to enlighten me if I have the goodwill and the open disposition that wants to know, to believe, and to obey. If simply knowing what Jesus says were sufficient, then, of course, we could say that Satan knows every single word that Jesus has said. That, however, is not transferred into anything else but a determined and sustained attempt to thwart, twist, and confuse every word that is spoken, to steal that word from the hearts of the hearers, and to bully them into following him down the road of disobedience.

Jesus promises to reveal himself to each of those who obey him. His whole purpose was to do the will of the Father and, by joining him in that attitude of obedience, we are assuming the whole ethos and life of the Trinity. The road back to the garden is one of obedience. It is not an easy road; because of original sin, obedience doesn't come naturally to us. It involves the cross, which is not heavy, but rather it is made up of the splinters of everyday living. Obedience is about following Jesus, about walking in his path. He is the Way and it is only by following him that we can make our way back to the garden.

Practical

In today's gospel, Jesus is near the completion of his work. He will soon be leaving us, and then the Spirit will come to complete the work which he began. It is no exaggeration to say that the most practical response I can make to today's gospel is to get my own modern-day translation of the gospels, put them in my pocket and, during some of those many empty idle moments we all have in our days, to take out that booklet, read a passage or two, put away the book, and reflect on what I have just read. If I don't have any of those idle moments, then I am too busy, and I'm so preoccupied with the urgent that I am neglecting the important.

In recent years there is no scarcity of Prayer Groups, Bible Study Groups, etc. I have long ago come to the conclusion that any one of us could benefit enormously by becoming part of one such group. I no longer think of a parish as being a community any more. The geographic spread is so wide. A parish is a community of communities and, in most parishes, there is not a night of the week when there isn't a meeting of some smaller Christian group, ranging from Vincent to Paul, to the Legion of Mary, to a Charismatic Prayer Group. I strongly advise each one of you to consider becoming a member of some such small group. Some of these groups, of course, through lack of anointed leaders, or through misdirected zeal, have broken away from the church, and have become 'house churches', or some other sorts of private entities. This is not always bad, but experience has clearly shown that, when such groups were not of God, they lasted for a while, and eventually went their separate ways.

Prayer is something that I always hesitate to define. It is such a personal thing, because it involves the action of God's Spirit within your heart. All I will say, however, is that, without prayer, all of what I'm talking about today will never come to anything. We are all too familiar with photos of young and old that look like moving skeletons, in the famine-stricken parts of the world. Without prayer, I am completely malnourished, and I don't have the spiritual energy to respond to any word that comes from God. 'Not on bread alone does man/woman live, but on every word that comes from the mouth of God.' How, when, or where you pray is entirely up to you, but you should never have any doubt whatever about the *why* you pray.

Story
The priest was new in the parish, so he set out to get to know his parishioners. He spent several hours a day visiting people in their homes, sharing a cup of tea and a chat with them. One day he was invited to a house for dinner. The meal was excellent, and the sense of hospitality was quite genuine. There was one thing that distracted him during most of the afternoon, and he decided to ask about it. All evening he heard the sound of running water. This bothered him, because he was afraid that a tap had been left on, and there was damage being done to some part of the house. When he drew attention to this, his hosts smiled, and explained the situation to him. When they decided to build their house many years ago, they discovered there was a spring (water) right in the centre of the building site. After some consideration, they decided what to do. They would develop the

spring as a natural fountain, and build their house around it. Thus, at all times, they had a sense of a gurgling spring of fresh life-giving water right in the middle of their house.

The priest reflected on this, and used it for several sermons about the idea of having Jesus and his Spirit at the centre of our lives, and how necessary it is for us to be aware of the presence of that fountain of living water within.

ASCENSION OF THE LORD

Gospel: Mt 28:16-20

Central Theme
Today's gospel is the very last two paragraphs of St Matthew's gospel. It makes no direct reference to the ascension, but it gives us some of the final instructions he gave his disciples before he took his leave of them.

Parable
I was speaking to somebody the other day who was very troubled over making a will. She had grown up in those times when making a will, or receiving what were called 'The Last Sacraments' were things that you put off until the very last moment. There was something very ominous about it. Indeed some of us may know families that were left completely divided because someone hadn't made a will. In today's gospel, Jesus has little to say, but he is very definite about what he has to say. This is in sharp contrast to the fact that, even at this last minute, some of his disciples still doubted.

Teaching
The first thing about the disciples is that at least they did what he told them to do. He asked them to meet him on the mountain, and they did that. Like any gathering of human beings, each had his own emotions. Some of them worshipped him, while some of them still doubted. Jesus didn't seem to have any great problem with that, because he knew that, when the Spirit came, all of those doubts would be ended. It would seem, indeed, that he was in a hurry to take his leave of them, so that the second part of his plan of salvation could get underway.

Notice that Jesus begins his few words by telling them that *he*, not they, have full authority in heaven and on earth. In an earlier account in Luke's gospel, he says, 'I have given you full authority over all the power of the evil one.' The full authority over everything, however, is something that he reserves to himself. Those who go in his name, do so with his full authority. The authority goes with the mission. That is why he adds, 'Go, therefore …'; in other words, because I have the authority, you can go wherever I send you. My power, my promises, and my Spirit will go with you, and will see you through. After telling them what to do, he concludes with the very clear and definite promise, 'And be sure of this: I am with you always, even to the end of the age.'

The mission of the apostles was a simple one. It was to teach others all that he had taught them. Just as he asked his disciples to obey him, they were to ask that others should obey his directions and instructions also. This is like when a doctor puts you on a course of antibiotics. The original sin was a lie. The Spirit is a spirit of truth. One of the rules connected with taking antibiotics is that it is essential to complete the course. Some people begin to feel well after a few days, and they discontinue taking the medicine and, of course, their condition gets worse. The programme of redemption and salvation must continue from generation to generation, until the end of time. With all the changes in the church and in society, the two things that have not changed are Jesus himself, and every word of his message. The Message and the Messenger have never, and never will change. People who are bothered about changes in the church today should be reminded that the only two things that matter have not changed at all.

Response

I am a follower of Jesus. I am not claiming that as some great merit, but with a sense of humble gratitude that he should have called me and, in my own way, I have chosen to answer that call. Some of the apostles worshipped him, and some of them still doubted. I can easily identify with both. Faith is always accompanied by doubt. If there never was a doubt, there would not be real faith. How many of us have ever wondered if the whole thing is a joke, and there is no reality to all those things we believe in, or hope for? I think most of us would have to admit to having those moments from time to time. There is great merit, however, in 'showing up', just as the apostles did in today's gospel. It may be all I can muster at a particular moment. It is like an alcoholic attending AA meetings. It is so difficult to convince such a one to grasp the following concept, and to hold on to it for dear life : 'Keep going to the meetings; keep showing up, day after day, and don't leave 'til the miracle happens.' For such people, the miracle always happens.

Most of us are in a situation in life that is quite unique to ourselves. The one thing we have in common, as Christians, is that each of us is offered a share in the power and authority of Jesus.

You could be in a wheelchair and be at peace, while someone else could be filled with zeal and enthusiasm as they bathe and wash the lepers. It is the same power, the same Spirit, the same mission. Jesus will never place me where his power, his Spirit, and his promises will not be there to see me through. The safest place for me to be in the whole world is to be wherever God wants me to be. Jesus was most powerful when he was nailed to a cross, and could do nothing, because that was where the Father wanted him to be.

The apostles were instructed to teach others all they had heard from him. We call this 'evangelising', or spreading the good news. Not everyone is called to be an evangelist. Paul tells us that some are called to teach, others to preach ; some are called to prophecy, others are called to work miracles. All Christians, however, are called to witness. Witnessing to the teaching of Jesus is done in silence, through the very way I live my life. I could be deaf and dumb and still proclaim the gospel. 'You write a new page of the gospel each day, through the things that you do, and the words that you say. People will read what you write, whether faithful or true. What is the gospel according to you?' Even sharing with another something you heard here today that you find helpful is to give witness. It must seem obvious to anyone who wishes to see, that the evidence of someone who is trying to live the sort of life that Jesus has taught us to live, must be a powerful witness, indeed. Some of the greatest witnesses to the gospel that I have ever known have not been the Mother Teresas of this world. They have been people like my own mother, or people I visited in hospital, or individuals I have known who work with the Simon Community, or who organise and care for those on the annual Pilgrimage for Disabled Children in Lourdes. These are the people who always bring me back to the basic teachings of Jesus.

Practical
One very real way of praying would be to take time out to have a look at my life, and the exact and actual situations within that life. Is there room, or am I conscious of a need for the authority of Jesus to be effective there? Even if my life is off the tracks, that, in itself, qualifies me even more for the power of his authority, and the evidence of his healing and forgiving power.

There would never be a war if somebody somewhere would only say, 'I'm sorry, I am wrong.' It can be very difficult, indeed impossible, for some people to admit that they are wrong. This is what Jesus is referring to when he speaks of obeying him. He himself had come 'to do and to teach' so, even on the cross, he was praying for those who were killing him. A characteristic of being a follower of Jesus is my willingness to forgive. This is not always easy. Even when someone has hurt me deeply, all I may be able to do is to be willing to forgive, and leave the rest to the Lord.

There seems to be a lot of loneliness and depression around today, or it may be that we are now more conscious or aware of it. There is a great difference between being alone and being lonely. I could be in the midst of a crowd, and be very lonely. On the other hand, it is said that I am never less alone than when alone. This applies especially to those who take the final words of today's gospel seriously, 'I am with you always'. Like a young mother, nursing her baby who is sound asleep, communication doesn't need words. If I am open to the presence and reality of the Lord in my life, then be sure that he will respond to that, and I will live with a conscious awareness of his presence.

Story
I can personally vouch for the truth of this story, which happened only yesterday. A young man in his mid-twenties was being introduced to his natural mother for the first time. Both were quite nervous, but the meeting went well. The mother told her son the details of her early life, and how, when she discovered that, as a teenager, she was pregnant, there was no way she could or would be allowed keep the baby. She had nothing to give the baby as she handed him over for adoption. She had a brown scapular of her own, which she took off, and placed it on the child. As she told her son this story, twenty-five years later, he reached under his shirt and produced the scapular. He had not known the story, but he had often wondered why his adopted mother always insisted on him wearing the scapular, and taking good care of it. Every time it broke, she repaired it with great care.

Just as the scapular was some sort of bond, so it is with the promises of Jesus as he leaves us to return to the Father.

SEVENTH SUNDAY OF EASTER

Gospel: John 17:1-11

Central Theme
Today's gospel is a jewel. What a privilege it is for us to eaves-drop on Jesus as he is deep in conversation with his Father. There is no better way to know the heart of a person than to be privy to what that person says to God in prayer.

Parable
Some years ago there was a very popular presenter of a child-ren's programme on BBC radio. He had built up quite a reput-ation for himself in the ways in which he could communicate with children, and how he had built up a large circle of faithful young friends, when his programme began each Saturday morning. One day, however, the whole thing blew up in his face, and thousands of young listeners were upset and hurt. He finished his programme in the usual fashion; all went well, and he was quite happy with himself. Another week over, and all went well. The sound engineer made a mistake and did not close down the transmission. Not knowing he was still on the public airways, the presenter shouted across to someone in the studio, remarking his utter distaste for the many spoiled brats he was supposed to entertain, and he followed this with several rude remarks about the whole lot of them. The man was sacked im-mediately, and his thousands of fans were deeply hurt and dis-illusioned. Despite everything that had happened up till then, those final remarks showed exactly just what kind of man he was, and what he really thought. When I listen to Jesus speaking to his Father in today's gospel, I am far from disillusioned.

Teaching
'And this is the way to have eternal life – to know you, the only true God, and Jesus Christ whom you have sent to earth.' That's a powerful sentence. How can I actually come to know God? The simplest way of all is to ask the Holy Spirit to enlighten my mind, and to bring me into a personal relationship with God. This may sound simplistic, but the ordinary word for that is prayer. I am not talking about, or thinking about saying prayers. I am talking about getting in touch with that hunger within the heart, that is part of every human being. St Augustine said, 'You

have made us for yourself, O Lord, and our hearts can never be at peace until they rest in you.'

Jesus has two things to say about his apostles. Firstly, he says that he has told them all about the Father, and he has told them all the Father told him to tell them. He also says that they accepted what he said, and that they know that Jesus has come from the Father, and that it was the Father who sent him. As I listen to these words, I cannot help remembering that, in spite of that, these are the very people who will, later on, deny him, betray him, and desert him. This is quite a comment on our human weakness.

The second thing that Jesus says about his apostles is that he sincerely prays for them. He asks his Father to 'keep them, and care for them ... so that they may be united just as we are.' Unity and love is at the heart of the Christian vocation. The work of the Spirit is to unite the members into the one Body of Christ. Once again, I think of this prayer against the background of all the divisions, and all of the conflicts that have taken place among those who claim to be followers of Jesus. It all seems such a contradiction. And yet, God's respect for our freewill is paramount. He will never ever coerce or force us to do anything. He will tell us what to do, and he will offer us the grace to do that. The rest is up to us. It is very obviously his sincere desire that we should live in unity with each other. He cannot compel us to do this, but he does speak, in another part of the gospel, of his wish that there should be one flock and one shepherd.

Response

To fully grasp the meaning of today's gospel, it is important that we remember the context. The words are spoken by Jesus to his Father. We cannot tell how they came to be written down. Obviously, the prayer was said out loud. We have several instances of Jesus being filled with the Spirit, and exclaiming a prayer of thanks to the Father. On many occasions we are told that he went off on his own up the mountain, or to a lonely place, where he spent the night in prayer. It is very significant that the apostles saw Jesus raise the dead, calm the storm, and heal the leper; but, of all the things they witnessed, their one request was, 'Lord, teach us to pray'.

It must be obvious that Jesus meant every word he said. Therefore, his message, and those to whom he entrusted that message, figured largely in his concerns. He gave them the message, they accepted it, and they knew from where it came. He prays that they be kept safe because, no doubt, Satan will do all within his power to thwart their every attempt to proclaim that message. As a Christian, as one of those who believes his message, and who believes that the Father sent him for such as me, I too am being prayed for in this prayer. Jesus actually includes 'all those you have given me'. You may not often think of Jesus actually praying for you. He speaks about asking the Father in his name. In other words, he is a go-between God, and I can pray in his name, and pray with his power and authority. It must be obvious then that prayer is more of what Jesus and his Spirit does in and through me, than anything I myself might do.

I cannot reflect on today's gospel and skirt around the issue of oneness, the need for unity. I can easily cop-out here, and see this as something for the churches to do. Unity embraces many things and many people. It begins within my own brokenness, and my ability and willingness to make friends with my own shadow, with that darker side of self that riddles me with guilt from time to time. It moves out from me to those closest to me. If I have peace within my own heart, it is so much easier to be a peacemaker in the lives of others. Jesus said, 'Happy are the peacemakers', not 'Happy are they who have peace.' 'Let there be peace on earth, and let it begin with me.' There is a Chinese proverb that says, 'If each before his own door swept, the whole village would be clean.'

Practical
Sunday after Sunday, when I think of something practical to do in response to the gospel of the day, I always find myself coming up with this one: buy a copy of the gospels, carry it on your person, and become familiar with it. I'm sure you'll admit, after all, that if the message is as important as we say it is, then, of course, we should do everything within our power to familiarise ourselves with it.

When you reflect on the gospel, you must surely have to face the question: can I claim that I really do know God, and Jesus Christ whom he has sent? How do you get to know anybody? One of the surest ways, of course, is to spend time with that person, to listen to that person, and to try to figure out how that person thinks and acts. This is only the beginning. When it comes to Jesus, there is, of course, the action of his Spirit, one of whose tasks it is to reveal Jesus to me. You cannot get to know someone

by listening to someone else talking about him. You have to talk
to him yourself, and listen to him as he speaks to you. Jesus said,
'No one knows the Father except the Son, and those to whom the
Son chooses to reveal him.' A very simple prayer is to ask Jesus
to reveal the Father to me.

Actually listening in when Jesus is praying to his Father is a
very simple and practical lesson on how to pray. I would put
that far in advance of all the books ever written on prayer. There
is a directness, a clear and definite statement of how he feels,
what he thinks, what his concerns and hopes are, and his deep
awareness of having the Father's full attention. When you speak
from the heart you speak to the heart. Prayer is really very simple when it comes from the heart, and when I mean what I say.

Story

This young lad was reared by the sea, and he spent most of his
spare time paddling around in boats, or mingling with the
fishermen at the pier. One day he found a piece of timber, and he
got an inspiration. He got a sharp knife and began to carve a toy
boat. His hands and his mind worked in conjunction, and he
found he was able to create something that he could visualise in
his mind. He spent a lot of time and patience and, eventually the
boat was completed. It was not finished yet, however. He decided to paint it his favourite colours, and to give it sails. He se-
lected a name for it, which he painted on both sides. It was a
thing of beauty, and a joy to behold.

It would not be a boat, however, if it never entered water, so
one day he brought it down to the pier, and placed it gently in
the water. He was filled with pride and joy at the sight of it, as it
bobbed up and down in the water. It was some time before he
realised what was happening. Because he had given it sails (free
will?), it came under the influence of a firm breeze, and it soon
had moved beyond his reach. Without thinking, he called it, because he had given it a name. Slowly but surely the boat moved
out to sea, and all the boy could do was look on helplessly. He
stood there for ages, hoping for a miracle but eventually he gave
up, and returned home with a heavy heart.

His mind was preoccupied with the boat for the next few
days, and the very thought of it was piercing his heart. He was
wandering around town one day and, as he was passing the
front window of a toy-shop, his heart rose in his throat. There in
the front of the window was his boat! He ran it to claim it, but

the shop-keeper left him in no doubt that the boat was his now, and, if the boy wanted it, he would have to buy it, like any other item in the shop. The boy was deeply troubled, and he ran home to tell his dad. The father listened with great attention, and then he spoke to the boy calmly. 'You now have a choice. If you want the boat, you will just have to pay for it, because legally it belongs to the shopkeeper, who bought it from one of the fishermen.' 'How much will it cost me?' asked the boy. 'I don't know,' said his dad, 'but I do know that if you want it badly enough you will be prepared to pay everything you have to buy it.'

The boy emptied every savings box he had, gathered every penny he could find, put the lot in a paper bag, and ran down to the shop. He placed the bag on the counter, and asked for the boat. The shopkeeper had a quick check on the money, and he then handed over the boat. The boy rubbed it, kissed it, and clutched it with both hands, as he ran all the way home to his dad. 'Ah, I see you got the boat. It's yours now, isn't it?' 'Yes, it is,' said the boy excitedly, 'It's mine now, and it's mine twice over. I made it and when I lost it, I gave everything I have to get it back. I won't let it go this time.'

The boy is Jesus, and you are the boat; he created you, and when you were lost he gave all he had to buy you back, so you are his now, you are his twice over.

PENTECOST SUNDAY

Gospel: John 14:15-16, 23-26

Central Theme
Today's gospel ties in the gift of the Spirit with obedience to Jesus. Original sin was one of disobedience, so the Spirit will be the antidote to that, in our salvation and redemption.

Parable
Obedience comes from the Latin word *obedientia,* which literally means to hold one's ear against. It is a special form of listening, like the native Indian holding his ear to the ground, or someone holding a bugging device to his ear, as he listens into a conversation from some distance.

Teaching
The kind of listening that is spoken of today is, in itself, a gift of the Spirit. The Spirit will remind us, will teach us, will inspire us. The Spirit will lead us, and guide our feet into the way of peace.

In asking for our obedience, Jesus does so for our good. There is always a little voice whispering within. Sometimes it's the human voice, sometimes the whisper of the evil one, and sometimes it is the voice of the Spirit of God. It is important to be able to discern the voices. When I have an open and generous heart, it is so much easier to recognise the voice of God's Spirit. If my attitude is right, and if I really want to hear that voice, then I can be sure that I will hear it. 'There are none so deaf as those who don't want to hear.' When Pilate asked Jesus, 'What is truth?' we are told that he walked away, and didn't wait for the answer.

Jesus places the Father fairly and squarely in the midst of today's gospel. It was the Father who sent him, and it is the Father who will send the Spirit. If we listen to the message, then the Trinity, Father, Son, and Spirit will come and make their home within us. What an extraordinary promise!

Response
My generation grew up on promises. We were always making promises to God … New Year's Day, Ash Wednesday, every retreat, etc. It is actually part of the conversion process when I stop making promises, and begin to listen to the promises of Jesus. There is not one 'maybe' or 'might' in all his promises. 'Heaven

and earth will pass away before my word passes away.'
Elizabeth said to Mary, 'All these things happened to you because you believed that the promises of the Lord would be fulfilled.' Today's gospel contains a very clear and central promise.
Jesus showed clearly that he had full authority over all the
power of the evil one. He gave constant witness to the fact that
he could subdue Satan, and rout him. Because I can be, and often
am, selfish or disobedient, it would be untrue to always put the
blame on Satan. Eve tried that one when she said that it was the
devil made her do it! Satan does, however, rejoice, and he con-
nives in our disobedience. Jesus gives me the authority he himself
exerted, and, if I wish to remain obedient to Jesus, I must get into
the habit of exercising that authority.

Quite often our failures come out of forgetfulness, or a failure
to be alert. 'Watch and pray', says Jesus. It is the work of the
Spirit to remind us, to bring to our minds the teaching and
promises of Jesus. The freedom of the Spirit to act in us is determined by the freedom we permit. The limits to the effectiveness
of the Spirit in our lives are the ones we set. We must not chain
the Spirit but, as Paul says, we should 'learn to live and to walk
in the Spirit'. Real prayer, when I shut up and listen to God, is
when the Spirit can speak most clearly to me. Real prayer is
'Speak, Lord, your servant is listening', and not 'Listen, Lord,
your servant is speaking.'

Practical
People of my generation are familiar with what we called 'examination of conscience'. It would be good to take a few moments
out to reflect on obedience, and how we consider ourselves in
that area, in relation to Jesus. We very easily could fail to identify
much of our behaviour as actually being disobedience. I know
what Jesus tells me to do. He is very clear in his teaching. If I
know, and do not do, then I am being deliberately disobedient.
Jesus equates this obedience with our expression of love for him.

Jesus tells us that the Spirit will never leave us. Just think
about that for a moment. I'm sure there are many times when
you feel very much alone, afraid, or confused. What a wonderful
thing it would be if we remembered these words of Jesus at such
times. Please think about this today. Again and again, in these
reflections, I repeat that a life without reflection is not worth
living. You have something very important, and really vital, to
reflect on here. Please take this with you into the day …

One of the outcomes of really taking today's gospel to heart, is that it should stimulate prayer. It is not for me to suggest what form that prayer should take. I think, if I listen attentively to what Jesus says, a prayer would come to my heart, and to my lips immediately. I don't speak of long prayers here. Rather do I think of short prayers from the heart; prayers expressing my longing for the Spirit, my willingness to be filled with the Spirit, to be led into obedience, etc.

Story

It is vital to remember that, of myself, I don't have what it takes to be a Christian. That is a gift of the Spirit. 'I will take out your hearts of stone, and give you hearts of flesh.' There was a crow one time that looked in very bad shape indeed. His friends were very worried about him as he lost weight, became withdrawn and depressed, and seemed to be zapped of all energy or enthusiasm for life. Some of his friends approached him one day, but he was very reluctant to talk to them about what was bothering him. After some persuasion, he opened up, and told them his problem. 'I had very few ambitions in life and, as my life enters its final stage, I realise I have accomplished very little of what I set out to achieve.' When pressed by the others, he gave one example of his ambitions. 'I always wanted to make a record.' When asked what he wanted to record, he replied 'Of me singing!' The other crows made the fatal mistake of smiling, something that deeply hurt and upset the poor crow. He became very emotional, as he screamed, 'Why couldn't I sing? Did you ever hear a blackbird singing? Well, I'm bigger than a blackbird, and I'm the same colour, so why couldn't I sing like a blackbird? If you knew the trouble I've gone to, to be able to sing like a blackbird. I went to the health-shop. I got whole-grain, vivioptol, Royal Jelly, Ballygowan, the whole sheebang. After all that I went up on a tree, opened my mouth, and all that came out was 'Caw! Caw!' Then I got a C-90 tape, and I went up among the blackbirds, and filled the full tape of blackbird song. I got a walkman (brain bypass?) and, as I flew around each day, or rested during the night, I had my headphones on, convinced that in some subliminal way I could learn to sing like a blackbird. Once again, though, when I went up on a tree, and opened my mouth, all that came out was 'Caw' Caw!' I then got sheet music, and went for voice-training, spending a lot of time, money, and energy in the effort. Once again, all I could produce by way of music was 'Caw! Caw! And now you're asking me why I'm depressed!'

The other crows were silent, not knowing what to say, as they withdrew, one by one.

Several months passed, when lo and behold, didn't the very same crows bump into the very same crow in the very same place! There was something extraordinarily different about him now, though. He seemed totally transformed, full of life, energy, and enthusiasm. When they asked what happened, he poured out the good news. 'After I met you the last time, I picked up a newspaper, and I read about a surgeon in South Africa, called Christian Bernard, who did transplants. The idea struck me like a thunderbolt. A transplant! That's what I needed. For the first time in my life, I realised that I could never sing like a blackbird if I didn't have the voice-box of a blackbird. I flew home, got on the phone, and made contact with Christian Bernard. 'I see here in the papers that you do transplants. What kind of transplants do you do?' 'Well, I do hearts, and lungs, and livers.' 'Did you ever do a voice-box?' 'No, actually, but it shouldn't be any more difficult than a heart.' 'If I went out there would you do a voice-box?' 'Yes, I could certainly attempt to. Come on out, and we'll see what can be done'.

I flew out to South Africa, and we kept in touch with the local hospitals and mortuaries, waiting for a blackbird to 'keel over', especially one with a donor-card. Finally, we got what we wanted and, at long last, I lay back and let someone else take over; someone who could do for me what I never could do for myself. I got the voice-box of a blackbird. When I had recovered, I flew up on a tree, and began practising with my new voice-box and, in no time at all, I was singing like a blackbird. And now, I discover that I just cannot sing any other way. And do you know what gives me added satisfaction? I know now that the whole-grain, the vivioptool, the Royal Jelly, the Ballygowan, the C-90 tape, and the sheet-music with the voice-training ... not one of those things, not one penny, or not one minute was wasted. Why I say that is, if I hadn't tried all those things, I wouldn't be totally convinced that they just didn't work. It was worth it all to learn such an important lesson.'

When I met Gordon Wilson, who touched the hearts of so many by his public forgiveness of those responsible for the death of his daughter in an explosion in Enniskillen, I thought of him as someone who had a transplant. I honestly believe that, if everybody belonging to him was killed, he would still forgive, because he couldn't sing any other way ...

TRINITY SUNDAY

Gospel: John 3:16-18

Central Theme
In his own words, Jesus tells us very simply and very directly why he came, why the Father sent him, and the results accruing to those who accept the truth of what he says.

Parable
The Trinity, of course, is pure mystery, and there is no way, through use of a three-leafed shamrock, or any other sign or symbol, that I can hope to explain a mystery; and this one, in particular. However, some of the following ideas may help. I have a glass of water, a glass filled with ice cubes, and a third glass filled with snow. In actual fact, each glass contains water in some different form or condition. God is spoken of as 'Father', because he is the source of life. He reaches out two arms of love to embrace and draw his children to himself. The first arm is Jesus. Jesus did what he was sent to do, and then he returned to the Father. The Father then sent the Spirit (the second arm), to complete the work begun by Jesus. Jesus paid the price to free us from bondage and slavery, and the Spirit leads us out into freedom from that same bondage and slavery. 'The Spirit will lead you into truth, and the truth will set you free.' It can help to think of the Trinity in terms of being embraced by God. After all, it is our eternal destiny to share in the life of the Trinity for all eternity.

Teaching
Thomas Aquinas tells us that when we speak of God there is only one thing we can be sure of: that we're wrong! No matter what we say about him, he is so much more than that. The only way we can get a 'handle' on God, if I may use that expression, is to quote John's comment that 'God is love'. Even though he is so much more than that, at least we know, when we say that, we are telling the truth. In recent years, it has become a feature of an Irish international soccer match to see someone in the crowd holding up a placard with 'John3:16' written on it. Those are the opening words of today's gospel: 'For God so loved the world that he gave his only Son, so that everyone who believes in him will not perish, but will have eternal life.' I'm not too sure that

111

the placard will change the hearts of those who see it but, at least, it presents us with the core of the gospel message, and, who knows, maybe the reminder could recall some of us to reflecting on that message.

Guilt is not from God. In Revelations 12 (the last book of the Bible), Satan is called 'the accuser of the brethren. He accuses them day and night before God.' A leading psychiatrist with the Eastern Health Board told me one time that he could discharge two-thirds of his patients from all the psychiatric hospitals in his care, if he could get them deal with their guilt. The tragedy is that most of that guilt has come from religion! 'The sin of this world is unbelief in me,' says Jesus. He states very clearly that he came to save the world, not to condemn it. All he asks is that I trust him, and take him at his word.

He says there is no judgement awaiting those who trust him. I could change the opening words slightly, and not change the message in any way. 'God so loved me that he gave his only Son, so that, if I believe in him, I will not be lost, but will have eternal life.' It is no exaggeration to say that, if I were the only person on this planet, Jesus would still have to come to redeem me, and the Spirit would have to come to lead me home to the Father. I know we're dealing with mystery here, but somehow I can accept the fact that God can actually give any one of us his complete and undivided attention, and his total love, without depriving anyone else of the same. It is difficult for our little minds to grapple with the idea of infinity!

Response

'Unrequited love' is a fanciful way of describing love that is given, but gets no response in return. OK, the whole idea and concept of love comes from God, who is the source of all love. Love, however, by its very nature, requires a response. It has the ability to generate itself. God's love for me actually generates in me some desire to respond to that love. Mother Teresa used to say that the hunger for love is a much greater hunger than the hunger for food in today's world. One of the many prayers to the Holy Spirit which has stood the test of time, contains the words 'enkindle within us the fires of divine love'. I'm sure I myself rattled off that prayer for years, and I never really understood how important it is. However, better late than never!

In the world of computers there is such a thing as a 'bug', and it implies that a file or folder has become corrupt, and that the computer needs an overhaul. I often think of guilt as being a bug in the system. It has no business being there, and it is certainly not life-giving. A sin is a sin, and I'm not suggesting that I should never feel guilty. What I am saying is that, when I accept Jesus as my personal Saviour, I give him the whole lot ... sins, guilt, and all. There is little point in asking him to forgive me if I am not prepared to forgive myself.

The Father sent Jesus. Jesus did what he was sent to do, and then he returned to the Father. The Spirit came to complete the work of Jesus. As Eucharistic Prayer IV says, 'That we might live no longer for ourselves, but for him, he sent the Holy Spirit as his first gift to those who believe, to complete his work on earth, and to bring us the fullness of grace.' In other words, in very non-theological language, the Spirit is the Executive branch of the Trinity among us. It is he who gets things done around here! For your spiritual life, the Holy Spirit is the Breath of God, and is as essential as the air you breathe for your physical survival.

Practical
Only God can do God-things. If you wish that your words and actions might be helpful to others, then ensure that you involve the Holy Spirit in everything. This short whispered prayer can precede a phone-call, writing a letter, or entering the home of someone else. Even at the very beginning of a time of prayer, whether that be private, or some community celebration, invite the Spirit to be in your heart and in your words. It is the Spirit who turns our words into prayer.

Imagine yourself sitting in front of a mirror and going to Confession to yourself! Do you think you could combine total honesty with total kindness? Both of these form the core of proper communication. I could be totally honest, while being brutally unkind; and I could be very kind, and yet be totally dishonest. As I look at myself in the mirror, it is important to remember that the biggest lies I tell are the ones I tell myself. I cannot ever be honest with you until I strive to be honest with myself. One dimension of your time in front of the mirror is that it will prob- ably confront you about making amends to someone else. This whole area of reconciliation with self, with others, and with God, is essentially the work of God's Spirit.

Do you really believe that God loves you? Do you have the courage to accept the acceptance of God? If I tell you that God loves you exactly as you are right now, I would be telling you the truth, but it would not be the complete truth. The complete truth is to say that God loves you exactly as you are right now, but he loves you more than that, or he'd leave you the way you are right now! 'Lord, I confess to you that I'm not as good as I ought to be, but I thank you that I'm a bit better than I used to be!'

Story
Let's just think for a moment about a young woman who is pregnant, and who is delighted that she is. She is a reflective soul, and she loves to spend some time on her own each day, contemplating the miracle that is happening within. As time goes by, she is more and more conscious of the stirring of new life within her, and her response is a whole-hearted and a grate-ful *yes*. Her prayer has never been more profound, even if she is not conscious that she is praying. She is in the midst, and in the process of creation; she is opening her heart totally to the possi-bility and to the potential. Her baby is already being created and nourished with love. This is a sacred time, and hers is a very sac-red call. There is a trust that is totally dependent on the process, and it is not a trust that she would have in herself of her own ability to see this through. That trust is nurtured by the love she experiences; it is that love that strengthens her trust. She just be-lieves that all will be well.

'For God so loved the world ...' When Jesus speaks of the great love of the Father, he immediately appeals for trust in that love. Jesus entered the womb of the world ... His coming among us was an expression of the Father's hug. 'They who see me, see the Father; they who hear me, hear the Father, because I and the Father are one.'

CORPUS CHRISTI

Gospel: John 6:51-58

Central Theme
Jesus speaks of himself as being food for us, sent from the Father in heaven. Unlike ordinary food, which just sustains life, this food gives a life that is eternal.

Parable
From the burning bush 'till the gentle breeze, God has made his presence known among us since the beginning of time. Being among us as eucharist is a very significant way of being present. The eucharistic presence is represented by bread and wine. Without wishing to be irreverent, if bacon and cabbage had an appropriate significance, it could serve as just another way of the Lord being present among us. Bread is the result of a process that begins with seeds of wheat. These are brought together and, after several stages of development, they end up as a unit which we call bread. Wine begins as a cluster of grapes. These also are processed and, again when the process is completed, they end up as a unit which we call wine. A group of people gather together in a church. Each individual is uniquely different. After a certain process, which is the work of God's Spirit, they become a unit, which we call church, or the Body of Christ. In communion, the Body of Christ is being nourished by the Body of Christ. If I stood on top of the altar here, and invited you all to gather around me, as close as you can, because I was going to whisper something to you, something else would take place of which you might be unaware. You would notice that the closer you come to me the closer you are to each other. When you ended up gathered closely around me, you would find that you were touching shoulders with each other. That is how community or the Body of Christ is formed. It is not a question of bringing people closer to each other; rather is it a question of bringing people closer to the Lord and, as a direct result of that, they end up being closer to each other.

Teaching
I think it was Fulton Sheen who said that the Old Testament was like radio, while the New Testament was like television. The Old Testament is like coming events throwing their shadow. Moses

leading his people through the desert, and the Red Sea, into the Promised Land is to be fulfilled when Jesus comes to make that a permanent reality. The daily manna, or bread from heaven, which they collected each morning to last them for that day is a fore-shadowing of the eucharist, the Bread of Life. 'Your fathers ate the manna in the desert, and they are dead. If you eat the bread which I am offering you, you will have eternal life ...'

Throughout history, God has spoken to his people through many and varied ways. He spoke to the prophet through the gentle breeze, and he spoke to Moses in the burning bush. The natives of Bethlehem weren't too excited to hear that a new baby had been born and, later on, Herod would treat him as a fool, and the soldiers would jeer him as a mock king. After the resurrection, Mary Magdalene thought he was a gardener, Peter thought he was a ghost, and the disciples on the road to Emmaus thought he was a stranger passing through. That he should present himself under the form of food and drink is nothing really wonderful for one who is often called 'The God of Surprises'. 'Not on bread alone do people live ...' He was referring to their deep-down real hungers. There is a hole in the heart, as it were, and, through the ages, many people have tried to fill that with everything other than God, and have never succeeded. Mother Teresa often said that the greatest hunger on earth was the need to be loved. It is not surprising, then, that God should choose to come to us in the form of food and drink.

I know it's not easy, but it is essential, that we grasp the full implications of what Jesus is telling us in today's gospel. 'I live by the power of the living Father who sent me; in the same way, those who partake of me, will live, because of me ... Anyone who eats this bread will live forever ...' That is an extraordinary statement, and one that requires serious and genuine reflection. To put it very simply and directly, if that statement is true, and if I believe it, then my heaven has begun. That's what Jesus means when he says that we have eternal life. In other words, the quality of life we now enjoy is an eternal quality; it is a life that will never end.

Response
When we speak about Jesus in the acclamations after the consecration of the Mass, we use the past tense. 'By your cross and resurrection you have set us free ...Dying, you destroyed our death, rising you restored our life ...' The eucharist we celebrate

now is a foretaste of the Eternal Banquet of heaven. There is a branch of scientific study called eschatology. It speaks of things that are, but are not full and complete as yet. We can speak of heaven as a reality, even though we must wait for another while, or another time, before we come into the fullness of the experience. You have heard the saying, 'Live, horse, and you'll get grass'. We are speaking of quite the opposite here. We are saying, 'Live life fully now, because you now have available to you the food of eternal life.'

The body is not me; rather is it a reflection of the real inner me. The body grows older, but the person living in the body remains a child. Eucharist is the food and nourishment for that inner person, for the real me, for my real hungers. There is a hole in the human heart that cannot be filled with anything less than God himself. Life is a journey, and eucharist is the food for that journey. In the past, we used refer to 'The Last Sacraments', or 'Viaticum'. Viaticum literally means 'food for the journey'. 'Unless you eat the flesh of the Son of Man you cannot have life in you.' Part of the mystery of eucharist is that it is both real and symbolic. Just as God was in the burning bush, so Jesus is in the bread; and, when I eat that bread, I receive Jesus into my body and into my spirit. Receiving Jesus under the form of bread is symbolic of the core element of stable food while, in actual fact, I am literally receiving Jesus in his totality.

'Jesus took the bread, gave thanks, gave it to his disciples, who distributed it among the people.' The sharing of a meal is central to the whole concept of eucharist. Breaking of bread, and sharing that with another is like the Indians passing around the pipe of peace as they sat around the camp-fire. It was a symbol of belonging and a declaration of communion or community. 'You will receive power from on high, and you shall be my witnesses …' In other words, I cannot expect the privilege without accepting the responsibility. Like Mary visiting Elizabeth, I too must carry Jesus within me to the people I meet on the road of life.

Practical
The word 'appetite' means some natural desire to satisfy our personal hungers. Because we are trapped within a human body, it is not so easy to be conscious of our spiritual appetites, of those hungers and desires that are not part of the emotions of the body. The ability to do this is what distinguishes us from the

animals. Jesus tells us that 'not on bread alone do we live', and Augustine says, 'You have made us for yourself, O Lord, and our hearts can never be at rest until they rest in you.' Going up to receive communion, even being present at eucharist is, in itself, a very deliberate statement. There is always the danger that we can come to take this for granted.

From a mere physical point of view, when I receive communion, I must, of necessity, open my mouth. What is most important, however, is that I open my heart. This is a most sacred moment, because it is a mutually agreed encounter between God and myself, between sinner and saviour. (This raises a question, without willing to be judgmental, on the habit some people have developed of walking out the door immediately they return from receiving Communion. Some may have good reason to leave at that time. However, for those who have no urgent or pressing business needing attention, this can be an opportunity for a few moments of quiet, sincere, and silent prayer.)

Jesus didn't come on earth to be locked in a tabernacle. Of course he is present in the tabernacle; but he is also present in the worshipping community. In fact, if I dare use the expression, he is more present (if such were possible) among the worshipping community than he is in the tabernacle. When I turn to those around me with a sign of peace, for example, I can touch him, hug him, hurt him, help him, or hear him. 'Christ be before me, Christ be around me …' I am standing full-square within the Body of Christ, and I am a living and significant member of that Body.

Story

I remember a simple incident that happened to me some years ago now. It was in the midst of winter, the weather was very bad, and I had driven to the extreme north of the country to say Mass for a Prayer Group. I had taken precautions to ensure that my car wasn't blocked in, because it was my intention to come off the altar, get out of the vestments, make straight for the car, and I would be approaching the outer ring road of Belfast before the choir would be finished their final hymn! As I rushed for the car, to my horror, I must confess, I saw an elderly lady standing by the side of the car. My initial thought was that she had suspected what I might have in mind, and was one ahead of me. I imagined myself having to listen as she told me her life story, or all the family problems. I resigned myself to the inevitable, and was not at all prepared for what happened when I reached the car. She produced a little boat-shaped basket, filled with beautiful little triangular sandwiches of all kinds, and the whole lot was covered with cling-film. 'I was thinking today, Father, that you'd have a long drive ahead of you after you finished here tonight, so I made you these to be eating as you go on your way. God bless, and may you have a safe trip.' For once I was lost for words! Food for the journey! (I still have the little basket here on my desk as I write.)

SECOND SUNDAY OF THE YEAR

Gospel: John 1:29-34

Central Theme
John the Baptist begins the work which we as a church have still to continue: to point to Jesus as the Saviour, to tell others who he is, and to encourage them to follow him.

Parable
Blessed Padre Pio is a man that is associated with a life of great and many sufferings. One of his greatest crosses in life was the excitement that ensued whenever he appeared. After Mass each morning, he used go up to the organ loft and spend several hours in prayer. Unfortunately, from where he was he could be seen by those in the church below. When they began pointing to him, and shouting requests to him, he always became quite agitated, as he pointed to the tabernacle, and withdrew from their sight. His role was to point to Jesus, to bring Jesus to people, and people to Jesus. As John the Baptist said, 'I must decrease if he is to increase.' A signpost points towards a place, but it cannot compel you to go there. To see a signpost marked 'Dublin' doesn't entitle me to claim that I have been in Dublin!

Teaching
John the Baptist has a very special place in the story of salvation that was to be revealed through Jesus Christ. Jesus said of him : 'I tell you there has never been a man, born of woman, who is greater than John the Baptist.' That is high praise indeed, especially coming from Jesus himself. John's role was to prepare the way for Jesus. We are all familiar with times like Advent, Lent, etc., times when we prepare to celebrate some special occasion in the life of Jesus. Naturally, it is easy to see that our celebration of the feast will be directly effected by the effort put into the preparation.

The language of John in today's gospel is unusually simple and direct. He is open and honest in telling us that he had no way of recognising who Jesus was, until he was given some clear evidence. He knew the Messiah was going to come, of course, but he had to wait for the sign so that he could identify him when he did come. The sign was the evidence of the Spirit coming upon Jesus and, indeed, he heard the Father's voice saying that Jesus was his beloved Son, and people should listen to him. A strong identification with Jesus, who he is, and why he has come, is a pre-requisite for anyone hoping to evangelise, or to be evangelised themselves. That is the role of the church. In some ways, the church has been seen to have almost replaced Jesus, and to point to itself as the means of salvation. All present attempts at renewal in the church have to do with correcting this misconception.

Baptism has to do with entering into membership, with cleansing and purifying, and with being named. All of these things are part of belonging as a member of the Body of Christ. Baptism is the beginning of a journey. John was the one who began that journey. His form of baptism was limited, because it was about initiation. When Jesus came he would move beyond water, and baptise with the Holy Spirit. This signified a permanent and eternal relationship within the life of the Trinity. The fact that a priest pours water on the head of a baby gives no guarantee that the baby will grow up to become a Christian. At some stage or other, the grown-up baby must say *yes* to that baptism, so that Jesus can anoint with his Spirit, and bring his work to completion within that person.

Response

One way of understanding renewal in the church is to think of us going back to the time of John the Baptist. It is a question of getting back to basics. We are human, we are continually changing and evolving, and we can so easily lose our way. I myself am a teacher by training, and so I am quite familiar with the concept of revision, and of returning to the basics again and again. (Correcting exams is one way of reminding a teacher that the information was not understood as intended, or that the message was interpreted as presented!)

We are all familiar with confirmation, even though we may not fully understand the full significance of what it means. The coming of Jesus was strongly confirmed again and again. Long before he came the prophets spoke of his coming, and what would happen when he came. We have the angel appearing to Mary, and to the shepherds at Bethlehem. At his baptism in the Jordan the Father's voice was heard, and the Spirit was seen to come upon him. In today's gospel we have John giving loud and clear confirmation and affirmation as to who Jesus is, and why he came. It is usually many years after our own confirmation before we ourselves begin to grasp just exactly what that is intended to signify. This might have greater power and significance if confirmation was withheld until we were in our late teens. We then would have a better idea what it means to be confirmed in my beliefs, and to feel confirmed and reassured about my way of life as a Christian.

John's introduction is very simple. 'Look! There is the Lamb of God who takes away the sin of the world.' I think it very important that we reflect on that statement. If Jesus takes away the sin of the world, then, of course, he can take away my sin. It can be meaningless to get caught up in generalities. For example, I can quote 'For God so loved the world that he gave his only Son', and never get around to accepting the fact that God so loved me that he gave his only Son.

Practical

How clear am I in my thinking about Jesus and the church? The gospel is about Jesus. Christianity is not about producing nicer people with better morals. I could be a pagan and be a good person. It is not about prayer and fasting. I could be a Muslim and do that. Christianity is about a person, Jesus Christ. The role of the church is very simple. When Jesus ascended into heaven, when he returned to the Father, he took the body he had with him. He sent the Holy Spirit to complete his work, and he asks us to provide the hands, feet, voice, etc., through which the Spirit can do that work.

How confirmed do I actually feel as a follower of Jesus Christ? How real is my sense of vocation, of being called? This is purely the work of the Spirit, and this will never become a reality in my life until I open my heart and my mind to the Spirit, and declare my willingness to be anointed by the Spirit. Just as John recognised Jesus, so I should be recognised as a follower of Jesus. You are familiar with the question that if we were arrested and brought to the nearest police station, where we were charged with being Christian, how many of us would get off scot-free for lack of evidence?

There is one pitfall open to all of us when we speak of church. We may fail to remember that *we are* the church. It is not a question of us sitting here, waiting for somebody out there, down in the bishop's house, in Rome, or somewhere else to change. If change is to be real for us it must begin within our own hearts. 'Let there be peace on earth, and let it begin with me.' Witness is at the heart of Christian living. The witness of the lives of the Christian Community is the evidence that Jesus is present among his people, and that his Spirit rests upon them. I must bring that one step further, look in the mirror, and ask. 'How do I measure up to the criteria of what it means to be a Christian?'

Story
It takes five years for the seed of a bamboo tree to show any growth above ground, and then it grows to a height of 90 feet in six weeks! Five years of preparation, of putting down roots, of spreading underground, so as to have access to plenty of food. And then, only then, does it take off.

This is an extraordinary fact that requires reflection. The time spent with John the Baptist was preparing the people to meet and follow Jesus. It was like a novitiate. We all need such preparation and formation. The journey moves from information, to formation, to transformation. Surely any failure to grow spiritually in our lives is the result of a lack of genuine preparation, of spiritual formation. To live in the warmth of God's love is a sure and certain way to grow.

THIRD SUNDAY OF THE YEAR

Gospel: Matthew 4:12-23

Central Theme
Today's gospel is about Jesus beginning his mission, calling his first disciples, and beginning to travel from place to place, to proclaim that the kingdom of God was close at hand.

Parable
As I write this we are approaching the Millennium. There is an obsession with preparation, even though there are divergent views on how to prepare. For those who are not Christian, the preparations must have a certain hollowness to them. I read an ad the other day for a New Year's ball priced at £1,000! This can disturb Christians, who feel the others are high-jacking the real reason for the celebration. I don't think that such negative reactions serve any purpose. As a Christian, I can make my own preparations, and let the others do whatever they choose. Part of being a Christian is to be like Jesus, to be a 'sign of contradiction', which frees me up from conforming to the dictates and norms of the world. The kingdom of God is not of this world. If, like Jesus in today's gospel, I have a very clear vision and goal, and I know exactly what I am about, my energy and enthusiasm for the task ahead will be dramatically increased.

Teaching
Today's gospel marks the beginning of the ministry of Jesus. John had been arrested, so that was the end of the ministry of John. The gospel tells us that instead of going to Nazareth (in other words, instead of going home), Jesus went to Capernaum. The show was on the road, as it were. As it happened, the prophet had foretold that this would happen. I don't think that the sayings of the prophets are what influenced Jesus. He was led by the Spirit, and that led him into the fulfilling of all the prophecies. Aren't they powerful words used by the prophet to describe what happens when Jesus appears among them? 'The people who sat in darkness have seen a great light, and for those who lived in the land where death cast its shadow, a light has shone.' Jesus would later refer to himself as the light of the world; and, in commissioning his apostles, he would tell them that they, now, were to be a light to the world.

The message of Jesus is a very simple one. 'Turn from your sins, and turn to God, because the kingdom of heaven is near.' I said earlier that the clearer my goal or vision, the higher will be the level of my energy in bringing that about. Sin is a false goal, an untrue vision, an empty promise. It is immediate, selfish, and is self-will run riot. It is the result of behaviour that is out of control, through a compulsion, addiction, or selfish whim. It can never satisfy because, outside the kingdom of God I am an exile, pining for home. Even in the depth of my sin the kingdom of God is very near. I just have to reach out, and Jesus is there.

When I was growing up the word 'vocation' was high-jacked by priests and religious. It is now being given back to the laity, and more and more laity are actually experiencing themselves as being called. There is nothing dramatic about this. It just means that I don't just stumble into the Christian way by default, without any clear path or pattern to follow. 'I have called you by name; you are mine.' 'You didn't choose me; no, I chose you, and I appointed you to go and bear fruit, fruit that would remain.' If the gospel is now, and I am every person in the gospel, then, through the gospel of today, I am being called.

Response
I mentioned earlier that, when I have a clear goal and vision to follow, my energy level in pursuing that is so much higher. When I was baptised, someone else said my *yes* for me. I cannot remember having any great enthusiasm about my confirmation, beyond the fact of the new suit, and the money from family and friends. There must come a time, however, when I am prepared to take personal responsibility for my own calling, and say my own personal *yes*. Because God is totally a God of now ('I am who am'), the only *yes* in my whole life he's interested in is my *yes* of now.

'Turn from your sins, and turn to God, because the kingdom of God is near.' In rugby football, when someone scores a try, that team is then given a conversion kick. In the ancient game of wrestling, when one succeeded in turning the other person right around into the opposite position, that was marked as a point or a conversion. Conversion has to do with crossing-over, with changing of direction, with a shifting of position. It means letting go of one situation or position, and moving to another one. It is basically about change. To live is to change, and to become holy or whole is to have changed often (Newman). The writer of the Psalms is continually calling on the Lord to change his heart. 'Create a new heart in me, O Lord, and put a right spirit within me ...' Having that attitude towards God is a necessary part of conversion. A constant declaration of my willingness to be changed is a central part of prayer.

Christianity is about a person, Jesus Christ. He is the pearl of great price that he speaks of, which, when someone finds it, is willing to sell everything he has to buy that pearl. The apostles in today's gospel just walked away from everything. This may seem highly insensitive to their father, and to their responsibilities to their families. There must have been some powerful magnetic force while in the presence of Jesus. There must also have been some great emptiness within the hearts of the apostles, because, certainly, not everyone who was in the presence of Jesus felt any call to follow him. Some were there out of curiosity, some to trip him up, and others were plotting his arrest and execution. The response of the apostles, therefore, must have come from a combination of their own inner hungers, and the charismatic power that came from being in the presence of Jesus. I imagine their own human condition was actually the first ingredient, because they had lived with that for many years before they ever heard of Jesus. I would suggest that, to have a deep personal encounter with Jesus, I could begin with my own human struggles, weaknesses, brokenness, and inability to manage life. No doubt that would help enormously, when it comes to listen to Jesus speak about forgiveness, compassion, and the special place of sinners in his plan of salvation.

Practical

I continue to stress one very important point, i.e. the gospel is now, and I am every person in it. I have a choice right now to be in two places. In my mind, I can be away back there when and where today's gospel took place; or I can be where I am right now, let Jesus enter that space, and have this incident encircle me. Supposing you personally heard the call to turn from your sins, and turn to God, can you actually identify something within yourself that would have to change? Some behaviour, action, attitude, etc., that would have to be faced up to, and removed? I am not suggesting that you yourself could actually do the removing, because, by yourself, you would not be able. What I am suggesting is that I am willing to bring it to the Lord, and declare to him my desire to surrender, and to have him change me.

While the apostles left their boats to follow Jesus, what is it that I would have to walk away from, before I would be free to follow? This could be anything from a wrong relationship, to an addiction, to a mental attitude. One seldom hears about the Seven Deadly Sins anymore. However, if I have a quick run down through those, I may find identification with one or more of them. Remember them? Pride, covetousness, lust, gluttony, envy, anger, and sloth. Translating those into modern language might give you a list like the following: Considering myself as superior to others; being jealous of what they have, and begrudging them their success; using others to meet your own needs, and confusing this with love; once again, we have that green-eyed monster of envy or begrudgery, and the inability to rejoice in another's success; anger is just another word for wounded pride, because someone dared to rain on my parade; and, lastly, we have the sins of omission, where I'm always going to get around to doing the good, but not just yet. The road to hell is paved with good intentions …

If I am not at all involved in evangelising others, this is a direct result of the fact that I myself have never been evangelised. I am not speaking of standing on a butter-box in the town square. Evangelising is something the Spirit can do through me, if I make myself available. 'Lord, may your Spirit within me touch the hearts of those I meet today, either through the words I say, the prayers I pray, the life I live, or the very person that I am.'

Story
There is a story told about Leonardo de Vinci's famous painting of the Last Supper. He searched far and wide for what he considered to be an ideal model for each person in the painting. He began with a fine-looking young man, full of life, and very anchored, and chose him as a perfect model for Jesus. He followed with other models for each of the apostles. Naturally, the work took several years. He left Judas till last, because he was having a problem finding someone who could represent him. Finally, he came across a bum, who was sleeping rough, who had all the appearances of being untrustworthy and, like Judas, would probably sell his soul if it brought him some money. Leonardo approached the man and persuaded him to come to his studio. While the work was in progress, both men came to the same realisation. This man had been in this studio before, representing

Jesus. He had gone astray, lost his way, and was now on Skid Row. It was a very great shock to de Vinci, and a moment of conversion for the man.

When Jesus called on people to turn from their sins, he also asked some of them to follow him. They were to become his pupils, people who would absorb his Spirit, and continue his work, when he went back home to the Father.

FOURTH SUNDAY OF THE YEAR

Gospel: Matthew 5:1-12

Central Theme
Today's gospel, what we call the eight beatitudes, is like a summary of Jesus' teaching. It is the gospel in a very condensed form and, therefore, requires a great deal of teasing out to get to the simple point by point message that it contains.

Parable
We are all familiar with political manifestos. These are statements about where the political party is at, what they stand for, what is in it for you if you vote for them, and what they intend to achieve if you elect them. Many people are quite cynical about politicians, and politics in general. No matter how sincere their promises are, many of them fail to deliver on those promises. Today's gospel is Jesus' Manifesto. The important thing for us to remember is that, in the words of Jesus, 'heaven and earth will pass away before my word passes away'. In other words this is a manifesto in which he certainly will keep his side of the bargain.

Teaching
There is a lot of teaching contained in today's gospel, and it would not be possible for us now to reflect on it at any great length. Let me try to put the beatitudes into very simple ordinary words, and that, in itself, might help us. They are blessed who are detached, and have a humble attitude. Even if they have great riches, they are not possessed by the riches, nor are they boastful and proud about them. Grief is the price you pay for love, so, if you have any capacity for love, then you will need to carry some tissues with you. If you never want to cry at a funeral, don't ever love anyone. The meek and the gentle are the very opposite to the bully, and they are the ones who are really powerful. Mahatma Ghandi and Martin Luther King refused to fight back, so the only way to stop them was to kill them.

They are good people who have a real desire for justice and fair play, and who are prepared to ensure that this is available to others. As you treat others, so you yourself will be treated, so if you want mercy, forgiveness, and compassion, then you must begin by giving this to others. A pure heart is not devious, deceitful, selfish, and cunning. A pure heart reflects an aspect of

God. Jesus did not say that they are blessed who have peace. Rather did he commend those who build bridges of peace and reconciliation between others, and between themselves and others.

Jesus warns us that, if we follow him, we will be treated like he was. There is a cost in Pentecost, and following him means taking up the cross. Right from the beginning when Simeon took the child in his arms in the temple, he announced that Jesus would be a sign of contradiction. Everything he said, everything he did, and everything he stood for, was a contradiction to this world and its values. Those with power, prestige, and control were very threatened by him. The religious leaders who ran the show, and who were the final arbiters as to what was right and wrong, were so threatened by him that they planned and succeeded in killing him.

Response
There is a certain sense of cleansing in today's gospel. It is about letting go of things in our lives that are not life-giving, and about becoming wholesome and free. It is a programme for living, a blue-print for inner peace and happiness. Religion runs the risk of being about rules and regulations and, ultimately, about control. Spirituality is totally the work of the Holy Spirit, and it is about surrender. Spirituality is about letting go, knowing that, in death, I must let go of everything anyhow.

To live life more fully, it is necessary to be as free from outside controls as possible. I can have wealth, but it need not control me, and drive me in a compulsive way towards accumulating more and more wealth. When I forgive someone, I am setting myself free. Having a resentment against another is a case of me drinking poison, and I'm expecting the other person to die! When I am authentic, or pure of heart, I become a life-giving person, and I mediate life to others. It's rather frightening to think that if I am inauthentic, I am mediating death to others.

When I take Jesus and his message seriously, and decide to follow him and to belong to his kingdom, then I can be sure and certain of meeting opposition. Quite a lot of that opposition will come from within myself. Self-preservation is a fundamental human instinct. Following Jesus involves dying – to self, to my creature comforts, to my pride, etc. If I let my head take over, rather than responding from the heart, then I risk getting sidetracked into endless cul-de-sacs. Prudence will advice me to hold back, and not get too involved. Procrastination will cause me to do nothing, really, because I will end up not doing anything today that I can put off till to-morrow.

Practical
This is one of those days when I wish I had copies of today's gospel, and a highlight marker, which I could give to each of you as you leave. I would ask you to read, and re-reread the passage many times. Then as parts of it become clearer to you, you could highlight those. The whole process, of course, could bear fruit only if the Holy Spirit is invited to lead me, to teach me, and to enlighten me.

Have you ever taken time out to reflect on how you are living your life? Part of the weaknesses of our human condition is that it blinds us to the reality of how we are. I could be a bully, and be the only one around who doesn't know that. Part of the disease of alcoholism, for example, is that it is the only disease known to man or woman that denies its own existence. Every dog in the street knows that John is an alcoholic, but he himself just cannot see that. It's his wife's fault, it's the stress of work, it's the need he has to take a break, and be good to himself, etc. Everything except the simple truth of looking at himself in a mirror, and saying, 'You are where you are right now because of yourself, and the things that you do.' It is a good thing, from time to time, to take the lamp of truth and go inside, and see what's happening there.

Today's gospel is all about blessings. It is about a whole shower of blessings, when I make myself available to receive them. I open my heart, and I ask the Holy Spirit to imprint the words of today's gospel on my heart. I accept the words as a guide to healthy and wholesome living, and a way to a life beyond my wildest dreams.

Story
Hilary Pole was a physical education teacher in an English second-level school. At the age of twenty-seven she was hit with a rare disease that crippled her, and she ended up where her mobility was limited to one sixteenth of an inch of her big toe. A professor in Oxford University devised and designed a special typewriter for her, and she began to practise typing within the limits of her condition. Very soon she was writing poetry and, strange as it may seem, all her poems had to do with the joy of

living. She became known nationwide, and was awarded an MBE by the Queen for her work. An example of her thinking can be gleaned from the following verse:

You ask me if I'm sad or bored,
Or if my life it is abhorred.
And I tell I am not;
That I can now accept my lot.
I remind your sadly shaking head,
It's my body, not my mind, in bed.

Today's gospel is about power from within … poor in spirit, meek, gentle, etc.

FIFTH SUNDAY OF THE YEAR

Gospel: Matthew 5:13-16

Central Theme
Today's gospel is about Christian witness. Christianity is about attracting, not promoting. The gospel is implanted by the very presence of a Christian living in that area.

Parable
When I was growing up, we didn't have fridges or freezers, as we have today. Every year my father killed a pig. The only way we had to preserve the sides of bacon over the months, until we could get around to eating the lot, was to pack the portions into boxes of salt. There was really as much salt as bacon in each box. One of the attributes of salt is to preserve, to keep food from going rotten.

I also remember from back then, we didn't have electricity. We had oil lamps, tilley lamps, hurricane lamps (for outside use) and, on occasions, we had a candle or two. I well remember the arrival of the electricity, and the excitement it generated among us kids. We would even have electric light in the cowhouse, as well as down at the end of the farmyard. This was exciting stuff for us country kids. To have light anywhere around the house, or outside the house, all one had to do was press a switch. This had profound effects on our daily life. We had a wireless that didn't need to have the battery charged every few weeks. We could do our homework in any corner of the kitchen, or in a bedroom. We no longer lived with the dangers (and the fumes) of oil lamps, of the spirits used in the tilley, or with the danger of a burning candle falling over, or left burning and unattended.

Teaching
I'm sure you can see that I can readily identify with today's gospel. Among the roughest and toughest ghettos there are some beautiful and very special people; and if they were not there, the whole area would be rotten. Most initiatives for self-help and for self-improvement in that area are the inspiration of these few. Neighbourhood Watch, Drug Awareness, investment in facilities for social and recreational needs are to be found in the toughest areas of the toughest towns. If you check into it, I'll guarantee you that the initiative and the impetus came from that

small group, who could well be called the salt of that area. Just as a pinch of salt can greatly improve the taste of food, so too much salt would destroy anything. That is why there can be such a benefit from the presence of just a few.

I'm sure you heard the saying that it's better to light a candle than curse the darkness. One candle doesn't give a great deal of light, but imagine a room in total darkness, and someone enters it bearing a lit candle. It is important to remind ourselves again that the kingdom of God is made up of tiny acts, and most of them are hidden. There is another saying that if each before his own door swept, the whole village would be clean.

Today's gospel is just beautiful in its simplicity. Earlier on, Jesus had declared himself as the light of the world. Today he tells us that we are to be the light of the world. I would rather be guided by a lighthouse than to be rescued by a lifeboat. Without preaching from a butter-box in the town square, I can preach the Christian message through everything I do, and every word I say. If the Spirit of God lives within me, then naturally, wherever I go, I bring the Spirit with me. When Jesus ascended into heaven, when he returned to the Father, with mission accomplished, he brought the body he had with him. He then sent his Spirit, and asked us to provide the body. He has no other feet, hands, or voice but ours.

Response

What good is salt if it loses its taste? What good is a light if you cover it and prevent the light from being seen? In today's gospel, Jesus tells us that we are the salt of earth and the light of the world. In other words, we have what it takes. The onus, then, is on us whether we make use of that or not. There is nothing automatic about being a Christian. It demands definite and personal decisions, and it demands that we carry out those decisions.

In today's world, about two-thirds of the people never heard of Jesus, or have not accepted his message. Of the third that do, a little over 50% would be Roman Catholics. Of those, about 10% are practising; and, of that number about 2% are practising out of personal conviction. And all of that is two thousand years later! This is where the question of the pinch of salt being effective comes in. I think if Jesus waited till everybody was ready and willing to listen to him, he would not have started yet. In the Old Testament, when the prophet begged God not to destroy the city, God said he would spare the city 'if you find me one hundred good men'. When the prophet failed to do, God asked for fifty good men. When the prophet failed again, God kept reducing the demands to twenty, to ten, and to five. God doesn't require a large army. He requires a definite personal commitment from a few and, with them, he can effect much good in that whole area.

Letting your good deeds be seen is not seeking public display or showing off. It simply means that, if I am a Christian, I should be seen to act and to live in a Christian way. 'By this will everyone know that you are my disciples if you love one another.' We are called to live the gospel, rather than just believe it or preach it. It's a strange thing but, if I went to live in a cave in the Dublin mountains, without telling anyone, and if I opened my heart to the fullness of the life of the Trinity, as offered by the Father, effected by the Son, and completed by the Spirit, there would be a procession of people climbing that mountain to visit me within a year or two. Real Christian witness is a very powerful instrument for influencing others for good. Not only are we the salt of the earth, and are we people who must let our Christian light shine brightly in today's world; we are also the living presence of the all-holy God, because we carry the Spirit of God within our hearts, we are members of the kingdom or the family of God, and we are God's touch-persons in the lives of others.

Practical
I'm sure you've heard the phrase 'street angel, house devil'. The first place I have to practise my Christian vocation is within my own home, among my own family. When I was a kid we were praying for the conversion of Russia, or we were collecting pennies for black babies in Africa. That was very safe, because it was a good and safe distance from home. Speaking of the various influences and effects of salt and of light, what kind of influence are you having within the circle of your daily living? Are you a life-giving person, who helps preserve and encourage goodness in others, and do you lighten the way and the burdens of others? We can so easily slip into the habit of taking others for granted and, while we would be concerned about atrocities and famine in far-flung places, we could completely overlook those who are closest to us.

There is one dimension of gospel living that we can so easily overlook. 'You write a new page of the gospel each day, through the things that you do, and the words that you say. People read what you write, whether faithful or true. What is the gospel according to you?' You yourself are the message. You can say all the lovely words you like, but if you don't believe them, and are not seen to practise them, you are wasting your time. I could preach the gospel even if I were deaf and dumb.

Have you ever come across people who seem to light up a room as soon as they enter it? They are people who are fully human and fully alive. They seem to wear antennae on their heads, because their sensitivity to others will immediately alert them to someone in the room who is out of sorts, is hurting, or uncomfortable. Because they themselves are fully alive, they transmit life to those around them. In his description of the General Judgement, Jesus has such people asking 'Lord, when we see you hungry and clothe you, etc. ?' Because of the kind of people they are, they are not conscious of the good they are doing. For them, to act in such a way has become a way of being. Such people are certainly the salt of the earth, and the light of the world.

Story

On 26 November 1965, *Time* magazine had a story that can give us all food for thought. An electrical fuse, about the size of a bread box, failed, resulting in 80,000 square miles along the US-Canadian border being plunged into darkness. All the electrical power for that entire region passed through that single fuse. Without that fuse no power could reach any point in that vast region.

The kingdom of God is built through the accumulation of tiny acts, most of which go unnoticed. We are all, unfortunately, too familiar with people gathering at scenes of atrocities and, as a statement of their abhorrence, they light and carry small candles.

SIXTH SUNDAY OF THE YEAR

Gospel: Matthew 5:17-37

Central Theme
Today's gospel contains five teachings of Jesus, on law, anger, adultery, divorce, and vows.

Parable
Without wishing to abuse the truth, I recall in general, the main thrust of a book called *Animal Farm* by George Orwell. There were no rules, no laws, nobody in positions of authority and responsibility. This was to be Utopia, where everything would go along as things should be, and nobody would dream of upsetting or rocking the boat, and everybody would live happily ever after. Unfortunately, the story doesn't turn out that way. Although the story is about animals, the point of the story is that, without structures, without rules to guide behaviour, without somebody taking responsibility to animate and lead the group, we also can descend into anarchy and self-destruction.

Teaching
Jesus doesn't want to do away with the law; rather he wants to fulfil it. He does not, however, want the law to become an end in itself. The law is there to serve the people, to guide and protect them, and it must not be used to control them and to oppress them. A man is in court for doing ninety miles an hour through a fifty-mile zone. He has broken a good law, which was put in place to protect, rather that to oppress people. Jesus tells us that all law comes from God and, therefore, for a law to be valid, it must be made for the common good. Jesus is more in favour of a law of love, rather than a love of law.

Whether his teaching has to do with anger, adultery, divorce, etc., what he is really speaking about has to do with love. He lays great stress on forgiveness. That's a very powerful word, when he speaks of bringing your gift to the altar, and then you remember that there's someone out there hurting because of you. Leave your gift to one side, go off and be reconciled with that person, and then come back to offer your gift. If we speak about loving God and loving our neighbour, then there must not be any contradiction here. It would surely be a contradiction to be reciting lovely prayers to God, while I'm not speaking to my neighbour. 'Whatever you do to the least of these, that's what you do onto me.'

He is very clear and definite when it comes to giving one's word. There's no need for solemn oaths, etc., if I am a person of my word. This was very important to Jesus. 'You are either for me or against me. Let your 'yes' be 'yes' and your 'no' be 'no'.' He himself is very emphatic about the sincerity of his promises to us. He gives his word, and he says that 'heaven and earth will pass away before my word passes away'. It is difficult to speak about adultery or divorce. I don't imagine any couple who got married with the intention of getting a divorce later on. I credit them with the very highest and best intentions and, as can easily happen, things just don't work out the way they had hoped. No alcoholic ever set out to become an alcoholic. This was something that crept up on him, as it were. Adultery can be wrong on grounds other than morality and sex. It can be a lie, because it can imply a commitment that is not there, and that one party, at least, has no intention of there ever being a commitment. The whole subject of today's gospel has to do with honesty, integrity, and genuine love.

Response

A sin is a sin. If God wanted a permissive society he would have given us Ten Suggestions instead of Ten Commandments. Having grown up in a church which had a preoccupation with sin that was bordering on the unhealthy, there is now a danger of the pendulum swinging in the opposite direction, to the other extreme, where we lose all sense of sin. I believe that the law of God is written in our hearts in such a way that we know rightly whenever we are wrong. (When I was a child I had a dog that looked very guilty after he did something he shouldn't. One look at him and you knew. As you approached him, he lay down, rolled over on his back, expecting to be scolded. If you patted him, he immediately jumped up, and leapt all over you, knowing that all was forgiven.)

We sometimes hear the saying 'My word is my bond'. It is good to be a person of your word. One of the most insightful comments of Jesus is that 'the truth will set you free'. The liar has to have a good memory! The facts are always friendly, because they never change. There is a saying of much wisdom which states that 'When everything else fails, try the truth, because it always works.' The essence of proper communication is to combine total honesty with total kindness. There are times when total honesty can be brutally destructive, and when total kindness can be totally dishonest. It's quite a struggle to get it right. It is an extraordinary gospel principle to strive to become authentic, to become genuine, to live and to speak the truth. Because original sin had to do with a lie, the antidote, the anti-biotic for that is the Holy Spirit, whom Jesus calls 'The Spirit of Truth.'

Sin, by definition, is a lie. Whether it be adultery, perjury, or self-righteous adherence to law, it can masquerade as virtue, as truth, as something other than the reality. Sin is not so much an act as the reason or motive behind the act. I could visit someone in hospital today because I feel sorry for him; or I could visit him because I want to rejoice in the fact that he is suffering. I could do the very same thing for very different reasons.

Practical

I must confess to being caught in a bind with today's gospel. It contains very clear and very definite teaching from Jesus, so that must surely merit our full intention. I myself, however, cannot bring myself to proclaim any sort of blanket condemnation of adultery, divorce, etc., and that bothers me in a way. Over the years I have known people who have been divorced, involved in adulterous relationships, etc., and I have known them to be very good people. It is difficult to condemn the sin without running the risk of judging and condemning the sinner. Most people that I know are quite aware of what's right and what's wrong. I don't think you can legislate morality. There is an in-built barometer in the human spirit that instinctively informs us when we're right or wrong. The biggest lies I tell in life are the ones I tell my-self. I will never be honest with you or with anyone else until I become honest with myself.

Today's gospel has a lot to do with honesty and integrity. The Spirit of God is a Spirit of Truth. Only the truth will set me free. It is a wonderful thing to strive to be authentic and genuine: to be a person of my word. That, of course, must begin with my-self because, as I have already said, the greatest lies I tell in life are the ones I tell myself. To paraphrase a sentence from Shakespeare, 'Be true to yourself, and then you won't be untrue to others.'

One of the most practical things I can do today is to check on my relationships, to ensure that I am not in a totally contradictory situation as I approach the altar. I often think that others should hear me say 'I'm sorry; please forgive me' more than God does. There would never be a war or, indeed, there might never be a divorce, if somebody somewhere was prepared to say 'I'm sorry. I was wrong.' It may sound simple, but it's very difficult for some people to admit to being wrong. In fact, our own pride can often blind us to the fact that we are wrong, and we fail to see things as they are. It's a wonderful freedom to be able to face up to the truth and, when we are wrong, to promptly admit it.

Story
One of the great wonders of the world is the Great Wall of China. It is said to be the only landmark on earth that is visible from the moon. It was built as a protection against invasion from neighbouring enemies. After all that mammoth endeavour, someone bribed the gatekeeper, who opened the gates and allowed the enemy through! So much for human endeavour!

The Christian life is a sign that should be seen from far and near. It is a sign of contradiction, of course, in that it insists there is another way of living than living with the values of a materialistic world. The only way to preach this message is to live it. 'You write a new page of the gospels each day, by the things that you do, and the words that you say. People read what you write, whether faithful or true. What is the gospel according to you?'

SEVENTH SUNDAY OF THE YEAR

Gospel: Matthew 5:38-48

Central Theme
Today's gospel is the teaching of Jesus about what is generally accepted as being the hallmark of the Christian, i.e. forgiveness and love. In one way it is nice, in a gentle or sweet way while, in another, it is among the toughest teachings in the whole gospel.

Parable
Gordon Wilson captured the hearts of the Irish nation some years ago when his daughter, Marie, was killed in an horrific terrorist explosion in Enniskillen. It was 'Poppy Day', an annual day when the British remembered those killed in the two World Wars. There was a monument in Enniskillen and Gordon and his daughter Marie were there with thousands of others for a service of commemoration. Suddenly a bomb went off right in the middle of the crowd, and the results were devastating, and the carnage was horrific. Marie took the full force of the blast, and for some time Gordon and herself were beneath the pile of rubble and bodies, while he spoke to her, and she herself actually uttered several words. She died, however, as they clung to each other. Right from the moment that Gordon Wilson was rescued from the rubble, he spoke of forgiveness for the people who had planted the bomb, and he asked for prayers for them. In his eyes, they were the ones to be pitied. He figured prominently in the Irish and English media. He crossed the divide to speak to those 'on the other side' of the conflict in Northern Ireland, and he offered his services as a mediator in any way that would help to bring reconciliation and peace. Because of his work for peace, and because of the glowing example of his powerful Christian witness, the Irish Government nominated him to be a member of the Senate. He worked tirelessly for peace and reconciliation, right up to his death a few years ago.

Teaching
The first thing I can say about today's gospel is that its teaching goes directly against everything that Jesus was taught as a child. With the Jews it was 'an eye for an eye, and a tooth for a tooth'. Your enemy was just that and no more, and was always to be treated as your enemy. Such a person could expect nothing else

but your hatred and opprobrium for the rest of his life. Their system of justice was arbitrary and ruthless, as we witness in gospel stories where the woman was being stoned to death, or when Jesus himself was crucified. The teaching of today's gospel is diametrically opposed to all of that.

Christianity does not ask me to become a doormat, or some sort of rag-doll that everybody can kick around the place. It doesn't ask me to become a wimp. Through the power of God's Spirit in me, I am asked to become extraordinarily strong, because it requires great strength of character, and great single-minded resolve to be able to forgive, or to turn the other cheek. Just think of the trouble many of us have in loving our friends! Today we are asked to forgive our enemies. I must never forget that, by myself and of myself, I just don't have what it takes to do what Jesus asks me to do. More about that later.

Jesus speaks of his Father in heaven as being a model for our loving. We are all children of God. He loves all of us equally. He loves us because he is good and, because God is love, he is not capable of loving any one of us less than 100%. Just think what a wonderful world it would be if all of us could be inspired with such love. We ask the Holy Spirit to 'enkindle within us the fires of divine love'. There is a lot of talk today about role models, and how important it is for the young to have people in their lives who live out the ideals and principles one hopes to instil in them. Certainly, as Christians, we have the role model *par excellence*, both in Jesus and in his Father.

Response

I'm sure most of us, upon hearing today's gospel, are faced with people and with situations to which this gospel speaks very directly. That's OK. No point in going on a guilt-trip. That's not what Jesus has in mind. He holds up to us the ideal, the call, and he offers us the power to be able to respond to that call; and then he is patient in awaiting our reply. There are times when the hurts are too deep, and the experience is too recent, to be able to even consider forgiveness. I have often come across people, and the best they could pray for was a willingness to want to forgive. That's a very good start. God can work miracles for those of goodwill.

'If you love only those who love you, what good is that? Even the pagans do that.' Today's gospel asks us to take that extra step, to walk that extra mile. Because of our own struggles, and because of our perception of church as being pre-occupied with rules, morality, and high moral ground teaching, we can easily overlook the simplicity of the gospel message. There are many people who would have no adherence to church, or to any form of structured religion, and yet who are totally enamoured and deeply struck by the simple message of Jesus. In a world of violence, revenge killings, and deep-rooted hatred, they dream of what things would be like if people listened to, and heeded the message of the gospel.

Jesus taught us one simple prayer. All Christians of all persuasions recite this prayer. In it, we call God 'Father' and, in fact we call him 'Our Father'. Over the years this prayer has continued to be said by churches of various denominations, even if they wouldn't dare to have any association with each other. It is often recited in a church where one member is not on speaking terms with another. Over the past year alone, on separate occasions I witnessed two husbands being supported at the graveside of their murdered wives, as they almost swooned with grief, only to read in the papers some days later that each of them had been arrested and charged with the murder. I know this may be an extreme example, but I use it deliberately to shock us into reflecting on what we do.

Practical
When it comes to the practicalities of today's gospel, there is little need for me to be very specific. I'm sure every single one of us can concretise today's gospel into some definite situation. 'To err is human, to forgive is divine.' When it comes to forgiveness, this is one area where we really need the Spirit to enter and to act. It requires a heart which we may not possess to be able to forgive and forget. Gordon Wilson, of whom I spoke earlier, was, indeed, a man of God. He was seen as such, and was spoken of as such by every person who knew him, or who knew of him.

In the beatitudes, Jesus speaks of the power of the meek, and the gentle. The bully cannot deal with the person who won't strike back. The only way the world could stop Mahatma Ghandi or Martin Luther King was to shoot them. They had a power, through their peaceful resistance and unwillingness to strike back, that threatened the might of the oppressor. It was Herod and the helpless baby all over again.

When I forgive someone, I set both of us free. There is extraordinary freedom in having a forgiving heart. Year after year we watch scenes of horror on our screens, in what is sometimes called ethnic cleansing, and often called genocide. This is the outcome of hatred, which comes out of a total unwillingness to forgive. What strikes us most, as we watch these horrors unfold on our screens, is the fact that it is the innocent who suffer most. Supposing the television set took control of the camera, and turned it on us, and followed us all around the house, what pictures would we be projecting from our own kitchens and living rooms?

Story

In the old days there was a very reliable way of catching monkeys in Africa. A hole was scooped out of a tree, and some nuts were placed in the hole. The monkey came along, discovered the nuts, grabbed a fist of them, only to discover that, with his fist full of nuts, he was unable to withdraw his paw. Extraordinary as it may seem, the monkey was so intent on getting the nuts that he would not let go of them, as the hunters approached, and threw a net over him!

Today's gospel speaks of letting go ... of resentments, unforgiveness, etc. There is extraordinary freedom in being big enough to forgive, and to let go of grudges.

EIGHTH SUNDAY OF THE YEAR

Gospel: Matthew 6:24-34

Central Theme
Today's gospel is about getting our priorities right. If we believe what Jesus tells us then, surely, we have no reason to worry about anything. St Paul tells us, 'Having given us Christ Jesus, will the Father not surely give us everything else?'

Parable
Catholics of my generation would be very familiar with the rosary, and the part it played in our formative years. Rosary beads were always hanging somewhere near the fireplace, and our grannies never seemed to leave them out of their hands. There is another set of beads, available today, which are called 'worry beads'. These beads are also worked through the fingers, one after another, the big difference being that there is no prayer being said. This is intended as some sort of distracting pre-occupation for those who are anxious or worried. Both sets of beads represent two ways of dealing with worry. One is to pray about it, and the other is to continue to worry about it. Today's gospel challenges Christians as to which beads they should use.

Teaching
There is a great difference between being rich and being wealthy. I could be very rich, and yet have no money. Of all the false gods we can have, money is the most popular. If wealth could bring happiness, then all wealthy people would be happy; but that is not so. I could lose myself and my soul to wealth, and end up knowing the price of everything and the value of nothing. Jesus tells us in today's gospel that we cannot serve God and money. He is not saying that we should not have money, that money is evil, or that it is incompatible with being a Christian. The problem arises when I come to answer the question, 'What is it that you love with all your heart, with all your soul, and with all your mind?' To that question some people could answer 'God', while others would answer 'Money'. It is in this situation that Jesus says, 'You cannot serve two masters. You cannot serve God and money.'

   Life is a gift from God and, with the gift, comes whatever it takes to live it. This may seem a contradiction when we think of the starving millions around the world, who have nothing to eat. It may not be of any great consolation to them to know that there is actually enough food in today's world for everybody. The real problem is that, while one half the world is dying of hunger, the other half is on a diet, trying to lose weight. If those who have, heeded today's gospel, the awful imbalance and injustice would be rectified.

God is the Creator of the universe, and that includes the birds of the air and the lilies of the field. Jesus refers to this when he wants to remind us of how God creates, and continues to take responsibility for his creation. Because of the fact that we have the gift of reason, however, we have a great advantage over the birds and the lilies. We have choices, and we can make decisions. Our heavenly Father knows our needs, and all we have to do is to trust him, and to seek to live in his kingdom, and 'everything else will be added to us'. Jesus taught his disciples one simple, short prayer. In it he told them to ask each day for what they need that day. Nothing more. Today's gospel ends with the words, 'Don't worry about tomorrow ... Today's troubles are enough for today.'

Response

Again and again in the gospel we are faced with decisions. The tendency of many people, when it comes to religion, is to begin some kind of discussion. Jesus is interested in decisions, not discussions. To put it simply, Jesus is either telling me the truth, or he's the greatest con-artist that ever lived! He is challenging us to make up our mind about him and his message. If I say the Our Father in the morning, when I ask for my daily bread, and then continue to worry for the rest of the day, then I am faced with a decision: I should either stop saying the Our Father, or stop worrying!

When I was growing up, I thought of false gods as being huge golden statues, with people bowing profoundly before them. I no longer think that way, thank God! There are false gods all around me. For one person it's money, for another it's power, and for someone else it's fame, and the good life. All trends in stock markets, political polls, or the latest fashions, are followed with slavish intensity. These gods claim complete control and absolute obedience. They rule the lives of people and, indeed, they often ruin the lives of people. There is an empty space within, there is a hole in the human heart, and that can never be filled by any or all of these false gods. Jesus tells us that we cannot serve two masters.

When Moses asked God what his name was, he was told 'I am who am'. God is totally a God of *now*. That is why Jesus speaks of the foolishness of worrying about tomorrow. In the only prayer he taught us, he told to ask for our daily bread, just what I need for today. There is a difference between what I need and what I want. We are all aware of things that we want, but don't really need. If God were cruel and sadistic, he would give me everything I ask for, and then have a good laugh! I often ask God for things that are not for my own good. Because God always answers prayers, there are times when the answer has to be *no*.

Practical

There are people who seem to be born worriers. They are always waiting on the other shoe to fall. If things are going well, it is the calm before the storm. For some of these people, this has become a way of life, and it is unlikely that they will change. Some of them, however, do get counselling and develop enough determination to decide that they have had enough. They have become sick and tired of being sick and tired. It is at such a moment that they may be ready to fall on their knees and hand the whole burden over to God. It is at such a moment, also, of course, that the miracle happens, and they find a life beyond their wildest dreams.

The only real sin I can commit, as a Christian, is not to have hope. St.Peter writes, 'Always have an explanation to give to those who ask you the reason for the hope that you have.' St Paul writes, 'Having given us Christ Jesus, will the Father not surely give us everything else?' I need to be constantly reminded, of course, that faith is a response to love, and it is only the work of the Spirit within my heart that enables me take Jesus and his promises seriously. I'm talking here about prayer. Prayer that is a cry from the heart, and not a whole string of words read from a book. It is not possible for a human being to fall on her face, cry out to God, and not be heard.

If I could make today's gospel my own, it would totally transform my life. All great evangelists, founders and saints, whether canonised or not, were people of solid faith. It was never a question of clenched fist, rugged jaw, or gritted teeth. Their faith was not in their own faith. They were able to stand back, get out of the way, and watch the Lord at work. It was like Mary at Cana. She didn't work the miracle, but she knew that Jesus could and would, if his help was sought. Jesus didn't go around healing anybody. He went around with the power to heal, and the person on the roadside had a decision to make. 'Do you believe that I can do this?' The answer, on occasions, was 'I believe, Lord; help my unbelief. Lord increase my faith.' I remind you again of the words of Jesus on another occasion 'The sin of this world is unbelief in me ... When the Son of Man comes will he find any faith on this earth?'

Story
The father decided to take the baby for a stroll through the park in the push-chair. It was a nice day, so he was enjoying the stroll. There was a football match on, so he decided to watch it for a while. He got so involved in the action that he lost complete account of time, and it was the sudden screaming of the baby that brought him back to reality. He looked at his watch, and was horrified to discover that it was over an hour past the baby's feeding time. He headed off, while the baby continued to scream. He kept saying, 'OK, Donald, you're OK, we'll be home in a minute. Calm down, Donald. You're doing very well, Donald. You'll be home in a few minutes.' There was an old lady sitting on the park bench, and she overheard the conversation. She approached the push-chair, looked into the pram, rubbed the baby's cheek, and said, 'Stop crying, Donald. Your dad is very good and he is taking good care of you.' To which the father replied, 'Excuse me, mam, but his name is Leslie, and my name is Donald.'

I cannot be a peacemaker in the lives of others if I don't have peace within my own heart. 'Let there be peace on earth, and let it begin with me ...'

NINTH SUNDAY OF THE YEAR

Gospel: Matthew 7:21-27

Central Theme
In every sense of the word, today's gospel is a solid teaching on exactly what Jesus means by being a disciple of his, and of doing as he prescribes.

Parable
It may sound strange, but religion was always been a cause of conflict and wars, right from the beginning. There is not a war anywhere in today's world that is not a religious one. As a pupil in junior school, I used listen with shock to the horrors attributed to Cromwell, as he sought to subjugate the Irish people. What shocked me most was when I heard that he was a deeply religious man and, every night, after massacring hundreds of the Irish 'Papists', he would go on his knees and thank God for the privilege that was his.

I have also come across people who adhered strictly all their lives to all the external trappings of their religion and yet, when the crunch came, when the cross arrived, when death approached, the whole fabric of their religion came apart, and they were certainly on very shaky foundations.

Teaching
Calling Jesus 'Lord', if he's not Lord, won't get me anywhere. 'I am the Good Shepherd. I know mine, and mine know me.' Allowing Jesus to be Lord in my life is a very different and, yet, a very simple thing. It is all a question of obedience. If he is to be Lord, then I must do things, and live my life according to the very clear guidelines he left me. 'If you love me, you will obey me ...'

There is a religious song called 'Jesus is the rock of my salvation, and his banner over me is love.' Jesus uses the word 'rock' several times. When he called Peter, he said 'You are Peter, and on this rock I will build my church.' Peter himself wasn't actually a rock, as his unfolding story shows, but he was to be the titular leader of a group of which Jesus himself would be the rock. When Jesus called Peter, he 'looked at Peter'. Later, when Peter denied him, 'Jesus turned and looked at Peter'. Peter saw that the look hadn't changed, and he knew that Jesus alone was the same yesterday, today, and always. Later, in one of his letters, he

149

would write 'Always have an explanation to give to those who
ask you the reason for the hope that you have.'

One translation of today's gospel has Jesus saying, 'Go away.
I never knew you. The things you did were unauthorised.' Jesus
is the author of our salvation. He has written the script. It is our
vocation to learn that script, and to live it out. 'Apart from me
you can do nothing.' As a Christian, I am someone who is sent,
who is commissioned to carry a message. That message is about
Jesus, and about the good news that he came to proclaim.

Response

Jesus asks a very important question in another part of the
gospel. 'Who do you say that I am?' If he is Lord in my life, then
that must profoundly change my whole approach to living my
life. If he is Lord, then, I am living in his kingdom. 'Seek you first
the kingdom of God, and everything else will be added to you.' I
have no reason to worry what the future holds if he holds the
future. Spirituality is about letting go, and death, at the end of
my life, is about letting go completely.

You will notice in today's gospel that Christian living is not
about what we do, as much as why we do it. I could be a pagan,
and be a good person, and do many kind acts. What is unique
about the actions and words of the Christian is that all of this is
done because Jesus has entrusted this mission to me. On several
occasions in the gospels Jesus was asked by what authority he
did what he did, and he always replied that he had come to do
the will of his Father in heaven. 'They marvelled at him, because
he spoke as one having authority.' Later on he would say, 'As
the Father has sent me, so I am sending you. If you love me, you
will obey me ...'

Jesus is the same yesterday, today, and always. That is why,
if my life is based on him and on his word, I can stand firm in the
midst of all the storms and trials of life. 'I will not abandon you
in the storm. I will come to you.' We can all be sure of the trials,
and the moments of testing, that is part of life itself. It is at such
times, more than others, than I can be most aware of Jesus' presence and his promises. It is often at such times that real growth
takes place in my life, rather than when everything is smooth,
calm, and under control. What to one person is a problem, to the
Christian can be an opportunity.

Practical
There is nothing automatic about Jesus or his message. Just because I was baptised is no guarantee that I will ever become a Christian. There comes a time when I must take personal responsibility for my Christian vocation and, with a generous heart, I accept Jesus as my Lord, and I ask for the anointing of his Spirit to enable me live and walk in his Way. Nobody else can do this for me. There is nothing profound or earth-shaking about this, although, indeed, it is an extraordinary moment of grace. The words I use matter very little. It is the goodwill in my heart that the Lord is seeking. Could that moment happen in your life today?

I said that there was nothing earth-shaking about this, yet it is a moment that will certainly bring profound change, and very real blessings into my life. These are changes and blessings that I will personally experience. I don't have to wait till the storms come to find that my faith is much deeper, and my conscious awareness and contact with God is more real. Jesus will no longer be some sort of 999 merchant, called in for emergencies only! I will find that he is included in every decision, and I consult with him on every issue.

Don't forget the crunch line in today's gospel. There is one thing you can be absolutely sure of. You are going to die one day, and come face to face with Jesus. Immediately the first part of today's gospel comes into effect. You either know him or you don't. There is a vast amount of material written about what happens, at such a time, to two-thirds of the world who never heard of Jesus, or who never heard his message. While acknowledging that there are solid, reasoned, and reasonable replies to such questions, they do not concern us now, because I am not speaking to those people at this time. I am speaking to us, about us, right here, right now. We all can slip into the habit of putting off till tomorrow something that should be done today. This question, however, is too serious for that. There are people walking around today, feeling strong, healthy, and well, and they will not be alive tomorrow. Not one of us can have any claim on tomorrow, which is a gift that God may or may not give us. We certainly cannot take it for granted.

Story
A certain clergyman was retiring, and he had put in train a whole series of plans in advance of that occasion. One of the

most important was his plan to build a bungalow on a piece of land he had acquired, overlooking the sea. He was looking forward to retiring there with his books, and to having time to engage in some of his favourites hobbies and past-times. He was quite gifted as a do-it-yourself handyman, and he decided to do most of the work himself. Everything went according to plan, until he came up against an unexpected problem. He couldn't hang a door! No matter how he tried it, he just couldn't manage to get the correct balance of hinges, saddle, jamb, etc. One day he gave up, and decided to go for a walk. He walked a mile or two when he noticed some new houses being built just alongside the road. He wandered in, and began to look around. To his great delight, when he came to one of the houses, he noticed that a carpenter was hanging a door. He stood to watch, something which made the carpenter feel uneasy, and he asked 'Can I help you?' The clergyman explained his predicament, and that he was watching to see if he could discover the secret of hanging a door properly. The carpenter thought for a while, and then, with a grin, he replied, 'I'll tell you what I'll do. I'll hang the doors for you, if you do something for me.' The offer was tempting, even though he was afraid what the catch might be. He agreed to accept the offer of help, whatever the condition. The carpenter said, 'I've been a member of your congregation for several years now. I sat and listened to you Sunday after Sunday, and there were many times when I wished I could speak out, and share with you what I thought. I'll hang the doors for you on condition that you allow me do something, where you are the listener and the onlooker, and where you will be unable to make any comment or to interrupt me in any way. This will be my turn to call the shots.' The clergyman smiled, as he agreed to this unusual request.

The carpenter put him into his car and they drove off down the road. They came to a gate, through which the carpenter entered, bidding the other to follow. Just inside the gate was a site for a house. The foundations were laid many years ago, it seemed, but they were now covered in weeds and nettles. The carpenter pointed to the site, while he simply said, 'Think about it.' The clergyman remained silent. They drove on down the road, and stopped in front of a beautiful modern building that was completed. The building was breath-taking, with manicured lawns, expensive drapes, and magnificent bay windows, and panelled front door. The carpenter led the way, opened the front door, and ushered the clergyman into the house. He was completely taken aback when he entered, to find that the interior of the house was just a hollow shell, no floors, no walls, no ceilings. This puzzled him greatly but, as he was not allowed speak, he just listened as the carpenter said, 'Think about it.' Like the story of the Three Bears, there is, of course, a third house. They reached this just around the next corner. This house really looked lived in, the grass could go with a clip, the curtains weren't hanging perfectly, and it could do with a coat of paint. The carpenter led the way, as they entered. 'I'm home, honey', he said, as he entered the front door. A woman appeared with a smile and a welcoming kiss, and two toddlers rushed towards him and leaped up into his arms. He produced some sweets from his pocket as he hugged them. The clergyman noticed a pair of shoes lying at the foot of the stairs, the picture in the front hall was slightly askew, and there were a few crayon marks on the wall. He was trying to take the whole scene in, when the carpenter turned to him and said, 'Oh, sorry … think about it.'

The following Sunday the clergyman gave the best sermon of his life, as he described the three different ways in which people accept the message of Jesus. Some of them put down a foundation during their childhood and school-time, but they do nothing more with it after that. Some others do a wonderful 'snowjob', where they are seen to be perfect and conforming on the outside while, within, there is an emptiness and a spiritual vacuum. The third group could do with a tidying-up from time to time, a visit to Confession, or an annual Mission; but, inside there is a tremendous amount of real love.

Think about it!

TENTH SUNDAY OF THE YEAR

Gospel: Matthew 9:9-13

Central Theme
Today's gospel is a gem, in that it gives us a simple little cameo of how Jesus dealt with sinners, how he related to them, and how he showed an undisguised preference for them. We must never confuse the difference between Jesus loving the sinner, while not approving of the sin. In another story, he told the woman taken in adultery, 'Neither do I condemn you. Go in peace, and sin no more.'

Parable
There was a very popular book around some years ago called *Joshua,* and I'm sure it is still available today. It is story about a man who is uncannily like Jesus in today's world. He came to live in this little town, he seemed different, and he soon had the attention of everyone. He made friends with the people of the town. The problem with each group was that he made friends with those whom they considered to be outside the circle. He went to church on Sunday, but he caused great anger when he went to each church in turn, including the synagogue. The religious people had a watch on his house, because he had very questionable late-callers, like alcoholics and the homeless. He wasn't actually crucified, but was run out of town. Some things never change …

Teaching
It's important that we understand what it means to be a sinner. It doesn't mean someone who is committing sin all the time. It is a state of being, a human condition, that is the result of original sin. If I let go of a bunch of keys, they will fall to the ground. That is caused by the law of gravity. On my own, I cannot lift myself out of the quicksand of my own selfishness. Jesus understands our human condition much better than we ourselves do. He can see things as they really are. That is why he came to redeem and save us, and certainly not to condemn us.

It is difficult for us to enter into the mind-set of the people who lived in the time of Jesus. Tax collectors, and all others who did not conform to the strict laws as laid down by the zealous religious leaders, were looked down upon, and treated as the scum of the earth. They were to be avoided at all costs, and one could be guilty by association in any way. Imagine how the Pharisees looked on Jesus when they saw the company he kept!

The final comment of Jesus in today's gospel should be written loud and clear on the outer and inner walls of all our churches. 'You can keep your sacrifices. I would much prefer you showed love, forgiveness, and mercy to each other. I came to heal the wounded, and those who are broken; I came to welcome, embrace, and forgive the sinners, whom you condemn. What I want is genuine love, not heartless prayers, and meaningless religious exercises.'

Response

Jesus came to call sinners. I will never hear that call unless I am convinced that I am a sinner, and that call is meant for me. Part of my sinful condition is that it blinds me to that very fact. It is so much easier for me to recognise the sinner in someone else. It is the work of the Holy Spirit to lead me into truth. 'He will convict you of sin', Jesus tells us. It may seem a contradiction to say that holiness is coming to believe and accept that I am a much greater sinner than I thought I was! If I stand in a spotlight, I can notice every bit of dust on my clothes. The closer I come to God, the more obvious my sins are.

There is nothing negative or self-condemnatory about all of this. It is simply a question of truth, an acceptance of how things are. When I think of sin, the first thing I must remember is that I am a victim of sin, original sin, something which I did not commit. If I cannot come to understand and accept this, I will never come to understand the things that I myself do. Once the alcoholic accepts his alcoholism, he can then see and understand why he did all the crazy things he did.

It can be difficult for those of us who were brought up on religion to genuinely relate to Jesus in our sinfulness. A leading psychiatrist told me one time that he could discharge two-thirds of his patients from all the psychiatric hospitals in his area, if he could get them to deal with their guilt, and most of that is the result of their religious upbringing. What a sad comment on what we have done with the message and the attitude of Jesus in today's gospel!

Practical

Jesus asks a personal question: 'Who do you say that I am?' If he is my Saviour then there are clear and definite ways of experiencing that. If I am riddled with guilt, remorse, etc., about the past, if I find it difficult to forgive myself for things I did, if I am not deeply conscious of my need to be a forgiving person, because I am a person who has been forgiven, then Jesus is not really my Saviour, I have not yet accepted him as my Saviour. This deserves immediate consideration, and I am speaking about *today*.

Do I fall into the trap of categorising people, slotting them into pigeon-holes, making a very clear distinction between whether John is a doctor or a docker? Jesus seemed to have a preference for all the wrong people! I don't have to 'hang-out' with marginalised people to treat them with respect. If the poor 'wino' has a hand out for money, I can treat him with respect, as I give him something. When I die, I won't be asked what he did with the money; rather I will be asked if I gave him something. Even stopping for a few words, asking him how things are, etc., can be more important than anything I may give him. Do you think Jesus would pass him by, and ignore him?

There are people who do not go to church, receive communion, etc., because they feel they are unworthy, and 'outside the pale'. Today's gospel stresses the fact that there is nobody outside the scope of God's love and acceptance. The more convinced I am that I am a sinner, the more at home I should feel in his presence.

Story

A man came into the doctor's surgery one day, and he was very worried. He explained his problem. 'Every part of my body that I touch is very very sore … my nose, my elbow, my head, my left hand.' The doctor gave him a thorough examination, x-ray, blood tests, etc. The man returned the following day for the results, and he was very nervous. 'Did you find out what's wrong with me?' he asked the doctor. 'I did,' he replied. 'What is it?' enquired the very worried patient. 'All that's wrong with you,' replied the doctor, 'is that your finger is broken!'

If I fully understood the nature of original sin, when I was the victim of someone else's sin, I will have a much clearer idea why I do what I do. I sin, not because I'm evil, but because I'm weak. Jesus understands that only too well.

ELEVENTH SUNDAY OF THE YEAR

Gospel: Matthew 9:36-10:8

Central Theme

Jesus looks around, assesses the situation, and he calls on others to join him in his crusade to minister to the many who are seen to be without leadership or direction in their lives. He gives a very clear mandate about what they are to present to the people. 'Go out there, and tell them the good news, and your words will be accompanied by the power I will give them.'

Parable

This is an extraordinary time in the history of the church. Religious life, as we have known it, is over. Religious life is a charism given to the church and, so, it will never be taken away, but it continues to evolve and to change with the times. All over Ireland today are ruins of monasteries, something that preceded the congregations of our day. A hundred years from now there will be something just as good but, at the moment, that is not yet evident. Jesus saw the need, so he called others to join him in the mission. This is what inspired every founder of every religious congregation and order in the church. There was a need that needed to be met, so a group of people were called to set up a congregation to meet the needs of the time. These needs are always changing, so the response of the prophet is to call others to join in some new venture. Every congregation or order in the church came from the cry of some individual who identified a need that was not being met and so a new congregation was born. That's what today's gospel is about.

Teaching

Today's gospel begins with a reference to the pity Jesus felt for those who followed him. They were like lost sheep, sheep without a shepherd, without any direction, goals, or purpose in life. He asked his immediate followers to join with him in praying to the Father for more workers, as the harvest was great and the labourers were few. Already he wanted to share his mission because, when he had completed his part of it, his followers would have to take over, and continue it.

He sent them with a message. It was a simple message, and, for someone at that time, among the Jews, it must have been a message for which they had long waited. 'The Kingdom is near.' It was not a message that would easily be accepted, because, with the limitations of our language and our difficulty in grasping the simple and the obvious, we have a real and serious problem with the language of God. At one point, Jesus said, 'Let your 'yes' be 'yes', and your 'no' be 'no'.' Nothing complicated; just a simple direct message. 'The Kingdom of God is near.' God is in your midst, if you open your ears to hear him, and your eyes to see him; above all, if you open your hearts to receive him.

Before sending out his apostles he endowed them with the power and authority they would need, if they were to continue his work. It was his work, and only God can do a God-thing. They were to be channels, not generators, or transformers. 'Make me a channel of your peace. Where there is hatred, let me bring your love ...' The mission is his and, as St Paul says, 'We are ambassadors for Christ.' An ambassador is one who represents someone else in a situation, and who says or does nothing without first consulting with the one who entrusted him with the responsibility.

Response
There is a lot of concern expressed today about the 'scarcity of vocations'. While this is understandable, it is not correct. More and more, the laity are becoming involved in areas which before had been the sacred preserve of the clergy. It is over twenty years since I wrote in a book called *It's Really Very Simple*, where I compared the church to the FA (soccer) Cup Final in Wembley, where 100,000 people, badly in need of a bit of exercise, were sitting down very comfortably, criticising eleven poor guys, badly in need of a rest! I longed for the day when they would come down out of the stands; even more, I longed for the day they would be invited to come down out of the stands!

There is a saying 'No involvement, no commitment.' People have to be allowed become involved before they can experience any sense of being committed. Jesus asks us to 'Pray the Lord of the harvest to send more labourers into his fields.' If I pray for this, I must be prepared and willing to respond to that myself. It's all too easy to sit back and wait for someone else to do something. There are three groups in any parish or society. There are those who cause things to happen. There are those who watch things happening. And, finally, there are those who haven't a clue what's happening!

'Give as freely as you have received.' As the song says 'Freely, freely, you have received. Freely, freely give.' God gives me nothing for myself. Life is a gift that is to be spent in the service of others. There is a book called *The Happiest People on Earth*, and it outlines a way of living the Christian life. The kingdom of God is near. The kingdom of God is as near as the heart of the nearest Christian. We are not all called to evangelise, but we are all called to witness. The life of a Christian is, in itself, the message. The messenger is the message. It sometimes happens, as in the case of Jesus, that some people don't like the message, so they kill the messenger.

Practical
There is a sense, in the gospel, in which Jesus is seen to be always 'on the go'. There was a sense of urgency about him. He was on a mission. 'There is a baptism with which I must be baptised, and how can I be at peace until it is accomplished?' Baptism, in this context, is the baptism of blood that would take place on Calvary. He kept calling his disciples to follow. 'Come, let us go ...' There are many incidents in the gospel when he is seen to be completely exhausted, even to the point of falling asleep in the boat, in the midst of a storm. There were other times when he felt sorry for his disciples, and brought them away from the crowd to have a rest. I don't think that I can honestly access my Christian vocation without considering ways and means of living it. In other words, it's not just a collection of ideas in which I believe. 'Faith, without good works, is dead.' Faith is in my feet, rather than some sort of mental assent in my head.

I should take a serious look at my surroundings, and ask myself a few honest questions. What difference is it making to these people among whom I am living now? If I were to die today, what would the legacy of my memory be? Most pictures of starving children, or displaced people are accompanied by a request for aid in coming to the rescue of those people. We are told that £3 a month will save the eyesight of someone; that £10 a month will help give a child a chance of survival, and of escaping from conditions that can only mean death. These requests are always followed by freephone numbers. Have any of those appeals moved or touched me enough to pick up the phone and reply? I am asking myself this question, as a Christian, while knowing that there should be no need to ask it.

Despite what has gone before, has the present use of the word 'vocation' come to mean anything personal to me? I have a vocation, as sure as the Pope has one, but am I willing to accept that call, and respond to it? 'Many are called, but few choose to answer.' It may be a cliché, but it is still true: All it takes for evil people to succeed is that good people should do nothing. If I am not part of the solution, I remain part of the problem. 'They that put their hand to the plough, and turn back, are not worthy of the kingdom of Heaven.' Jesus puts it another way. 'You are either for me, or against. Let your 'yes' be 'yes', and your 'no' be 'no'.'

Story
One Sunday the priest announced that the church was dead, and he would conduct the funeral on the following Sunday. This aroused great curiosity in his listeners, as they turned up the following Sunday, unsure what was going to happen. Sure enough, there was a coffin in the sanctuary, with the lid up against the wall, over to the side. Before beginning the 'funeral Mass', he invited the congregation to come up one by one, to view the remains. They streamed up in single file and, as each looked into the coffin, there was a look of surprise on each face. The coffin was empty, and the bottom of the coffin was a mirror. As each looked in, it was that person's face that was reflected back to them. They got the message, as the priest made full use of the liturgy to enthuse them to become involved, and to take responsibility for their role in the life of the church.

TWELFTH SUNDAY OF THE YEAR

Gospel: Matthew 10: 26-33

Central Theme
This is a very powerful statement from Jesus about the cost of discipleship, and the expectations he has, and the promises he makes to those who follow him.

Parable
Over the past thirty years, the history of Northern Ireland has been one of violence and tribal warfare. One of the things most evident was how the Godfathers of violence continued to recruit young people to their cause. The training must have been extraordinarily intensive, because many of these young men gave their lives for what they were told was a just cause. Some who deserted the ranks, or who failed to follow the line of action dictated, were often summarily executed and, in the cases where they were suspected of collusion with the enemy, this execution was preceded by savage torture. It is against that backdrop that I present the gentle, but firm message of today's gospel. No threats, just a simple call to rally to his call, and to trust his promises to those who follow him.

Teaching
Jesus is asking us to trust him. He is asking us to throw in our lot with him, and he promises to see us through. There is a cost in Pentecost. We cannot pick and choose the Christian message like some kind of à la carte menu. If we choose to follow him, we should not be surprised if this brings us some of the negative reaction that he himself encountered. Fear can make cowards of us all. There are people who wouldn't even dare bless themselves passing a church, for fear of what the others on the bus might think!

His reassurances about the Father's care and provision for us is very definite, and very simple. The God who cares for the lilies of the field, and the birds of the air, will surely take full care of his own children. I remember reading a children's story one time, when the birds just couldn't understand why people should so often be crippled with fear. The birds quoted Jesus' words about the Father taking care of them, and they also knew that he made the same promise to us. Unfortunately, it's so much easier for us to make promises to God, often promises that we cannot fulfil, than to believe the promises he makes to us. 'Heaven and earth will pass away before my word passes away.'

There is a strong word in today's gospel about the need to give witness to our beliefs. My silence, when I should speak out, is sometimes moral cowardice and, in doing so, I am denying that I am a Christian. From earliest childhood, I was always puzzled by Peter's denial of Jesus. How could he possibly do such a thing? He had seen Jesus raise the dead, calm the storm, and he got a glimpse of his glory on Mount Thabor. As I went on in life, it was much easier to identify with Peter, as I recognised a tendency within myself to save my own skin at all costs. We have a phrase about 'fair-weather friends'. When everything is going my way, it is easy to believe in God, in myself, and in others. However, it is when the going gets tough that the tough get going.

Response
There is a disposition of heart that is necessary before the words of Jesus can enter. To read a passage from the gospel requires a completely different attitude and openness than reading something in a newspaper. The message of Jesus is more Spirit than words. The Spirit enters my heart through the words that I hear. Today's gospel, like any other passage from the gospel, can go right over my head if the Spirit is not present in my heart, giving me a way of hearing that is so much more than simply using my ears.

Faith is very difficult to define. It has little to do with knowledge, and has nothing to do with religion. Faith is a response to love. When Jesus speaks today about how the heavenly Father cares for each of us, his intention is to provoke a response of faith, rather than just agree with what he is saying. From my own experience, and I cannot speak for anyone else, the problem with my response is that it can be slow in coming! I often need to hear it many times before I really hear it. To hear it includes responding to it.

There are several core messages in today's gospel. Two of the most important ones are the call to trust the Father's care, and the importance of giving witness to my discipleship. No doubting, no denying. It is amazing how many times Jesus presents his message in a single-minded, clearly defined way. He leaves us in no doubt what he means, if we choose to listen. In one part

of the gospel Jesus has some words to say that we could be reminded of here. He says that 'When I come, I will not have to
judge them. The words that I have spoken will be their judge. If I
had not come and spoken, they would have an excuse for their
sins.' This does 'box' us in a little bit, doesn't it?

Practical
At the moment of death I will stand before God, totally naked in
every sense of that word. Nothing hidden, no pretence, no denial. The canvas of my life will be completely laid out before
him. In the words of today's gospel 'Everything will be revealed,
and everything that is secret will be made public.' Why should I
wait 'till I die for that to happen? I can stand before God, like
that, any day I wish. To do so is a wonderful way of praying.
'Here I am, Lord.'

Can you identify something in your life that you feel, as a
Christian, you ought to do, but are not doing? Sometimes I can
be timid about joining the SVP, or some voluntary parish group,
because of moral cowardice, afraid of what someone might
think or say about me. My pride can get in the way, and I
haven't the same freedom to pontificate on a high stool down in
the local pub, if I am seen to be one of 'them'! For every one who
is involved, there are plenty of others willing and ready to criti-
cise them, and to say 'Who do they think they are?' They are
Christians, they are members of this community, members of
the Body of Christ, who are actively pursuing their Christian
vocation, as best they can.

We are familiar with the question 'If all of us were arrested,
brought down to the police-station, and charged with being
Christian, how many of us would get off scot-free for lack of
evidence?' In today's gospel, Jesus is once again saying 'It's
make-up-your-mind-time.' 'Blessed are the pure of heart, for
they shall see God.' Purity of heart is about being single-minded,
sincere, truthful, and faithful. It's about ridding the heart of all
the human deviousness that can so easily become part of our
behaviour. If I am a Christian, then my options in life are drastic-
ally changed. Examine your heart today and, in all honesty, be
your own judge about whether you take Jesus seriously or not.

Story
I remember saying Mass for a Padre Pio Prayer Group in a certain cathedral in Ireland. There was a huge congregation, and

everything was highly organised, with ushers, readers, music, etc. In the midst of my words of wisdom, Angela (not her real name), the town drunk, came up the middle of the church. She had several shopping bags that she always carried with her, and she was shouting something that I couldn't understand. All eyes in the congregation turned towards her, and there was an air of silent shock among the people. She made her way up to the very front seat, shouted at the people there to move in, and she flopped down, with bags falling in all directions. She continued to shout at me for a while and, eventually, she dropped her head and fell asleep. Immediately, I switched from what I was saying, pointed in her direction, and continued to speak about how I had felt just then. I didn't mention her name, nor was I specific enough to provoke her attention, should she be only dozing. I told the people of how worried I was, not at what happened, but at what might have happened. My one fear was that someone, with the best of intentions, might have attempted to remove her from the church or prevent her from entering in the first place. We were a Padre Pio Prayer Group, and one of his claims to glory was that he had the wounds of Christ on his body. I told them that, if they ever came across the Body of Christ without the wounds, they could be certain it was a phoney. Angela was one of the wounds, and to remove her would have put me in an impossible situation because, in conscience, I could not continue with the Mass.

Angela helped teach us more about Christianity that night then anything I might have said, with whatever sermon I had prepared.

THIRTEENTH SUNDAY OF THE YEAR

Gospel: Matthew 10:37-42

Central Theme

Jesus makes a direct connection between the Father, himself, others, and ourselves. What we do for one, we do for all. A kind deed done for another is registered in the books of heaven as having been done to God himself.

Parable

Looking back on my own life, I have plenty of memories. One of those has to do with members of my family emigrating. At one stage or other, eleven out of thirteen of my siblings had to go abroad, in search of employment. One very important person, in each situation, was the person each was going with, or the person each was going to. Each needed a helping hand to get started, by way of temporary accommodation, work, etc. As the years went by, and each of my siblings became self-sufficient, there was always a special love and appreciation reserved for those who were there for them, when help was needed. When someone helped one member of the family, that person gained and earned the love and appreciation of everyone else in the family.

Teaching

On first reading, today's gospel comes across as harsh, and un-feeling. Once more, Jesus presents us with a straight choice. He issues a call, and the onus is on us to respond to that call. His own life is the blue-print. He spent his life in the service of others. He himself lived the message he spoke, and he never asked his followers to do anything he himself was not prepared to do. Following him meant taking up a cross.

The word 'cross' is often not understood too well. We speak of someone losing a job, losing mobility, or losing a loved one, as having a heavy cross to bear. These are not crosses, because these things happen to pagans as well. A cross is anything I have to do as a result of my decision to follow Jesus. To become a Christian is to have lopped off all other options. The word 'decision' comes from the Latin word *decidere*, which literally means to 'lop off'. To follow Jesus is to take up the cross of service every day. It is a cross that is made up of splinters, and those who spend their lives in the service of others are the happiest people on earth. 'My yoke is sweet, and my burden is light'.

The reference to the cup of cold water, given in Jesus' name, should give us thought for reflection. Every good deed is recorded, nothing goes unnoticed. The kingdom of God is built up in two ways, by tiny acts, and most of them are hidden. Jean Vanier says that most of the greatest movements for good in the history of the world have been brought about by the quiet prayers of totally unknown people.

Response

The problem with today's gospel is that it is so much of the Spirit that it is difficult to speak about it in human words. The call that Jesus utters can only be heard by the heart. No glossy posters, or slick TV ads can get this across. When today's gospel first happened, the apostles were looking at Jesus as he spoke, and his voice reached them. Today, because of my own Pentecost, the voice comes from within me. I can read the words of today's gospel, but I have to listen to them with my heart.

Life is a gift given to us for the service of others. If I save it for myself, it remains un-invested, and produces nothing. I had a funeral some time ago of a young man who died in an epileptic fit. He was spastic, and was frequently hospitalised. He died aged 31. His whole life was spent in the service of others. His funeral was an extraordinary experience, and it began with a five-minutes standing ovation. This was from members of every possible branch of disabilities, because he had spent his life raising funds, pushing wheelchairs, visiting the sick in hospitals, and serving as a Scout Leader. To him could be applied the following quote from Harry S. Truman, former President of the US: 'I always remember an epitaph which is in the cemetery at Tombstone, Arizona. It says 'Here lies Jack Williams. He done his damnedest.' I think that is the greatest epitaph a person can have – when he gives everything that is in him to do the job he has set before him.' My words at the funeral were 'He did the very best with what he had.'

It is interesting to note that Jesus seems more interested in charitable deeds than in religious practices. Describing the General Judgement in Matthew 25, he speaks of bread, water, clothes, visits to prisons, etc. There are no questions about how many prayers you said, or how often you went to church. Today's gospel even stresses the importance of giving someone a cup of cold water.

Practical

Look at your life, and distinguish between what is a cross, and what is a misfortune, or a disaster. Remember that the cross is always redemptive, and it always produces life-giving blessings. Walking the Christian Way is to take up the cross of service every day; it is about sharing, listening, forgiving, helping, etc. If you are a Christian, you have no choice, because there is only one way to live the Christian life.

The word 'welcome' is repeated several times in today's gospel. Hospitality is very much part of Christian living. Jesus tells us 'what you do to others, I will take as having been done for me'. We extend hospitality to Jesus every time we welcome another into our homes. I may not have much to give by way of food or drink, but the quality of the hospitality is not measured by the amount of what is given. It would be a really worthwhile exercise to examine how I would rate myself on the scale of hospitality. It would, indeed, be interesting to know how others rate us in this area.

Whatever I invest in life, through my service of others, takes on an eternal value. Whatever I keep for myself, when I die, it dies. It is in giving that we receive, and the richest people are not the wealthiest people. My richness comes from my generosity in sharing what I have. Like Scrooge in Dickens' novel, the miser is always miserable. Today's gospel goes to the heart of what it means to be a good friend and neighbour; something that is within the capabilities of any one of us.

Story

Ruth went to her mailbox, and there was only one letter. She picked it up, and looked at it before opening it. Then she looked at the envelope again. There was no stamp, no post-mark, only her name and address. She read the letter.

Dear Ruth,

I'm going to be in your neighbourhood Saturday afternoon, and I would like to visit.

Love always,

Jesus.

Her hands were shaking as she placed the letter on the table. 'Why would the Lord want to visit me? I'm nobody special. I don't have anything to offer.' With that thought she remembered her empty kitchen cabinets. 'Oh, my goodness, I really don't have anything to offer. I'll have to run down to the shop and buy something for dinner.' She reached for her purse, and counted out the contents. Four pounds and fifty pence. 'Well I can get some bread and cold cuts, at least.' She threw on her coat, and headed out the door. A loaf of bread, a few slices of turkey, and a carton of milk; leaving Ruth with the grand total of sixty pence to last her till Monday. Nonetheless, she felt good as she headed home, her meagre offerings tucked under her arm.

'Hey, lady, can you help us, lady?' Ruth had been so absorbed in planning the meal that she had not noticed two huddled figures in the alleyway; a man and a woman, both of them dressed in rags. 'Look lady, I have no job, and we're both living out here on the street, and it's getting cold, and we're really hungry. If you could help us, lady, we would appreciate it.'

Ruth looked at them both. They were dirty, they smelled bad, and she was sure they could get some kind of work, if they really tried. 'Sir, I'd like to help you, but I'm a poor woman myself. All I have is a few cold cuts and some bread, and I'm having an important guest for dinner tonight, and I was planning on serving that to him.' 'OK, lady, I understand. Thanks, anyhow.' The man put his arm around the woman's shoulder, turned, and headed back into the alley. As she watched them leave, Ruth felt a familiar twinge in her heart. 'Sir, wait!' The couple stopped and turned, as she ran down the alley towards them. 'Look, why don't you take this food. I'll figure out something else to serve my guest.' She handed the man her grocery bag. 'Thank you, lady. Thank you very much.' 'Yes, thank you.' It was the man's wife, and Ruth could see now that she was shivering. 'You know, I've got another coat at home. Here, why don't you take this one.' Ruth unbuttoned her jacket, and slipped it over the woman's shoulders. Then, smiling, she turned and walked back to the street; without her coat, and nothing to serve her guest. 'Thank you, lady. Thank you very much.'

Ruth was chilled before she reached her front door, and she was also worried. The Lord was coming to visit, and she had nothing to offer him. She fumbled through her purse for her keys, and, as she did so, she noticed another letter in the mailbox. 'That's odd. The mailman doesn't usually come twice in one day.' She took the letter out of the box, and opened it.

Dear Ruth,

It was so good to see you again. Thank you for the lovely meal. And, thank you, too, for the lovely coat.

Love always, Jesus.

FOURTEENTH SUNDAY OF THE YEAR

Gospel: Matthew 11:25-30

Central Theme
This is a beautiful gospel passage, in which Jesus tells us the kind of heart he has, and the kind of hearts we should have, if we are to be open to his message. It is a very consoling gospel, because it speaks of humility, gentleness, and rest.

Parable
I remember, some years ago, when Mother Teresa received the Nobel Peace Prize in Oslo. The 'powers-that-be' didn't know how to deal with her! They sent two limousines to the airport to meet her, one for her, and one for her luggage! She arrived smiling, with her personal belongings in a shopping bag, and the welcoming committee was completely at a loss what to do. They would have no problem at all with heads of state, and other dignitaries but, with this little frail woman who had some sort of extraordinary aura about her, this made them feel powerless, and they were in awe in the presence of a power and a strength with which they were totally unfamiliar. That is what Jesus speaks of today.

Teaching
Please notice that part of today's gospel is not spoken to us at all! It is Jesus speaking to his Father. I often think that, if you really want to get to know someone, it would be easier if you could eavesdrop on their prayers! How they speak, and what they say gives an insight into what's going on within. The prayer in today's gospel is like a whispered exclamation of gratitude. Jesus is truly grateful about the nature of his message. It is for the child-hearted, for the ordinary punter, and not for the intellectuals, and the worldly-minded. It makes little sense up in the head, because it goes against the thinking and values of the world, and it confounds those who know the price of everything and the value of nothing.

Jesus repeats his oft-spoken message that he, and he alone, is the only way to the Father. He came with a message from the Father, and he is the only one who knows that message, and can deliver it. Genius is the ability to discern the obvious. The message is so simple that only God could have inspired it. The Jews

169

were expecting a Messiah who would be endowed with worldly might, and he would lead them to earthly power and glory. This has no value in the eyes of God. Jesus said that the meek possess the earth, that the lowly are raised up, and that to live in his kingdom requires the heart of a child. Even as I write I know that you, the reader or the listener, don't want some kind of theological dissertation. You want a simple message that touches your heart, and inspires your thinking. If the thinking is clarified and simplified, the actions that follow are simple and clear.

Today's gospel contains a beautiful invitation. Jesus invites us to come to him if we want peace, if we want solid teaching, if we want salvation, or freedom from the bondage of our humanity. 'Let me teach you', he says. Come to him, just as you are, and he will lead you to a life beyond your wildest dreams. This life is not about going to heaven, or something that is promised after we die. It is promised and offered now, because the road to heaven is heaven.

Response
Today's gospel certainly calls for a response. It should evoke a kindling of the heart, and it should offer us a clear way out of our turmoil and struggles. We can all distinguish between being intellectual and worldly-wise, and being childlike. Jesus speaks to the Father, and he speaks about the Father in today's gospel. If God is Father, then we are called on to become like children. Being like children is to live within the limits of what we have, what we know, and what we can do. It is a time of learning and discovery and, especially, is it a time of dependency. For those of us blessed enough to have had a normal childhood, it is so much easier to understand what that means.

Jesus speaks about knowing the Father, rather than knowing about him. We are invited into a relationship, an attachment, a sense of belonging. We have to think of God as Father, and to speak to him as Father. Prayer would be so simple and spontaneous if we could speak to the Father as a child speaks to his/her earthly father. Not all fathers are good at listening, nor are some of them good at giving time and space to their children. This can make it all the more difficult for us to relate to the full meaning of such a relationship. Jesus tells us that he will inform us about the Father, and he will reveal the Father to us. Jesus is always on 'stand-by', as it were, waiting on us to be ready.

We all experience weariness, and heavy burdens from time

to time. There is a tendency to file God's phone number under 'Emergencies Only', and to turn to him when everything else has failed. God would love to be in on the act so much quicker. He is our Father and, having given us life, he wants to be involved in every dimension of our lives. Coming to Jesus is coming to the Father. Jesus tells us that his burden is light. It is not a question of exchanging one burden for another. Responding to his call, or invitation, is a source of great blessing and real joy. Responding to his invitation is to share in his life. The people who do this are the happiest people on earth.

Practical
When you get a chance, a quiet moment, today or soon, go down into your heart and see can you find the inner child there. Remember it is only the body that grows old. The person within is always a child, who always likes to be loved, needed, and praised, and who still whistles passing the graveyard. If you can get in touch with that inner child, your heart is ready to be open to God. If you read today's gospel with that sort of open heart, it would really enter into you, and your heart would burn. The children of God are heart-people, not head-people. Down in my heart I know, even when I completely fail to understand it in my head. For those who don't understand, no words are possible; and for those who do understand, no words are necessary.

Have you ever asked Jesus to reveal the Father to you? 'Jesus, please reveal the Father to me.' To use this as a mantra, to be repeated again and again throughout the day, is bound to bring you into a new experience of God. Jesus, who knows our innermost hearts, will see clearly whether I'm serious or not and, therefore, whether to answer or not. You can easily become one of those to whom Jesus chooses to reveal the Father, as he says in today's gospel.

It is not possible for a human being to fall on her/his knees, cry out to God, and not be heard. The next time you feel 'down', go aside somewhere and, remembering Jesus' invitation in today's gospel to 'Come to me', call out to him from your heart. He will hear you, and respond to your plea. Then you take up the yoke of service, do something for someone else, and you will soon be distracted from yourself and your burdens. 'I will give you rest … You will find rest for your souls.' The only way to know this is to do it. Take him at his word, and be open to him keeping his promises.

Story

The father and mother brought Junior with them to the super-market on a Thursday night, to do the weekly shopping. They filled up the trolley and arrived at the check-out. The girl looked at them, waved them forward, and said 'It's OK, everything is free today; no charge.' Imagine the reaction of the parents! There is no way they believe this, as they begin putting items on the conveyor belt. When the girl insists that it is all free, and there's no charge, the father checks to ensure that it's not April Fool's Day. Then it dawns on him. Candid camera! He smiles as he looks around, and continues to transfer his shopping from the trolley to the conveyor belt. When the girl insists that there is no charge, the parents begin to get annoyed. A joke is a joke, but they are in a hurry, and they can't be standing around here all day.

In the meantime, where is Junior? He heard the magic word 'Free' and, by now, he has grabbed another trolley, and is dashing around the supermarket, grabbing boxes of sweets, crisps, etc., off the shelves! He has no problem at all with things that are free, and he sees the situation as an opportunity, rather than a problem!

Unless you have the heart of a child, says Jesus, you will never understand what I am telling you.

FIFTEENTH SUNDAY OF THE YEAR

Gospel: Matthew 13:1-23

Central Theme
Today's gospel contains a core teaching of the gospel message. It is about his message being given to us, and the ways in which we respond to it. His message is given, it is available to all. When he has spoken, he stands back and awaits our response. That response can range from a full response, to a half-hearted, lukewarm one, to none at all.

Parable
Where I am living at the moment, there is a small garden out front. I always got the impression that it is very scruffy-looking! Over the years, various people have thrown a few fists of seeds here and there, but it brought little or no improvement. Over a month ago, a resident here, with some gardening expertise and enthusiasm, removed the whole top sod. He then proceeded to dig up the soil, to let the air at it. He fed it some nutrients, and he drove small holes all over it, to let both the air and the rain enter into the soil. He then raked, smoothed it, and removed all the stones, etc. It was then that he sowed a good quality seed. The garden is totally transformed, and I feel good every time I look at it.

Teaching
The first point is a very simple but central one. 'The sower went to sow his seed.' He just scattered it here, there and everywhere, with a certain sense of prodigal generosity. Having done that, his task was finished. What happened the seed after that was not his responsibility. That depended on what kind of ground received the seed. The conditions of the ground varied, from place to place. Where the right conditions existed, the seed took root and grew into a harvest. It is exactly like that with the message of the gospel. We often speak of someone 'having a heart condition'. Well, in this case, it really does depend on the condition of the heart of the hearer. Every invitation from God has RSVP written all over it. Even 'no' is a response!

Some of the ground was as hard as a rock; other places were very shallow and had no depth, while other areas were taken over by briars and weeds. There were, however, certain places that were just right for sowing, and the seed got a chance to grow. Have you ever noticed that, after a shower of rain, part of the ground is quite dry, while another part has a pool of water on it? It is the same with human beings. Some people are really open, and the rain can enter freely, while another person is so shut off that the water has to lie on the surface, evaporate, and return to the clouds from whence it came. Beneath the driest desert there is plenty of water, but it is only in very rare places that the water is able to reach the surface. So it is with people …

'You have been able to understand the secrets of the kingdom of heaven, but others have not.' It is only when they came aside with Jesus that the apostles were given special insights into Jesus as a person, and into the message he spoke. It was at one such time that he taught them to pray; it was at another that they saw him glorified on Thabor; and yet again, it was thus when they saw him in agony in the garden. Prayer is about spending time with God. It is about listening to him. 'Speak, Lord, your servant is listening', rather that 'Listen, Lord, your servant is speaking.' All of this is part of the openness of the good soil. Prayer is a hunger, and the soul has a real hunger for God, and his word. 'You have made us for yourself, O Lord, and our hearts can never be at rest until they rest in you.'

Response
Everything that comes out of today's gospel is an invitation to respond. Jesus was speaking to people who were familiar with farmers sowing seed, and the various and varied outcome of that work. They knew exactly what he was talking about. Being the brilliant teacher that he was, he brought them from the known to the unknown. He was speaking to them about something new and wonderful, while using images with which they would be familiar. There is his offer, and my response. His offer is sure and certain, and can be relied on. The big question is: What is my response? What condition is my heart in, to receive the word of God with gladness?

We are not saints! None of us can claim to be perfectly ready to receive God's word. It is consoling, then, to notice that what Jesus called good ground produced different levels of results, some 30%, some 60%, and some 100%. Even the 30% was considered good ground. The thing about it is that the ground produced something. It didn't lie completely idle, and produce nothing. The message is for 'those of goodwill'. In another story about talents, Jesus tells us that the person who received five talents produced five more; the person who received two talents produced two more; while the person who received one wrapped it in a cloth, and did nothing with it. He was held accountable for what was entrusted to him.

'To those who are open to my teaching, more understanding will be given, and they will have an abundance of knowledge.' We are speaking about a personal contact with Jesus here. These are the times when we come aside. Life can be difficult, and sometimes out of control. Not to have the spare moment is not to be living, but to be driven or dragged. If I'm too busy for those quiet moments, then I'm too busy. There are as many ways of praying as there are people. It is more a question of getting in touch with and acknowledging my inner hungers, than of the time spent or the method used. Anybody can pray, and praying is so much easier and so much more natural than saying prayers.

Practical

When it comes to God and to his word, I must be prepared to go downstairs into my heart, because it is only there that I will meet him, and hear him. 'Be still, and know that I am God.' 'It is in silence and quiet that you will preserve your soul.' I can have all the theories and knowledge in the world but, if I do not give God time, open my heart to him, and invite him to live in my heart, nothing will happen. 'You are the potter, we are the clay.' 'You are the sower, I am the soil.' Are you aware of the conditions within your heart, as you reflect on today's gospel?

How do you rate yourself as a listener? To be a good listener is a wonderful blessing for others. You have one mouth and two ears, so you should listen twice as much as you speak. We often hear the remark 'Take the cotton wool out of your ears, and put it in your mouth!' Jesus speaks of people who do not listen. 'Speak, Lord, your servant is listening.' A very worthwhile experience is to sit quietly in a spot where there are no distractions, to close your eyes, and to try to listen with the heart. On the first few occasions you may hear nothing. Please take my word for it, and act on it: if you continue this experiment, you will hear, and that hearing will lead to prayer.

Unlike the soil which is suitable for sowing only at certain times of the year, there is no time constraints on hearing God's word ... like today, for example. There are so many things in our lives that we are 'going to get around to' sometime! 'If today you hear his voice, harden not your hearts.' If you read this, or hear this, now, then consider what you should do about it. It is worth reading the text of the gospel a few times, so it would be good to have a gospel, or a Mass leaflet, so that you can do that. All I can do is repeat the offer of the gospel. Your response is as important as if you were actually there listening to him with the crowds. It is a personal message, however, or at least the response has to be personal. Think about it.

Story
A working man set out to work every morning with his lunchbox under his arm. In the canteen at lunchtime, he went through the same exact ritual day after day. He opened his box, took out the sandwiches, opened one of them, and muttered 'Oh, no! Not cheese sandwiches again!' One day his mate had enough of this, so he said 'Look, dummy, why don't you ask your wife to put something else in the sandwiches?' 'What wife? I'm not married,' came the reply. 'Well, who makes the sandwiches?' 'I do,' he said.

My life is the way it is because of me. The Lord has scattered the seed, but I may not have the proper condition of heart to receive it …

SIXTEENTH SUNDAY OF THE YEAR

Gospel: Matthew 13:24-43

Central Theme
Today's gospel is very rich in its teaching. Jesus uses images like fields, wheat, mustard seed, and yeast, to illustrate to his listeners what the kingdom of God is like. In today's gospel, we see Jesus the teacher at his best.

Parable
A very important issue in today's world is that of health, polution, global warming, etc. Some people are concerned, while many are indifferent. We feel we are losing something, and there is no simple solution as a recovery. An individual can feel powerless, and feel the problem is too much for any one person to tackle. The fact is, however, that the solution must begin with some individual. 'If each before his own door swept, the whole village would be clean.' 'Let there be peace on earth, and let it begin with me.' While no one of us can remove the weeds, each can be like the yeast, which effects where it is mixed, or we can begin some growth that can lead to greater things. We may begin as a tiny mustard seed, but we have all known wonderful people who were giants. Belonging to the kingdom of God imposes responsibilities on all of us.

Teaching
What God creates is good, like the wheat sown in the field. Unfortunately an enemy (the word Satan means 'enemy') has sown the weeds of sin, sickness and death in our humanity. These are not part of God's creation. The reality is that it is only the Creator who can recreate. Jesus came to remove the weeds of sin, sickness and death. We must know our place here, because only God can do a God-thing. We say 'Lamb of God who takes away the sins of the world … Lord, you are the source of our healing … Dying, you destroyed our death.' Jesus came to remove the weeds, because any attempt by us to do so would only make matters worse.

Jesus is a brilliant storyteller. His stories are simple, but the message is profound. Using the effect of yeast, when placed in the dough for baking, is a very simple way of describing the profound change that the Christian can have on his/her surroundings.

As a Christian, you are the message, because Christianity is about attracting rather than promoting. 'You shall be my witnesses ...' We cannot underestimate the effect of Christian living in the world. For example, missionaries going to India today would be more concerned about the witness of their Christian living than about 'converting' anyone to Christianity. I still have to bear witness, even if there's no chance that anyone would want to become Christian. Jesus gave the witness of his life, and he left the rest to us. Not everyone who listened to him actually followed him.

'Learn to live and to walk in the Spirit ...' This is a learning process. It is slow, gradual, and on-going. I have seen mustard seeds, and they were so tiny that I could not pick them up with my fingers, but had to use a strip of cellotape to hold them on the fly-cover of my Bible. I also have seen mustard trees in the Garden of Gethsemane, and I was amazed at the size of them. This is surely a powerful image Jesus uses, when speaking to people who would have been familiar with the items in question. It certainly is a very slow growth, but it also is a very sure growth. We are told that our faith can grow like that, if we exercise it. I learned to walk by walking, and to talk by talking. I learn to trust by trusting, and my faith grows the more I exercise it. In fact, like the mustard tree, in whose branches the birds of the air find shelter, other people can find consolation and encouragement through my faith. When the people lowered the man through the roof, in the gospel story, it is possible that he was unconscious and incapable of having faith. However, Jesus marvelled at their faith, and he healed the man.

Response
Each of us has to face up to the reality of the presence of weeds among the wheat in our lives. Each of us has to accept the reality of sin, sickness, and death. In a way, I suppose, I could say that we are all cracked! The Spirit, however, enters our hearts through the cracks of our brokenness. The presence of Jesus in my heart must make a fundamental difference. I throw open the canvas of my life, right out to the edges, and I allow him see the sin, the sickness, and the fact that I have to face up to the certainty of death. I hear him say 'Your sins are forgiven ... arise and walk ... I have overcome death.'

My presence within the community has got to make a difference. Every brick in a wall is important, whether it is at the base, or on the very top row. 'Bloom where you're planted ...' It is constantly evident in a parish, for example, that there are some people who contribute enormously to the vibrancy of parish life. They are the yeast, they are the salt. Without them the community would be greatly impoverished. Not everyone listens, therefore, not everyone responds. 'Many are called, but few are chosen ...' Many are called, but few choose to respond. A community is like a mirror taken off a wall, dropped on the ground, and shattered. Each person in the community is entrusted with a piece of that mirror. Each person represents some aspect of God's reflection. It is only when each is ready and willing to make that piece available, that the community can reflect the full face of God.

It is an extraordinary thing that the only sure thing in our lives is that we shall all one day die, and yet there is a tendency to keep that well at the back of our mind. Many people are not sure how to approach the whole issue. Should we face up to it now, or keep our heads below the parapet, and wait till it approaches us? Jesus speaks about the general 'round-up' at the end of time. There are a few places in which he speaks of what we call the General Judgement. There will come a time when we cannot hide anymore. No more denial, no more pretending, no more rationalising. We will stand naked before God, with the canvas of our lives wide open before him. He will separate the sheep from the goats. The sheep follow the shepherd, while the goats have to be driven by the goat-herd. God doesn't send me anywhere when I die. Rather does he eternalise the direction in which I choose to travel now. The decision is mine, because I have free will. One thing is certain: I can never say that I didn't know!

Practical
Because of the whole evolution in today's world, with the growth of materialism, etc., in a post-Christian era, I am either a mystic or an unbeliever. A mystic is someone who reflects on life, and ponders the tensions, while facing up to them. We live in a world of 'quick-fix'. Soon we will not repair cars, machinery, etc., but just replace the part that is causing problems, and everything will be up and running in record time. We replace a pair of shoes rather than go to the cobbler. We cannot do that with the weeds of original sin in our lives. The mystic faces up to reality, is not in denial, and is open to the work of re-creation, which only the Creator can do. Can you get your head around

the concept of what it means to be a mystic? I could easily accept
the teachings of Christianity, and not believe in God at all. I can
live with the ideology of Christianity, while not having any
great faith in redemption, salvation, and transformation. What
are my thoughts on that?

Look around you, and see if the world where you live is any
better because you are part of it. The best place to begin is my
own heart, and then in my own home. When I was a kid we
were praying 'for the conversion of Russia'. That was safe, because it was far enough away! It really made no demands on me.
When I put myself on the line, however, against the background
of today's gospel, there is no escape. If I read this gospel very
slowly twice, once for the head, and again for the heart, and I
take it as being directed personally to me, what do you think my
reaction should be? Do I really need any sermons on it? I don't
think so. The easiest way to avoid doing something is to talk
about it long enough! Jesus, however, calls for decisions, not discussions.

'We shall all one day die' is OK, but 'I shall one day die' can
be uncomfortable. It is much easier to keep it in the first person
plural. Without wishing to be morbid, what do you think God
might see if you stood before him now, in death, and out of the
body? It has been suggested that there could be a meeting at the
moment of death between the person that I am, and the person
that God created me to be. I hasten to add that God loves me exactly as I am, but the complete picture is that he loves me more
than that, or he would just leave me the way I am! Sometime,
when you get a chance, let your imagination bring you before
God as in death. Reflect on your thoughts, and see if you get any
inspiration, or can glean any insights. This is part of being a
mystic, and it can deepen my consciousness as a believer.

Story

A young lad was passing a sculptor's yard somewhere in Italy.
He was on his way to school. He noticed a huge block of marble
in the middle of the yard. For the following few months, as he
passed by, the front doors were closed, but he could hear the
sculptor chipping away. After several months, he passed by,
and saw that the front doors were open. He stood transfixed in
amazement. Where the block of marble had been, stood a giant
sculptured tiger. It was so life-like, with powerful muscles, and
a real sense of aggressive movements. He stood looking at it for

a while, and then he approached the sculptor. He tugged his coat, looked up into his face with awe, as he whispered 'Excuse me, sir, but how did you know there was a tiger in there?'

Jesus looks at each of us, and he sees the possibilities. He cannot begin, however, without our openness and goodwill ...

SEVENTEENTH SUNDAY OF THE YEAR

Gospel: Matthew 13:44-52

Central Theme
Today's gospel contains three simple illustrations to help us grasp what the kingdom of God means. It is not a question of explaining it, because the reality would be beyond our comprehension. It is a question of using illustrations to enable us to get some concept of what Jesus is talking about.

Parable
There was a man one time who had a huge block of marble. His pal asked him what he intended to do with it, and he said that he was going to sculptor an elephant. 'But you are not a sculptor', said his pal. 'I know that, but I thought if I chipped off everything that doesn't look like an elephant, I might succeed.' Jesus said 'Seek ye first the kingdom of God ...' In searching for something, it is necessary to have some idea of what it looks like!

Teaching
The first parable is about finding a treasure in a field. Jesus is appealing to their common sense. Supposing one of us found some very precious item in a field, we would surely love to have it in our possession. We cannot take it, however, because it is buried, and it would require an amount of digging to get it out and, anyhow, that would involve stealing something that is not ours. One of the ways around it would be to investigate the possibility of buying the field. If I buy the field, all that it contains becomes mine. What Jesus is telling us here is that, once the coin drops and we realise what an extraordinary treasure we are offered, we should be motivated enough to give up everything else to get it. 'Seek ye first the kingdom of God, and everything else will be added onto you.'

The second parable is almost a repeat of the first, except it is addressed to a different audience. The first one was for farmers, this one is for fishermen. We have legends of the extraordinary lengths people have gone to, to discover the Holy Grail, or to retrieve the gold on the Titanic. This is a full-blooded commitment, and nothing, short of death can deter those who go searching. The difference with the kingdom of God, of course, is that it can easily be found. 'It has pleased your Father to give you a Kingdom.'

Once again, Jesus uses a fishing practice to illustrate the workings of the kingdom. We can interpret it in many ways. One simple thought is that I throw the net across the sea of my soul; I gather everything there is, good, bad, indifferent. I then sit down and begin to sort out my catch. There is much to be disposed of here, which includes getting rid of the wreckage of the past, and throwing out the leaden weights of addiction, compulsion and sin, that weigh me down and prevent me from living life to the full. In a way, it is like the programme of Alcoholics Anonymous. When the alcoholic puts down his last drink, that is 10% of his problem solved. There's still 90%, and this has nothing to do with alcohol. The alcoholic drinking was but a symptom of the underlying cause.

Response

If I may continue speaking about the alcoholic for a moment. When the recovering alcoholic discovers and experiences sobriety, it becomes the top priority in his life. If he gives that his full attention, everything else in his life will come right. He can forget his name, his address, or his dinner, but he must never forget that he is an alcoholic. Going to meetings, reading the literature, helping other alcoholics, all of this becomes a driving force in his life, and now he is more committed to sobriety than he ever was to alcohol. When I find the kingdom of God …

Many of us grew up with stories and legends of Yukon and the gold rush in California. Many people left Ireland to travel there, and join in the frantic search for gold. Many of them perished in the cold, and horrific conditions. Nothing could deter them, as they were driven by their desire for the sparkler. That is exactly what Jesus is pointing to in today's gospel. If we know where the gold is, we will dig with our bare hands, if we have to.

The parable of the net being cast into the sea has often been used to speak about the end of the world, and the General Judgement. I don't have to wait till then for the net to be cast. There is an approach nowadays that's becoming more prevalent, and it generally has to do with working on oneself. People attend psychiatrists, join Self Help groups, or get a spiritual director. It has to do with clearing the wreckage of the past, and with developing healthy skills for living. It is about finding the treasure of inner peace, and of getting rid of all those things that adversely effect that inner peace. Peace is what I experience when my relationships are the way they ought to be. There is no problem in life that is not a relationship one. I am not getting on too well with God, myself, or with others. There are people who cannot relate properly to food, alcohol, money, etc., and they find themselves in a situation where the tail is wagging the dog!

Practical
There are three rules in the kingdom of God that are diametrically opposed to the values of this world. The first is *Jesus is Lord*. If I live in the kingdom of this world, my god can be money, success, pleasure, or power. There are people who are completely driven by the Stock Markets, opinion polls, or tam ratings. If I live in the kingdom of God, then I am driven by the person and teachings of Jesus. Are you conscious of what drives you in life? What sustains you in your living?

The second rule in the kingdom is that every person is on this earth with as much right as anyone else. The most disabled person is on this earth with as much right as the greatest genius that ever lived. Those who live with a worldly mind-set have no problem with abortion, euthanasia, or ethnic cleansing. Half the world is dying of hunger while the other half is on a diet, trying to get down the weight. We have all witnessed racism, bigotry, and intolerance. What a wonderful thing if I could rid my heart of all traces of such. 'Live and let live' is a good motto for living.

The third rule in the kingdom is that it is the Holy Spirit, living in me, who alone can make this possible. If I live in the world, I can get my power from social status, political clout, or bigger and better Star Wars. If I live in the kingdom, it is only possible through the power of the Holy Spirit. 'The kingdom, the power, and the glory are yours …' If I supply any of the power, I will be tempted to steal some of the glory. 'Learn to live and to walk in the Spirit,' says Paul. I have a friend whose daily mantra is 'Come, Holy Spirit.' This prayer is going on in his heart all day long. It helps remind him where his power lies. Worth considering, eh?

Story
An elderly man, whose memory was beginning to lapse, decided to take the car, and travel to a new shopping centre on the other side of town. His daughter tried to dissuade him, but to no avail. She insisted, however, that he take her mobile phone, just in case he had problems. An hour or two later, she was listening to the traffic report on the radio. It told about a bus broken down on

the Artane road, and traffic lights that had failed in Inchicore. The reporter went on to speak about word that had just come in about a car travelling in the wrong direction, against the flow of traffic, on the M50. 'Oh, my God, I hope dad is alright.' She rang him, and warned him about the car travelling the wrong way, as he would have to travel on that motorway. 'Tell me about it,' he replied, 'there are hundreds of them coming the wrong way!'

Living in the kingdom of God often involves going against the flow of traffic. You will meet people actually moving away from the very thing you are looking for ...

Gospel: Matthew 14:13-21

Carry on from here (handwritten)

Central Theme

① This is one of a few different accounts of miracles in the gospel, involving loaves and fishes / It matters not if all accounts are about the same event, or that it happened on more than one occasion.

Parable

② Easter week is the annual pilgrimage to Lourdes for thousands of children from all over Europe. Because of the age and condition of the children, there is not a heavy schedule of religious events. On one of the days, there is a trip to a mountain, with picnic baskets, sports activities, and the combined musical talents of thousands. I remember, on one occasion, being with a group on the mountain, when we were approached by the leader of another group, telling us that they had a serious problem. They had left all the baskets of sandwiches back in their hotel, and they had nothing to eat. The response was extraordinary. The word was passed from group to group, and in a very short while this particular group had much more than they needed. The interesting thing is that, while having given part of our food to them, we ourselves had more than we needed. Love in action is very powerful …

Teaching

The first thing we notice in today's gospel is that the crowds had a hunger much stronger than that for food. They followed Jesus, listening to every word he spoke, and in none of the stories does it say that they were bothered about food for the body. In today's story, it is the apostles who expressed their concern. In another story, we are told that Jesus 'looked at the crowd, and felt sorry for them, because they had been with him for several days, and had nothing to eat'. Mother Teresa said that the greatest hunger in today's world is for love, and not for food.

Jesus puts the apostles on a spot. When they express their concern about the people, Jesus tells them to feed them themselves. This, of course, is impossible in their eyes, and they tell him so. He was trying to show them, and all of us, a very basic lesson: 'Whatever you have is enough. Just let me have it, and I will do the rest.' At Cana, all they had was water, and that was all he needed. He would do the rest. One of the saddest phrases in the gospel is in another version of this story, where one of the apostles says 'We only have a few loaves and some fish, but what is that among so many?' The tendency then would be to put the loaves and fish back in the bag. Mother Teresa would never have started if she had that attitude.

There is power in the actions of Jesus. He looks towards heaven, says a prayer, and begins distributing the bread. Before he called Lazarus forth from the tomb, he raised his eyes to heaven, and said 'I thank you, Father, that you have heard me.' It was his constant contact with the Father that inspired his actions. At his baptism in the Jordan he had heard the Father's voice saying 'This is my beloved son, in whom I am well pleased.' He lived constantly with the Father's approval, even when everyone else rejected him. What a lesson this is for all of us! In commissioning his apostles, later on, he would tell them to feed the hungry. Because he came 'to do and to teach', that is why he fed the hungry before sending his apostles out to do the same.

Response
Hungry people make up a large part of today's world. We can become immune to the pictures of emaciated bodies, of children with bloated stomachs, or of thousands of hands in the air, reaching out for the one item of food being offered. This should disturb us. Unfortunately, it is much easier to press the remote control and change channels. In another version of this miracle, we are told that 'Jesus looked at the crowd, and felt sorry for them, because they were like sheep without a shepherd ...'; and then he did something about it. For his listeners, because of their everyday experiences, and their long traditions, culture, and way of doing things , the idea of a flock of sheep without a shepherd would be shocking beyond belief. It was always understood that the shepherd was one who would die in protecting his sheep, if necessary.

Some of us can be frozen into inactivity, because of what we call our limited resources, either in terms of earthly goods, or physical ability. We may not see how each of us is a vital part of the solution. Even a cup of cold water is upheld in the gospel as something that will gain an award. Whatever you have is enough. I celebrate eucharist every morning in a nursing home

next-door to where I live. The residents are elderly, with many
confined to wheelchairs. Many of these people ran the show for
many years, either at home, or in the workplace. All that is gone
now, however, and the danger is they may begin to see themselves as being of no value anymore, because their usefulness is
no longer as evident. That is why I have to repeat, like a daily
mantra 'Whatever you have is enough.' You may be limited to a
quiet prayer for the hungry people of the world, or for those
who are trying to feed them. You may ask God to touch the
hearts of those who have more than they need, so that they
might be inspired to share with those who have nothing.
Whatever you have, whatever you can do, give that to Jesus, and
let him work the miracle. Jean Vanier says that some of the
greatest miracles for good in today's world have been brought
about by the quiet prayers of totally unknown people.

When Jesus told the story of the sower who went out to sow,
he describes him as throwing the seeds in all directions. He
threw fists of it here, fists of it there. That was his task. Whether
the wheat grew or not depended on the conditions in the place
where it fell. In today's gospel, Jesus was prodigally generous in
delivering bread and fish so that the people could eat. He wasn't
putting any conditions on the giving. He didn't demand a
declaration of belief in him before providing the food. He acted
like he told us his heavenly Father acts, when 'he lets rain fall on
the good and on the bad.' He had fed them with his words, and
then he fed their bodies. We are told that 'he had compassion on
them, and he healed their sick.' He was interested in their welfare, both soul and body. He was both a friend and a miracle-
worker.

Practical   So very, very appropriate & applicable

Today's gospel is very applicable to the world in which we live.
We are called to 'complete his work on earth'. There are still
many people searching for what Jesus had to offer by way of
peace, salvation, and hope. They are also hungry for food to
keep them alive. I cannot be a spectator in today's world. Those
emaciated bodies and those swollen stomachs must pull at my
heart, demanding a response. I may not be able to do much on a
material level, but we all can do something. The door-bell rings,
and it's some homeless person looking for a cup of tea and a
sandwich. I may be busy, and the person is a nuisance. I have to
make a decision. If I have taken the message of Jesus to my heart,

there is only one decision to make. To make the effort is to carry the cross of service to others.

Most of us have more than we need of money, clothes, food, etc. We may not have as much as we *want*, but we have more than we *need*. There is a struggle here, and there is a tension from which we cannot escape. 'Whatever you do for the least of these, I will take as being done for me.' The decisions to walk in the Christian Way removes many of my options and choices. Christianity is much more than just saying prayers. It is also a call to action. It is a call to do as Jesus would do. I cannot read today's gospel and remain indifferent or detached.

'It is in giving that we receive.' When we give, we discover that we are not at a loss. It is an extraordinary paradox, but it is literally true. I will never know this until I try it. How do you consider yourself in the whole area of responsibility for the welfare of others? We are all familiar with the SVP, Trócaire, Concern, Goal, etc., and we may admire what they do. We must go beyond admiration, however, and become willing to imitate, and follow their example. Christianity is about witnessing, and in the witnessing is the invitation to 'go and do likewise'. The opposite to love is not hatred, but indifference. If God is love, and I am indifferent, then I must seriously examine where God is in my life. This is a fundamental and basic question that must be asked, and it must be answered.

Story
There is a story told about a parish in the south west of Ireland. The parish priest was annoyed by some of the local farmers who came in the back door on Sunday, insisting on standing there, and who disappeared before Mass was over. He decided he would do something to correct this bad habit. He would have a parish mission, the first week for the men, and the second for the women. The word got out around the village, and the guys decided to boycott the mission. On the opening night the missioner came out on the altar, complete with biretta, sheaf of notes, turnip watch, and a crucifix. He got a shock when he looked down the church to see just one man in the whole church. This man lived out at the back of the mountain, he hadn't been in town all week, and he hadn't heard about the boycott. The priest didn't know what to do, so he approached the man, asking him what he thought he should do. It is well-known that, in that part of the country, it is very difficult to get someone to answer a

question. 'Ah, sure I wouldn't know, Father. I'm just a simple
man, and I live out at the back of the mountain. But I'll tell you
what, though, Father. I have fourteen hens, and when I call them
in the morning, if only one of them comes, I'll feed her.' 'Oh, I
see,' said the priest. 'I get your point.' He returned to the pulpit
to feed the one solitary hen that showed up! He began with
Adam and Eve, and he worked his way through to the Second
Coming, about an hour and a half later! Down he came to the
man again. 'Was that OK? Were you happy enough with that?'
And here again we have another question! 'Ah, sure Father, I
wouldn't know that. I'm just a simple man, and I live out at the
back of the mountain. But I'll tell you what. I have fourteen hens,
and when I call them in the morning, if only one of them comes,
I'll feed her ; but I certainly wouldn't give her the full bucket!'

In today's gospel Jesus gives them much more than they
could possibly eat ...

NINETEENTH SUNDAY OF THE YEAR

Gospel: Matthew 14:22-33

Central Theme

Today's gospel is one of several incidents when Jesus calmed a storm on the Sea of Galilee. It has several extra nuances, because it tells us about Jesus going aside to pray, how he walked on the water, and how poor Peter fared when he attempted to do the same. It is a gospel that has much to teach us.

Parable

I'm sure we all have seen a sheet of paper on the wall near a phone, with emergency numbers on it. There's the fire brigade, the ambulance, the doctor, etc. It is useful, and very advisable to have these at hand. I have never seen God's name on this list! And yet, he is often called on in emergencies only. The apostles were lucky that he arrived on time.

Teaching

The opening of the gospel is quite touching. It speaks about Jesus sending his apostles away, where they could have a rest, while he would stay back and deal with the crowds. He then went off to be alone, to spend some time with the Father. He showed wonderful concern and sensitivity for others, but he also had to have time for himself. Many good people fail in this second part. I can become so busy with the work of the Lord, that I haven't time for the Lord of the work. There is something very gentle and impressive about these opening comments. It gives us a glimpse of just how beautiful a person he must have been for those who walked with him in life. That is the same for us today.

To the Hebrews, water was a symbol of death, as well as life. They had to pass through the waters of the Red Sea to enter the Promised Land, just as we have to pass through death to enter eternal life. Jesus came to remove the weeds of sin, sickness, and death. By walking on water, he showed that he had authority over death. Later on, after his resurrection, he would keep appearing among his apostles to convince them, beyond doubt, that he was alive. He told them on several occasions that he would rise from the dead. Death was 'the final enemy', and it was essential that they be convinced that death had been conquered. Their mission was to be witnesses to his resurrection. 'Dying, you destroyed our death ...'

Peter was always ready for a 'dare'. If Jesus could walk on water, then Peter was ready to try that too. It was as if he were saying, 'Lord, could I have the freedom over death that you have?' Jesus invited him to come on, and try it. Peter did that, and, when he kept his eyes fixed on Jesus, he succeeded. Once he took his eyes off Jesus, however, and became conscious of the wind and the waves, he lost his nerve and began to sink. 'Keep your eyes fixed on Jesus, the author and finisher of our faith ...' Jesus faced Peter with the fact that he hadn't trusted him, as if Jesus was going to let him drown. How often do we hear those words from Jesus, 'Oh, you of little faith; why did you doubt?' It is interesting to see that as soon as Jesus stepped into the boat, the wind stopped. Quite a dramatic lesson!

Response

Most of us have seen films based on the life of Jesus. The persons playing the part of Jesus were almost identical in every case. It would have been fascinating to have met Jesus in the flesh. We must be touched by his gentle thoughtfulness in the first part of today's gospel. A friend is someone who is willing to walk another mile with us. We are told that 'he came to do and to teach'. He did the kind act first, and then he told them to love one another as he loved them. For those who witnessed his actions, this must have seemed an impossibility.

When I reflect that the gospel is now, and I am every person in it, then I must surely experience myself in a storm of one kind or other, and I cannot see how I can remain afloat, or regain a balance in my life. Alcoholics, manic depressives, etc., experience this all the time. It must be really difficult for those who feel alone, either because they do not believe in Jesus, or they choose to ignore him. The sea of life can be very intimidating at times, and my boat is very small. It is essential that I make room for Jesus in that boat. It is not possible to call out to him, and not be heard.

Peter had a spontaneity that often got him in trouble. He certainly was the only one in that boat who would dare step over the side! Jesus must have smiled at Peter, while being pleased with the trust he had in Jesus. Human as he was, he lost his nerve, and he got quite a fright. However, he knew where to call for help and, once again, he was not disappointed. He still had a lot to learn, but he was willing to have a go, and to learn, even through his mistakes. Experience is a good school, although the fees are often very high!

Practical

I'm sure we all know people who are just naturally kind, thoughtful, and active in service. I know one lady who, when she visits a house, she is happiest if she can find a tea-towel, and help with the wash-up. She just has to be doing something. She seems to be at her best when she gets an opportunity to roll up her sleeves and help in clearing up after a meal or a party. I see that in Jesus at the beginning of today's gospel. I also admire the balance between taking care of dismissing the crowds, and going off by himself, to be alone. There is a simple lesson there for all of us. It would be a well-worthwhile exercise to take some time out to reflect on what I see in my own life in this area.

Please don't keep Jesus' phone number under 'Emergencies'! Practise involving him in everything you do. 'Lord, please walk with me today. May your presence within me touch the hearts of those I meet today, either through the words I say, the prayers I pray, the life I live, or the very person that I am.' Learn to walk with the Lord. Imagine him entering every door just ahead of you. Don't wait for the storm to call for help. I would rather be safely guided by a lighthouse than be saved by a lifeboat.

Give some thought to the words we use in the Mass : 'Lord, by your cross and resurrection, you have set us free. You are the Saviour of the world ... Dying you destroyed our death; rising you restored our life ...' Notice these statements are in the past tense. We speak of something that has already happened. Peter did not have the advantage of hindsight that we have. When I think of death, I can reflect on stepping over the side of the boat. The secret is to keep my eyes fixed on Jesus, and I won't be troubled by the wind and the waves. Jesus has made all things possible for me, and I must be willing to claim my inheritance from the legacy he has left. I have an onus to accept the gift of salvation, and this puts a further onus on me to witness to that truth, and look saved!

Story

There was a disastrous drought in one of the southern states of the US some years ago, and much of the crops were lost. The state was declared a disaster area and, while the government was coming to the help of the farmers, all churches began to pray for the rains to come. One night a mother was putting her little girl to bed. She was saying her night prayers. The mother suggested that she pray for rain, but she refused. This puzzled her mother, so she tried several different ways of broaching the subject, but each attempt was firmly turned down. The mother couldn't figure out why she was so insistent on refusing to pray for rain, so she came right out and asked her. 'Mammy, I have two dolls on a bench in the back-garden, and if you go out and take them in, I'll pray for rain.'

If she prayed for rain, she expected it to rain! You could imagine Jesus saying 'Thank you for your faith, and for not doubting my promises.'

TWENTIETH SUNDAY OF THE YEAR

Gospel: Matthew 15:21-28

Central Theme
Today's gospel is a beautiful vignette of faith in action, and in a way is quite puzzling. Jesus seems to ignore the woman, and then be offensive, before he yields to her persistent faith, and answers her prayer.

Parable
Over the years we have all witnessed the stories of those who were wrongly imprisoned for many years, before their pleas of innocence were listened to, and they were finally released. It must be really traumatic to be accused in the wrong, to be sentenced to prison, and to be vilified in the press when, all the time, the person knows that he is innocent. The sheer persistence, and a stubborn refusal to give up, must have taken a heavy toll of those who were in such a situation. I sometimes reflect on what they must be thinking when they are released, and recall the chilling words of the judge who lectured them, before passing sentence. The woman in today's gospel loved her daughter so much that she just would not take 'no' for an answer.

Teaching
The woman in today's gospel is an unusual woman. Firstly, she was not a Jew, and yet, in approaching Jesus, she called him 'O Lord, Son of David.' This was a mark of reverence for who he was and what he was. Obviously, it was her love for her daughter that drove her to overcome every barrier, and to persist in any search, if that could save her daughter. As far as Jesus was concerned, she was on a trump card here, because she was doing exactly what he would ask anybody to do. She was driven by love, and that was sure to find a response within the heart of Jesus.

It is difficult to understand why Jesus seemed to ignore her, and even to insult her. I can only imagine that he was teaching his disciples a lesson. It was they who asked him to send her away, because she was a persistent nuisance. He may have wanted them to discover that she was much more than that, and that her faith was something they may not have witnessed before. It was as if he knew that her love for her daughter was so

195

strong that she just could not be put off. He adopted the official Jewish line against such people, because they were considered no better than dogs, while the Jews were the children of God. The woman wasn't going to get sucked into a discussion or a debate; she looked to Jesus for a decision, and she was not disappointed.

One can almost imagine Jesus throwing his hands in the air, and giving up! The apostles were right; get rid of this woman! There was only one way to get rid of her, however, and that was to give her what she was looking for. Despite all that had gone before, one can easily imagine Jesus smiling, and with warmth in his voice, he told her to go on home, that her daughter was healed. There is a saying nowadays, 'Don't invade my space'. Well, she had come at him like a JCB, went through everything in the way, and she came away with what she came to receive. I could imagine Jesus saying 'What a woman!'

Response

Let's look at this woman again. She is not aggressive, or demanding anything as her right. She is powerless, the daughter she loves is dying, and she has nowhere else to turn. Like the apostles in the boat in the midst of the storm, the point of experiencing our powerlessness and helplessness is the point at which we can come face to face with Jesus. He is the only one who will continue to be there for us. 'I will never leave you, or abandon you in the storm.' 'If you have found him, never let him go', is a line from a song of some years ago. The first Step in a Twelve-Step Programme is 'We admitted we were powerless over alcohol, and that our lives had become unmanageable.' This clears the way for an appeal to a Higher Power.

The power this woman had came from her love, and from her humility. She didn't see herself as deserving anything, and she was prepared to be grateful for the crumbs that fell from the master's table. The combination of her love and humility insulated her from the slings and arrows of others. She was single-minded in her quest, and she never took her mind off what she wanted. Surely this makes for a powerful prayer of intercession. There are several incidents in the gospel like this, such as Bartimeus, the blind man. Even though those around him told him to keep quiet, he continued to call out to Jesus, until Jesus stopped, and called him to come to him, where he was healed. At another time, Jesus asked a man 'Do you want to be healed?'

It is obvious that this woman wants her daughter to be healed, and with her love and humility, there's no way Jesus could continue to ignore her!

This woman may not have done much homework or research on Jesus before approaching him. However, for whatever reason, she seems to have got the 'measure' of him, and this prompted her not to take 'no' for an answer. She was a Gentile and he was a Jew; he was a man, and she was a woman. In those days each person had a place on the ladder of life, and they were expected to stay within those boundaries. It was because her love for her daughter was boundless that she probably would have followed him into the Temple, if she had to! Jesus didn't go around healing people; rather he went around, and he healed when he was stopped and asked. Bartimeus was told 'Jesus of Nazareth is passing by.' Bartimeus had a choice. He could call out to him, and stop him; or he could die a blind man. The woman in today's gospel is a very clear example of someone who has enough faith, hope, and love, to enable her to keep going, and not give up till the miracle happens.

Practical
A friend of mine is an alcoholic, and when he began attending AA meetings at the beginning, he found it very difficult. However, one old-timer who had been around the block for many years, brought him aside and gave him a word of advice: 'Just keep showing up at the meetings, and don't leave until the miracle happens.' He has followed that advice, and he has now been sober for many years. If a child asks Santa for a bicycle around about early October, and he never mentions the word 'bicycle' again, I doubt if he will get a bicycle. If he really wanted a bicycle, he would mention that fact from time to time and, as Christmas approached, it would become a regular topic of conversation. When you ask God for something, he can read your heart, and know whether you really want what you ask …

There are many instances in the gospel where people brought their sick to Jesus to have them healed. The centurion came for his servant, who was too ill to travel. Jairus came for his daughter, and the woman in today's gospel came for her daughter, as well. It is certainly a very strong lesson about how our prayers of intercession can benefit others. I know one lady who said a Rosary every single day for twenty-three years for a brother of hers who was an alcoholic. The most impressive part of this is that her brother, who is now sober, has never known this, and is still not aware of it. Praying for others can be real love in action ...

We live in a world of 'quick fix', of instant cameras, and of global communication at the push of a button. We cannot approach prayer of intercession in that way. There must be an element of perseverance in our prayer. 'Ask, and you will receive; seek, and you will find; knock and the door will be opened to you.' How often I fail to find a lost object on my first search. I begin again, and I retrace my steps, and look for areas I may have overlooked first time around. The depth and length, and thoroughness of my search depends on how precious the object I have lost. I have spent hours searching for something, and I have experienced the joy of finding. If I approached prayers of petition in this way, I certainly stand a much better chance of getting an answer.

Story

Most of us have learned to live with 'automated answering services' now as a necessary part of our daily lives. But have you ever wondered what it would be like if God decided to install voice mail? Imagine praying and hearing the following:

Thank you for calling heaven.

Please select one of the following options:

Press 1 for Requests

Press 2 for Thanksgiving

Press 3 for Complaints

Press 4 for all other inquiries

I am sorry, all of our angels and saints are busy helping other sinners right now. However, your prayer is important to us and we will answer it in the order it was received. Please stay on the line.

If you would like to speak to:

God, Press 1

For Jesus, Press 2

For the Holy Spirit, Press 3

If you would like to hear King David sing a Psalm while you are holding, Press 4

To find a loved one that has been assigned to heaven, Press 5, then enter his or her social security number (PRSI), followed by the pound sign. (If you receive a negative response, please hang up and try area code 666.)

For reservations at heaven, please enter J-O-H-N followed by the numbers 3-16.

For answers to nagging questions about dinosaurs, the age of the earth, life on other planets, and where Noah's Ark is, please wait until you arrive.

Our computers show that you have already prayed today. Please hang up and try again tomorrow. This office is now closed for the weekend to observe a religious holiday. Please pray again on Monday, after 9:30 am.

If you are calling after hours and need emergency assistance, please contact your local parish priest.

TWENTY-FIRST SUNDAY OF THE YEAR

Gospel: Matthew 16:13-20

Central Theme
'Who do you say that I am?' is probably one of the most important questions in the gospel. In today's gospel we are told that the
apostles were asked that question. Today, that question is being
put to us.

Parable
The story is told that Jesus put this question to a very learned
theologian one time, and the reply he got was : 'You are the
eschatological manifestation of the ground of our being, the
kerygma, in which we find the ultimate meaning of our inter-
personal relationships.' Jesus exclaimed : *'What?'* I will find the
answer to this question within my heart, and not in some theological threatise ...

Teaching
Jesus puts some personal questions to his apostles. 'Who do you
say that I am? ... Will you also go away? ... Do you love me
more than these?' Notice in today's gospel that he begins with a
general question: 'Who do people say that I am?' They give him
several answers, and before they are finished, he comes with the
vital question: 'But you, who do you say that I am?' It matters little
what others say, but he needs to know what his disciples say.
Every place he went he taught the people, but they were different people each time. The apostles, however, were present to
hear all of his teaching. Surely they should have a much clearer
idea than the general public.

Peter steps into the breach with the correct answer : 'You are
the Messiah, the Son of the living God.' It is interesting that Peter
could give this answer with such conviction while, later on, he
would deny him and desert him. Most of us can identify with
Peter, who shows more of humanity than any of the other apostles. Perhaps he knew this up in his head, but it had not yet
arrived down in his heart. Knowing who Jesus is, is not faith,
because even Satan knows who Jesus is. Knowing it in the head
is nothing more than mental assent. It is when I begin to act on
that knowledge that it becomes faith.

Jesus commends Peter, however, for his answer, and he says

that it is the Father who has revealed this truth to him. He then goes on to confirm Peter as the one on which he would build his enterprise. There follows a real outpouring of trust and of promise. The church will be built on Peter, and it will remain safe from all the attacks of the evil one. It will continue to live with his promises, and he will accept whatever the church does in his name. Later on, when Jesus ascended into heaven, he brought the body he had with him. He then sent the Spirit to complete his work. Our roles, and the role of the church, is to provide the body, so that the Spirit can work through us.

Response
'Who do you say that I am?' The answer to that question will not be found in a book. Rather will I find it in my heart. There are three parts to the answer. The first has to do with the past. If Jesus is my Saviour, then I can safely, and with total confidence, entrust to him the room of my past, with all its sins, brokenness, and hurts. If Jesus is Saviour in that room of my past, there is no place for guilt, self-condemnation, or regret. 'Lord, give me the serenity to accept the things I cannot change ...' St Thérèse of Lisieux had such confidence in God's love and mercy, that she said if she committed every sin that has ever been committed, she would die, trusting totally in his mercy and forgiveness. Regarding the first part of the answer to today's question, if there is part of me back in the past, with guilt, regret, hindsight, or self-condemnation, then I can answer 'Well, Lord, you certainty are not my Saviour.'

The second part of the answer has to do with the future. If Jesus is Lord, then I have no reason to fear the future, because he is in charge. I don't have to worry what the future holds, if he holds the future. Just as I should not be in that room of my past with guilt, neither should I be in the room of my future with worry. 'If you follow me, you will not walk in darkness, but will have the light of life.' I need not worry what the future holds, be that a wheelchair, cancer ward, or cardiac unit. If he is Lord, then every morning I will accept the gift of that day, batteries included. Each day brings its own daily bread, and I am asked to live my life, one day at a time.

The third part of the answer has to do with now. God is totally a God of now. 'I am who am.' Just as he is Saviour in that room of my past, and Lord in that room of my future, so he must be God in the room of today. 'For with God nothing is impossible.'

It is very easy for us to slip into the trap of trying to play God. Accepting the things I cannot change means that I am powerless over persons, places, or things. Allowing God be God in my life makes all things possible, and brings me to a life beyond my wildest dreams.

Practical
The first thing I would suggest is that you take some time out, go into the room of your past, and spend some time there. You are a product of that room, because your past, either through nature or nurture, has made you the person you are today. The room could be cluttered with the wreckage of the past. You will find hurts, scars, unforgiveness, resentments, etc., there. You will find the roots of all your guilt, and of all your fears and phobias. By using your creative imagination, you can open the door and invite Jesus to come in and to take over, as Saviour. You can watch him as he takes out the whip of cords, and begins to rid this temple of everything that is not from him. When he has exorcised this room, healed the hurts and scars, and washed away the sins in his precious blood, you can ask him to remain on there as your personal Saviour, so that his work there will be ongoing, as each of my todays become yesterdays. When this is done, you should come out of that room, and leave it to him. The only value the past has are the lessons it taught me. I would be very wise, compassionate, and understanding of others, if I learned the lessons from that room of my past.

The second thing I want you to do is to look at the room of your future. You cannot enter this room, of course, because it would be total darkness, as you cannot foresee the future. However, you can imagine Jesus coming out of that room, putting his hands on both your shoulders, and saying gently to you: 'I know everything that's in this room. You have a choice. You can struggle on alone into the darkness of the future, or you can allow me take charge of this room, and each morning I will hand you one day at a time from it. I know what's in this room, even down to the number of days that are left. If you let me be Lord, I will never lead you where my grace and my Spirit will not be there to sustain you. I will never hand you a day which you and I together will not be able to handle. The decision is yours ...'

The third thing I ask you to reflect on is to look at today; indeed, at this very moment. The only *yes* in your whole life that

God is interested in is your *yes* of now. What part has God in your life today? Do you feel that you are plodding along all alone? Turn to Jesus and invite him to walk with you today. 'Jesus, I invite you into my heart today. Please make your home there, feel at home there, and be at home there. May your presence within me today touch the hearts of those I meet, either through the words I say, the prayers I pray, the life I live, or the very person that I am.' You'll never walk alone ...

Story
One Sunday morning, a priest, in the middle of his homily, held up a 20 pound note. He asked if anyone wanted it. Many hands shot up. He then crumpled it in his fist, making a small ball of it, held it up again, and asked if anyone still wanted it. Again the hands shot up. He tore it in two, held up the two pieces, and asked if anyone still wanted it. And yet again the hands were raised. The priest then went on to speak of the offer Jesus extends to us. If we could appreciate the value of it, our response would be clear and definite. If we didn't understand it too well, we would seek some spiritual direction, go on a Retreat, or buy a book. Hopefully, we would call on the Holy Spirit to lead us into the fullness of the truth being presented to us, because Jesus promised that 'the Spirit will lead you into all truth, and the truth will set you free.'

As I said earlier, the answer to the question in today's gospel is to be found within our hearts ...

TWENTY-SECOND SUNDAY OF THE YEAR

Gospel: Matthew 16:21-27

Central Theme

In today's gospel, Jesus tells his disciples what is going to happen to him, and he invites them to follow him, while explaining to them some of the ramifications of their decision to do so.

Parable

Fr Damien the Leper was a member of my own Congregation. What he undertook was something entirely new in the Congregation at that time. He knew the risk he was taking, and he eventually paid the full price for his courage and bravery. Since that time others in our Congregation have been inspired to follow his example, and to travel down that road. We have confrères working with lepers in Calcutta and, as recently as a few years ago, one of our priests was withdrawn from Damien's island of Molokai, because he too had contracted leprosy.

Teaching

It is worth noting that, from early on, Jesus told his disciples that he would be killed, but that he would be raised on the third day. It is interesting, because, when it did happen, the disciples didn't seem to be ready for either event. Even on the morning of his ascension, we are told that some of them doubted. They still had a problem at taking him at his word. And it was in believing his word that Jesus depended for the success of his mission. 'Heaven and earth will pass away before my word passes away.' He himself was the Word of God, and when he spoke a word it could be accepted and acted on. 'The sin of this world is unbelief in me.'

The contribution of Peter, and the strong reaction of Jesus, is well worth looking at. Right from the start of his mission, Satan had done everything within his power to thwart his plans. He put Jesus through a severe testing in the desert. His attacks took several forms, but today's episode is particularly cunning. Satan is using Jesus' own right-hand man to do his dirty work for him. Peter is completely innocent, because he acts out of love and concern. He doesn't want to see Jesus walking into the hands of his enemies. However, he cannot see the scenario as Jesus can, and so he doesn't realise that this is all a part of the Father's plan for Jesus. Later on, on the way to Emmaus, Jesus asked the disciples, 'Did you not read what the prophets said, that the Son of Man must suffer, and be delivered into the hands of his enemies, who would kill him, but on the third day, he would rise from the dead?'

After his confrontation with Peter, Jesus lays it on the line for his followers. He makes it very clear what following him will entail. He speaks in apparent paradoxes, because I'm sure the disciples never heard such thinking in their lives. How could you find your life by giving it away? Was it necessary to sacrifice one's own personal ambitions to be a follower of Jesus? He then goes on to make a distinction between what is most important, and what is less important. You can abandon your earthly dreams, and sacrifice your bodily comforts, but you must never lose your own truth, your authentic self, your own soul. He then goes on to bridge the gap between his earlier prediction about his death and resurrection, to tell about his final coming in glory with all his angels. It will all end in eternal triumph, and those who follow him will be part of that. It seems, once again, that the apostles failed to grasp the great truth behind what he was saying.

Response
Reading today's gospel two thousand years after it happened gives us a great advantage over the disciples. The facts of death and resurrection have been fulfilled. We should have no problem, then! Our problem can arise when we try to bridge the gap between what happened to Jesus, and what must happen in our lives. When we take the gospel story and apply it to our day, we discover that we are the ones who now have to die, and then be raised from the dead. We believe that it happened to Jesus, but it's not so easy to believe that it will happen for us. Incarnation is not a once-off event that happened to Jesus. Bethlehem, Calvary, the tomb, the Pentecost room, all this must be on-going within our hearts.

Prudence and over-caution can stultify us, and freeze us into non-action. To live is to take risks, and the person who never takes a risk cannot claim to be fully alive. I can eat as much as I want and put on weight, and the chances are that no one will say anything. However, if I fast, I will get all sorts of advice about being careful, about minding my health, and about the dangers of going down that road. Some years ago, one of our young priests decided to go on the mission to Mozambique. I was present when a friend of his tried everything within his power to dissuade him from doing this. There was such a need for young priests in Ireland, etc. Today's gospel is now …

The latter part of today's gospel holds some very solid teaching for all of us. We are called on to consider what is involved before we make any decisions. What good is it for any of us to gain the whole world, and lose ourselves in the process? If I were to play back the tape of any normal day, and line up in order how I spent my time and my money, it would give me a picture of where my priorities lie. If there is a football match on the television, I'll arrange my time in such a way that I have a chance to see it. Nothing wrong with that. However, I may find that I didn't have time for someone who called on me, or I may not have time to take the few quiet moments to be alone with God, and my reflections. If I am that busy, then I'm too busy. Jesus tells us that we will be judged by our deeds. Carrying the cross has to do with being at the service of others. Having time for others is a very important part of being a Christian.

Practical

'You see things from a human point of view, and not from God's.' Taking time out to reflect gives me an opportunity to see things from God's perspective. In prayer I come before God exactly as he sees me, and I accept his love and acceptance. Faith is to have the courage to accept God's acceptance. I must make a clear distinction between saying prayers and praying. Prayer is what God does and says when I give him an opportunity. It is essential that I develop a reflective spirit, and I cannot do this without giving time to it. After a while it becomes natural, and I can have a reflective heart in the midst of city throngs.

Am I aware of the place of the cross in Christian living? It's not about suffering all the time, or about enduring a burden, without seeking help or advice. Jesus tells us that his yoke is sweet, and his burden is light. The kingdom of God is built up by tiny acts of kindness, and most of them are hidden. I have to develop a generosity of spirit that prompts me to be there for others, even if that inconveniences me. It is about dying to myself for the sake of others. It is about giving, and about walking that extra mile with another. Like Jesus, we are called to be 'basin of water and towel people'. The selfish person lives in solitary confinement, because I am the only person in my life.

I suggested above that I might look at the priorities in my day. This enables me to discover what god I serve. Some people are completely taken over by the god of money, pleasure, or power. This is what motivates everything they do. They know the price of everything and the value of nothing. If money brought happiness, then every wealthy person would be happy, and we know that is not true. The happiest people on earth are those who serve others. There's a vast difference between being wealthy and being rich. I could be a really rich person, and have very little money. I need to check my priorities, to select what is most important in my life, and to make what changes are necessary to become a life-giving person for others. Today's the day for stock-taking!

Story

The mother had to go out to the shop, so she asked her children to set the table for dinner when she was gone. They did as they had been asked, but they added a nasty sting to the tail of their giving. They got a piece of paper, and wrote on it, 'For setting the table £2.' When the mother returned, she spotted the piece of paper, picked it up, put it in her pocket, and said nothing. She went into her bedroom, deeply hurt and disappointed. She got an A4 page, and began to write. 'For giving you life, and for carrying you within me for nine months. For going through the pains of childbirth, so that you could be born. For nursing you, and caring for you night and day for several years. For sitting up with you when you were sick at night. For dressing you and feeding you. For bringing you to school, helping you with your homework, and for bringing you on holidays. For buying you presents at Christmas, on birthdays, and at many other times. For loving you, and for giving you everything I possibly could. *Total Bill: Nothing!*' She returned to the kitchen, placed the sheet of paper on the table, and began preparing dinner. The children read what was written, and they began to cry. They went over to her, hugged you, and told her they were very sorry for being so selfish.

They learned something about love, and about giving ...

TWENTY-THIRD SUNDAY OF THE YEAR

Gospel: Matthew 18:15-20

Central Theme
Today's gospel gives us an interesting insight into how a Christian community can relate to those who deviate from the norms of that community. It also tells us about the powerful results that attend a community where harmony reigns, and where Jesus is to be found.

Parable
We are living at a time of public enquiries, tribunals, and accountability measures being introduced to root out corruption and dishonesty wherever it is. The church is very much involved with this, relative to cases of sexual abuse against its members. When the truth about clerical sex abuse began to emerge, the powers-that-be in the church were caught unprepared. There was no policy, because there seemed to have been no great awareness of a problem. By now exact procedures have been drawn up, precise instructions are available to all involved in dealing with sex abuse and, like the advice of Jesus in today's gospel, there are very clear steps to be followed.

Teaching
The first part of today's gospel speaks of accountability. It certainly is not about 'policing' my neighbour. Any action that might be taken is to be done in love, and out of a concern for the individual, and for the Christian community. Rather than being an accessory to the wrong, I am asked to take responsibility, and to share my concerns in a certain order. If I know the errant one, I may speak to him/her myself; and if that is not successful, I may then ask others to support me by following up on my initiative. 'All that's needed for evil people to succeed is that good people should do nothing.' We hear a lot of stories today where people were defrauding a system, or behaving in a way that would lead to harm for others; while we also hear that many others were aware of this but, because of moral cowardice, chose to turn a blind eye to what was going on and do nothing. Condoning a wrong-doing is to contribute to the wrong-doing.

Some people find it very difficult, if not impossible, to confront another with the truth. It requires moral courage, a genuine concern for the moral welfare of others, and the ability to speak my truth in love. If the other refuses to listen, even after you have got others to support you in your endeavours, then, having done your duty, you can follow an official route and let the powers-that-be take over and act. Your first attempt was to help, in love, and to prevent a bad situation becoming worse. There comes a time, though, when you must walk away and let the chips fall where they will. Jesus told his disciples that when they entered a town with his message, if the people refused to listen to them, they should shake the dust of that town from their feet, and move on.

The concluding paragraph of today's gospel has two gems of hope and consolation. If two or more of us ask God for something, and we are of one heart and one mind, that request will be granted. He goes on to tell us that where two or three gather in his name that he is there in the midst of them. What a joy that should evoke in the heart if the reality of that truth sank in. When he ascended into heaven, he took the body he had with him. He sent down the Spirit, and he asked us to provide the body. It follows then, of course, that where the body is gathered, the Spirit is present, and where the Spirit is, there are the Father and Jesus as well.

Response

The gospel is about love, and love is what should motivate our actions. My love for the community, the message of Jesus, or for my neighbour must be the primary motive in any attempt to point out to another the error of his ways. It is not a judgement or an authority thing. It is a question of caring enough for truth, or the welfare of another, that causes me, at times, to face up to painful situations, and to make painful decisions. If there is love, this should motivate me to overcome the moral cowardice that can freeze us into inaction.

When I cannot influence a serious situation, I must follow through by going to someone else for advice or support. Eventually, this may have to be an authority figure, as a last resort to correct a bad situation. There is great sensitivity needed here, because I should never interfere in something that is not my business, or my concern. Sometimes I may have to stand back and let an alcoholic hit Skid Row, and possibly die. I must avoid the temptation to play God, because I am powerless over persons, places, or things. It is only when the common good is being adversely effected, or there is an apparent injustice being done, that I should speak out in love. This is not a question of being a 'nosey Parker', or interfering in something that is not my business.

As a Christian I should have a genuine respect for the community dimension of that. If Jesus has positively endorsed the value of those who gather in his name, I must keep this in mind when I share in community gatherings. The Spirit is given to the community as the Body of Christ, and I am 'plugged into' the power of that Spirit when I am part of the Christian community. There is no flying solo within the Christian community. As the church is evolving at present, there is a greater call for people to take responsibility for their part within the life of the church. The word 'vocation' which was once the preserve of the clergy and religious, is now being restored to the laity as their right. I have a Christian vocation, whether I choose to live that in the married, single, clerical, or religious life. My baptism is much more important to me than my ordination.

Practical

Part of the revelations in recent Tribunals of enquiry has been the fact that so many others were aware of what was going on, and they chose to remain silent. In doing so they were complicit in the wrong-doing. I should look at my life as a loving critic, to ensure that I am not being an enabler in any wrong-doing. 'Fear makes cowards of us all', Shakespeare wrote. Moral courage, inspiring us to honesty, is a precious quality, and it should be part of the stock-in-trade of every Christian.

In being a loving critic of my own life, I may discover areas where others drew my attention to something in my conduct that was hurtful to others. Resentment is a luxury that a Christian cannot afford. 'There are none so blind as those who don't want to see, or none so deaf as those who don't want to hear.' I have met many people who lived to become eternally grateful to someone else who alerted them to the destructive nature of their behaviour. It takes generosity of spirit, and an openness to truth, to enable us listen to the truth of others. It is a real sign of maturity and humility to be able to reflect, without bitterness, on what another has pointed out to me. None of us like being corrected or having to face up to some unpalatable truths.

I may attend Christian community gatherings, or be part of

an active Christian community, and not fully appreciate the extraordinary truth that Jesus is present among us. I should have a sense of reverence when present at such gatherings. It makes a fundamental and profound difference when I have this awareness. It means that I'm not just present in body, but that my whole being is present at that gathering. If I do this, I will soon discover the enriching graces of such a presence. It is vital that I check the level of my involvement and awareness as a member of the Christian community.

Story
A young mother had a way of cooking ham that intrigued her husband. She would take the ham, and cut off a section of it from both ends, before putting it in the dish that went into the oven. One day he asked her why she did this, and she said she did it because her mother always did it. The next time he met his mother-in-law he decided to make further enquiries. He asked her why she always cut off the ends of a piece of ham, and she said that, for many years, she had quite a small dish, and the ham didn't fit into it! He discovered that his wife had continued to do something for which there was no reason, logic, or explanation.

Today's gospel calls on us to reflect on our actions, and to discover the motives behind our behaviour. Have you heard about the priest who dreamt he was preaching a sermon, and he woke up to find that he was?

TWENTY-FOURTH SUNDAY OF THE YEAR

Gospel: Matthew 18:21-35

Central Theme
Today's gospel is a very clear teaching on forgiveness, and we can no longer say that we weren't sure what Jesus' teaching was. He tells us how the heavenly Father will treat those who refuse to forgive a brother or sister from the heart.

Parable
On far too many occasions over the years, we have had tit-for-tat murders in Northern Ireland. The revenge being sought usually came from some element of the paramilitaries. On many occasions the families of those killed begged that there be no revenge killing, and were very public in proclaiming their willingness to forgive those who had killed a son, a father, or whoever. Gordon Wilson, whose daughter Marie was killed in the Enniskillen bomb during a commemoration ceremony at the cenotaph, was one of the most outstanding examples of Christian forgiveness. He became a witness to the whole country, and was co-opted into the Senate by the Dublin government.

Teaching
Jesus was a brilliant teacher. He used stories a lot, because it was a very simple way to get across a message. Peter had asked him a question, which must have been about a topic being discussed among them. He asked how often should he forgive his brother if he sinned against him? Peter went on to hazard a guess at the answer, by suggesting seven times. In this he was being generous, and he probably expected to merit Jesus' approval. Imagine his amazement when Jesus replied, 'No! Seventy times seven.' This was an expression meaning 'endless' or 'indefinitely' among the Jews.

I almost feel like saying 'Yes, you heard correctly. He said that you must keep forgiving, and there must never come a time when you draw the line, and say "no further".' Quite obviously, this is impossible for us, when someone continues to hurt us, take advantage of us, use us. Yes, indeed, it is impossible for us. All things are possible for God, and for God only. Even while he was dying on the cross, Jesus was asking the Father to forgive those who were killing him. It is only through the presence and action of the Spirit within my heart that I have any hope of ever becoming and acting as a Christian. When Jesus calls on us to forgive without end, he also offers us what it takes to do that. He will never ask us to do something, or to go anywhere where his Spirit will not accompany us, and his grace sustain us.

Jesus draws a simple parallel between both men in today's gospel. The basic message is that we must forgive others because God forgives us. St John, in one of his letters, says 'Little children, let us love one another, because God has first loved us.' In the one prayer he left us, Jesus taught us to ask God to forgive us as we are willing to forgive others. If forgiveness doesn't go from me to others, it ceases to come from God.

Response
Nowhere does the gospel suggest, and nowhere am I suggesting that forgiveness is easy. Some people have been deeply hurt and traumatised. Nobody was more unfairly treated than Jesus. It is easy to confuse forgiving with forgetting. I cannot be expected to forget what happened to me, and many people carry the horrible memories of their pain to their graves, even if they have long ago forgiven those who hurt them. 'To err is human; to forgive is divine.' I may need counselling or some self-help group to enable me heal the wounds, and let go of the anger and resentment.

The first step on the road of forgiveness is a willingness to forgive. If I have the will, God will give me the power. Even while still hurting, I can get to a point where I am able to pray for those who hurt me. This is a giant step, and it is the first step along the road of recovery. It takes a big heart to be able to let go of the need to seek revenge, and to get even. By myself it is too much for me. I cannot do it on my own; that is why I must come to a point where I am willing and ready to turn the whole thing over to God.

When I forgive I free myself from the prison of resentment and anger. The person who is hurt most is myself, when I refuse to forgive. There is an extraordinary healing in forgiveness, because it opens my heart to the forgiveness of God. We are all in need of forgiveness, especially from God. What a blessing it is to know that I am forgiven by God. The only way I can be sure of this is that I myself become a forgiving person. Forgiveness becomes a way of life for the Christian. This is surely the work of the Spirit, and it is clear evidence of the action of the Spirit in my heart. If you want to be free, and to live a wholesome life, then you must have a forgiving heart.

Practical
Today's gospel should cause us to search our hearts. Forgiveness is a very wide issue. It is more than just forgiving others. It includes forgiving myself, and it may even include forgiving God because of some tragedy or disaster in my life. When I am ready to look in a mirror and give myself absolution, only then am I ready to come to God for forgiveness. Otherwise, I could find myself asking God to do something that I myself am refusing to do.

We have all heard the phrase 'burying the hatchet', but there is a tendency to mark the spot, so that the hatchet can be dug up at short notice, when needed! Forgiveness does not exclude remembering the pain, or experiencing a twinge of anger at a moment of recall. It means that, at such times, I am willing to pray for those who hurt me, so that the pain will go away. It is an on-going process and, like any wound, it takes time to heal. Opening my hands and letting go, means that my hands are open to receive many wonderful blessings from God.

For the Christian, there is no way around forgiveness. I can justify and rationalise anything but, at the end of the day, I just have to forgive. 'Forgive us our trespasses as we forgive those who trespass against us.' I must reflect on the short prayer Jesus asked me to say. It doesn't give me much choice, does it? Forgiving is a very high level of loving, because it costs me. If a couple knelt down before me to get married, and they hadn't much sense, and even less money, I would still go ahead with the ceremony, if I thought they had enough forgiveness in their hearts. If they have enough forgiveness, their love will last, because it is through thousands of acts of forgiveness that love grows. Today's gospel certainly gives us some very serious reflection material.

Story
It happened on a huge ranch somewhere in South Dakota. The mother was preparing some food, while her toddler son was amusing himself with some building blocks. It was a dark evening, and there was quite a storm outside. Her husband was down in the farmyard with the other workmen. The mother was so engrossed in her work that she failed to keep an eye on the

child, who had by now made his way to the back door. When she was finished her work she called him to feed him, and he didn't respond. She wasn't worried, thinking he may be asleep on a couch, he could have made his way upstairs, or downstairs to the cellar. It took some time for the coin to drop, and for her to realise that he was not around. She began to get anxious as she ran from one end of the house to the other, calling his name. It was then she spotted the back door open.

She ran outside into the rain and the darkness, frantically calling his name, but, apart from the storm, there wasn't a sound. She spent some time running around the outside of the house, before he decided to phone the farmyard, and call for help. Her husband and the workmen arrived immediately. The house was surrounded by huge fields of wheat, which was nearly twice the height of her son. They ran into the wheat, with torches, calling his name all the time. After some time, they called the police, as they continued the search. Eventually they had to give up, and resigned themselves to wait for the light of dawn. Many of the neighbours arrived to assist in the search. They ran every which way through the wheat, but to no avail. Finally, one of the policemen called them all together, and he said to them 'We're all running all over the place, without plan or order. The child is so small that he could be within yards of any one of us but, with the tall wheat he is not visible. Why don't we hold hands, form a straight line, and move down sections of the field, one after the other.' They did this, and it wasn't long until they found him. He was lying in a gully, and he was unconscious, after being exposed to the elements all night. The policeman picked him up in his arms, and ran towards the house. The mother was at the door, and the child was handed to her, but it was too late. The tiny flame of life was extinguished, and he was dead in her arms. She sat on the back porch, clutching her dead baby in her arms, as the others looked on in a state of shock and helplessness. Suddenly, from somewhere within the mother came a scream. 'Why, oh why, didn't you people hold hands sooner?'

How many more people have to die in Northern Ireland, Jerusalem, East Timor, before people begin to forgive each other, and hold hands ... ?

TWENTY-FIFTH SUNDAY OF THE YEAR

Gospel: Matthew 20:1-16

Central Theme

Today's gospel tells us that it's never too late for God. There is full wages offered to all of us, whether we have served him all our lives, or we have turned to him at the eleventh hour.

Parable

Thérèse of Lisieux tells about a criminal being executed, and he stubbornly rejected all offers of spiritual help from the prison chaplain. She was very concerned about him, and she became very determined, in prayer, to obtain some change of heart before he died. An extraordinary thing happened that had a profound effect on her understanding of God's love and mercy. Just before he was blind-folded, and placed beneath the guillotine, he snatched the crucifix from the chaplain's hands, and kissed it reverently. He continued to clutch it, as he was put into position, and the blade fell. It is never too late for God.

Teaching

I know someone for whom today's gospel is a great consolation. She has led a good life, but she still gets great reassurance from this story. On the other hand, I have met people who are annoyed by this story! They have been on the side of God all their lives, and they seem to resent the fact that someone else can live it up all his life, turn to God at the last moment, and join them with equal reward in heaven! I have been asked about the 'good thief' on Calvary, who asked for help and was offered heaven right there. I have also heard others questioning the justice to the brother of the Prodigal Son. He had worked hard, stayed at home, and yet it was his profligate brother who got the party!

If I don't grasp the scope of love, then I will never understand the mind of God. It is said that God created us in his image and likeness and that we have returned the compliment! 'God's ways are not our ways.' Jesus, in the story, quotes the man as saying, 'Can't I do what I wish with my money? Are you angry because I am kind?' We should be truly grateful that God is so generous and so forgiving. If God was to err I'd prefer him to err on the side of mercy! He understands the human heart, and what is important that those who were called at the last moment, answered that call. 'Live, and let live' is a good motto. Those who began working in the morning got a full day's wages. What the others got should not concern them. But we all know that if this happened in an industry here on earth, there would be pickets outside the factory the following morning!

Jesus uses this story to tell us about love, mercy, and forgiveness. It is not the amount of work we do; it is the spirit that we bring to the work. He calls, and we answer. Because of our human condition, we are not always ready to follow the inspirations of God. In another place, Jesus speaks about a man who had two sons, and when he asked them to do some work, one said he would, but he didn't, the other said he wouldn't, but he did. It's how the story ends up that matters. Everyone in today's gospel ended up working in the vineyard, no matter for how long. His blessings are reserved to those of goodwill, who act on that goodwill.

Response

I can place myself in the vineyard of the Lord, no matter what age I am, or how I have lived my life up till now. The only *yes* in my life that God is interested in is my *yes* of now. 'Today, if you hear his voice, harden not your hearts.' We are all called. We may hear the call at different times, or we may dilly-dally with our response, and eventually accept the invitation. 'Many are called, but few are chosen' could be interpreted as 'Many are called, but few choose to respond.' The heart of today's gospel is hope, because I could easily put myself outside of God's love through guilt or a sense of unworthiness.

There are calls within calls. I have come across people who were called to a particular way of life and, at a later stage they got a second call to specialise in some specific form of Christian ministry. I know priests who worked at home, and then felt called to work in the Third World. I have known married people who, when the family was reared, felt called to set up a half-way house, or to work with the house-bound. God is always calling us, and it is important that we listen, so that we can hear and heed that call.

I love today's gospel. I find it difficult to specify why exactly that is so, but it has something to do with everybody getting a fair chance from a patient and loving God. I find that I use it a lot to give people hope, who may have given up on themselves achieving anything in life. It is never too late for God. 'Behold, I stand at the door and knock.' That knock is not a once-off thing, but is constant and persistent. 'You have made us for yourself, O Lord, and our hearts will never be at peace until they rest in you.' I will not have peace until I heed that call. I may resist it as long as I want but, eventually, and hopefully, grace will win out, and the response will come. It is only then that I will realise what I have been missing all those years.

Practical

The fact that I was born into a particular religious persuasion, or that I join a worshipping community once a week, doesn't automatically mean that I have answered the call. At my baptism someone else spoke for me; at confirmation I may not have had much of a personal choice either. There comes a time, however, when I must answer that call in a personal and deliberate way. I should reflect on the ramifications of that response before I make it. In Charismatic circles, they have a programme called 'Life in the Spirit Seminars'. There is a teaching one night a week for four weeks, which is accompanied by prayer, praise, and sharing. On the fifth week there is a ceremony called 'Baptism in the Spirit', which is a resume of baptism and confirmation, when people pray with me for an outpouring of the Spirit, which will enable me respond fully to my Christian vocation.

On the following two weeks there are other talks on the practicalities of living the Christian life, and of answering the call. I have seen elderly people with tears rolling down their cheeks, as they confessed that, until now, they had no idea just what the whole Christian vocation was. They thought it simply meant going to church on Sundays, and saying a few prayers now and then. You may not be the kind of person who would be attracted to Charismatic Prayer Groups, and there's nothing wrong with that. However, no matter how it happens, you must be baptised in the Holy Spirit. In other words, you need to travel from your head to your heart, from academic knowledge to experiential knowledge of God. That will happen when you are ready to fall on your knees and sincerely ask for it.

I said earlier that I love this gospel. I would be happy if you loved it too, for whatever reason. It gives a wonderful insight into how the Lord works, and how he sees things. We are all equally important in his eyes, and we are all offered full wages, no matter when we join the workforce. It would be good to reflect on this gospel today, and to get in touch with whatever that reflection evokes. What I have written here is intended as a stimulant to reflection, and it must be taken from there by the reader or listener. In a way, it is yet another call … a call that must be heard.

Story
A young man was getting ready to graduate from college. For many months he had admired a beautiful sports car in a dealer's showroom and, as his father could well afford it, he told him that this was what he wanted. As Graduation Day approached, the young man awaited signs that his father had purchased the car. Finally, on the morning of his graduation, his father called him into his private study. His father told him how proud he was to have such a fine son, and told him how much he loved him. He handed his son a beautifully wrapped gift box. Curious, but somewhat disappointed, the young man opened the box, and found a lovely leather-bound Bible, with the young man's name embossed in gold. Angrily, he raised his voice to his father, and said 'With all your money, you give me a Bible?', as he stormed out of the room, leaving the Bible behind.

Many years passed, and the young man was very successful in business. He had a beautiful home, and a wonderful family, but he realised his father was very old, and he should call to see him. He had not seen him since that Graduation Day. Before he could make arrangements he got a telegram, telling him his father had passed away, and willed all his possessions to his son. He needed to come home immediately and take care of things. When he arrived in his father's house a sense of sadness and regret filled his heart. He began to search through his father's papers when he saw the new Bible, just as he had left it years ago. With tears, he opened the Bible and began to leaf through it. His father had carefully underlined a verse, Matthew 7:11, 'And you, being evil, know how to give good gifts to your children, how much more will your heavenly Father give to those who ask him?' As he read these words, a car key dropped from the back of the Bible. It had a tag with the dealer's name, the same dealer who had the sports car he had so desired. On the tag was the date of his graduation, and the words *Paid in full*.

I am so grateful that it's never too late for God …

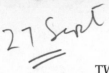

TWENTY-SIXTH SUNDAY OF THE YEAR

Gospel: Matthew 21:28-32

Central Theme

Today's gospel points out the difference between talking the talk, and walking the walk. It tells us that what we do is more a test of what we are, than anything we say.

Parable

I met a friend of mine last week, and he was full of enthusiasm for a new venture he had undertaken. He is a relatively young man who has a particularly vibrant sense of the spiritual. He wanted to do something to help others, by way of saying thanks to God for what he and his family had. He went along and offered his services to the St Vincent de Paul Society, an offer that was eagerly snapped up. He enjoys the work, and he feels really good about his decision. It is interesting to note that he first got the idea several months before that, when a colleague said that he was thinking about joining the SVP! So far, for his colleague the thought has not been translated into action.

Teaching

Today's gospel is very simple, and it is easy to get a lesson from it. In another gospel Jesus says, 'If you love me, you will obey me.' The gospel is a call to action now. One young man told Jesus that he had to bury his father first, another had bought a farm, and he had to inspect it, etc., etc. Excuses, excuses, excuses! The excuses are funny, if they weren't serious. There is no hint that the first guy's father is sick. When his father dies twenty years from now, there will be somebody else to bury. The second man would hardly have bought a farm first, and then go to examine it! If I don't want to do something, I'll always find an excuse to avoid it.

There's nothing more powerful than an idea whose time has come. There is no scarcity of ideas, but there can be a real scarcity of goodwill to put those ideas into practice. The Christian message is intended to galvanise me into action. The best way to avoid doing something is to talk about it long enough. Jesus wants decisions rather than discussions. There is such a thing as a moment of grace. It is just like the story about Bartimeus in the gospel. He was a blind man, sitting by the side of the road, he heard the commotion, and asked what was happening. Someone told him that Jesus of Nazareth was passing by. Immediately Bartimeus grasped the moment. 'Jesus, son of David, have mercy on me,' he shouted again and again. The people around him tried to silence him, but there was no way he was going to let this moment of grace pass. He continued shouting until Jesus stopped, called him over, and healed him. There's many a moment in our every day when 'Jesus of Nazareth is passing by.'

Jesus really incensed the Jews when he told them that tax collectors and prostitutes would enter heaven before them. He explained how this was so. The tax collectors and prostitutes listened to John the Baptist, and changed their ways, while Jesus' listeners continued to be stubborn, and refused to listen to him. At another point in the gospel, he warned them that, just because they could claim Abraham as their father, it didn't give them an automatic claim to anything. If anything, they would be judged all the more severely, because they had a religious background, were familiar with the scriptures, and they should have recognised his teaching as coming from God.

Response

'Faith without good works is dead,' St James tells us. What we believe is evidenced through our actions, not our words. Jesus asks us to ensure that our 'yes' is 'yes', and our 'no' is 'no'. He calls on us to make a decision, and to act on that decision. 'Come, follow me,' he asked the apostles, and they left their boats and followed him. Sheep will follow the shepherd, while goats have to be driven by the goat-herd. Today's gospel is speaking to us today, and our response must be made today.

Like the Jews, we cannot claim that all is well just because we associate ourselves with a particular Christian denomination. I can have a baptism certificate in my pocket, and not be living a Christian life. I can fully accept the concepts of Christianity as an ideology, and not believe in God. Jesus came to lead us to the Father, not to give us some nice little ideals and ideas for living.

Christianity is not about producing nicer people with better morals. I could be a pagan, and be a nice guy. It is not about prayer and fasting. I could be a Muslim, and do all of that on a regular basis. It is about a person, Jesus Christ, who leads us to the Father, into the fullness of the life of the Trinity. His message calls for obedience to his teaching and thinking. He came 'to do and to teach'. Our vocation is also about doing and teaching. We are not all called to be evangelists, to stand on a box in Hyde Park, preaching the gospel. However, we are all called to be witnesses to his life, death, and resurrection. Our Christian life, lived in obedience to his teaching, is our message.

Jesus has some harsh words for the religious leaders of his day. They refused to believe John the Baptist, and to obey his call for repentance. By so doing, they rejected the message, and so lost their priority as God's chosen race. The public sinners, whom they condemned and marginalised, will enter heaven before they do. They heard the call, but refused to respond; therefore the onus for such unbelief rests with them. The same is true for us today. We can never claim that we didn't know. We are guilty of what used be called 'culpable ignorance'. If I refuse to respond, I become irresponsible. There will come a day, however, when I will be held responsible.

Practical

At the moment of death, I will come face to face with God, naked, and with no place to hide. The denial, excuses, and delaying will be over. Might I suggest the following: In my reflection, I can imagine that moment, and try to visualise what it might be like. I can do that every single day. Hopefully, it will motivate my response now, while I still have time. I can spread out the canvas of my life right now, and allow the Spirit of truth to reveal to me what is to be seen.

When I reflect on the two sons in today's gospel, how do I see myself relative to each of them? I may find a little bit of each in me, and that is not bad. The idea is that I continue to renew my commitment to Jesus, and I continue to open my heart to the fullness of his message. I depend on the work of his Spirit within my heart to lead me into all truth. With my human resources alone, I can easily have many blind spots. My mind and my eyes can be very selective in what I see, and in what I accept as true. I cannot rely on human wisdom, because there is some sort of basic rebelliousness within us, because of original sin, and it is only the Spirit of truth who can lead me into truth, and guide my feet into the ways of peace.

Maybe I could do with a change of attitude towards those who seem to be outside the community of believers. I may see them in this way, because I compare myself to them, and they are seen to be lacking by comparison. Have they had the chances that I've had to hear the message of the gospel? Indeed, have they had any spiritual formation at all? They certainly will not be condemned or rejected by God, just because they have never heard the message. If I have heard the good news, and have an opportunity to put it in practice, and to live it, this should lead to compassion, understanding, and tolerance, rather than pride, judgement, and bigotry. I should examine my conscience, as I hear Jesus speak about the tax collectors and the prostitutes in today's gospel.

Story
An Afro-American was standing outside an evangelical church in one of the southern states of the US. It was many years ago, and the church was for whites only. Just then Jesus came along, and asked him what he was doing there. The man told him that he loved listening to the singing, and that was why he was standing outside the door listening. He went on to explain that, because of his colour, he could not enter the church. Jesus smiled wryly, and said, 'I know how you feel. I myself have been trying to get into that church since it was opened!'

Gospel: Matthew 21:33-43

Central Theme
Today's gospel contains some home truths for the Jewish religious leaders. If they continue to reject what is being offered them, it will be taken off them, and given to others. The Jews were considered to be God's chosen people, but this title could be taken away from them, and offered to others, who will accept it.

Parable
When an American spy-plane was forced to land on Chinese territory, it precipitated quite a diplomatic conflict. Each side blamed the other, and the Americans refused to apologise and to admit that they had transgressed. The Chinese made the most of it, and things began to look nasty. One of the weapons that the Americans used in the negotiations was to withdraw the title of 'favoured nation status' that had been conferred on China some years ago. This title gave them access to American markets, industries, etc. To lose that status would have been a major blow to the bludgeoning economy of China. At present, there is still some kind of stale-mate going on, but it is generally accepted that the US would never risk alienating such a powerful emerging nation as China, and so the 'favoured nation status' provision will continue.

Teaching
I wrote a book some years ago called *Jesus, the Man and the Message*. Despite the many thousands of books written about Jesus over the centuries, I was really enthused by the personal insights I gained during the writing, and especially the reflection that accompanied the work. He obviously was 'meek and humble of heart', but his pursuance of truth enabled him to be very firm when that was needed. There was no comprising the message he came to deliver. While he stepped outside the Jewish law in his dealing with sinners, sick, and outcasts, he was also quite firm and unrelenting when dealing with stubborn, perverse, and unheeding religious leaders. Today's gospel is a good example of the latter.

Today he tells his own story through a parable, and his listeners knew only too well what he was saying. He asked a question, and they themselves said what should happen to those who refused to accept the messenger. Out of their own mouths he was condemning them. Throughout the years God had sent prophets and holy men to call the people to turn back to him. Many of the prophets ended up as martyrs. In the fullness of time, God sent his only Son, and he suffered the same fate. While claiming to be religious leaders, and people of God, they acted with a pride and arrogance that came out of their conviction that they alone knew the truth, and they alone knew the way to travel. They were not for turning.

Jesus leaves them in no doubt when he tells them that the kingdom of God will be taken from them, and given to those who will produce proper fruit. In saying this, he was certainly drawing their wrath upon himself and, rather than listen to him and discover that they needed to change, it was easier to kill him. If you don't like the message, shoot the messenger. Jesus is really stepping into a field of landmines in today's gospel, but he hadn't come to condone wrong-doing or to confirm untruths. He knew the price he would have to pay, but this did not deter him. There are several such incidents in the gospel when one feels that his fate is sealed, and he has gone a step too far. He knew what he was doing, however, and the story he chose to tell in today's gospel is certainly an accurate foretelling of all that was to come.

Response
It could be very easy for us to sit back and consider today's gospel as something that was meant for the religious leaders in Israel. I remember being at a Billy Graham rally in Shea Stadium, New York, where he was holding forth about the evil of prostitution on 34th Street. Of course, we were all sitting there, feeling quite smug, because he wasn't speaking about us! I cannot do that with the gospel, however, when I remind myself that the gospel is now, and I am every person in the gospel. I can have my own form of righteousness and there are times when I hear a sermon, I'm sorry that such-a-one is not here to hear this! I have every reason to consider myself a chosen disciple, because the Lord has been very good to me. I had ideal formation as I grew up, had the privilege of a good education, and I'm now fully engaged in gospel ministry. It would be so easy for me to look towards others as the people who are in need of conver- sion! That would be a sad scenario, because I would not be

personally touched and effected, as I read today's gospel. This gospel is for every one of us, and I must reflect on my own life against the background of what Jesus is presenting to me today. Religious pride is one of the more serious forms of pride. It blinds us to reality, and prevents us seeing the beam in our own eyes, while we point to the splinter in the eyes of others.

St Paul spoke about the danger of him 'having preached to others, and I myself becoming a castaway'. When I stand before God at the moment of death, all the masks will be removed, and all the truth will be exposed. 'To whom much is given, of him will much be expected.' The person with five talents will be expected to return five talents extra, while the one with two talents will be held responsible for a return of only two talents. I cannot accept God's choice, and his great love, without attempting to return that love with whatever time and talent I have. St Thérèse of Lisieux was so enthralled by God's love for her that she set herself the task of spending her whole life in returning that love with every ounce of her being.

Practical

The fact that you are reading this now is some indication that you are open to the word of the Lord. It is important that you appreciate this gift, because we cannot accept the gifts of the Lord, without accepting responsibility for how we use them. When Jesus speaks of the seed falling on good soil, he said that some produced 30%, some 60%, and some 100%. Even the thirty per cent was considered good soil, because it produced something. I am expected to do the best with what I have. I should hold myself responsible for the gifts God gives me, which, of course, includes time, talent, money, etc.

I believe it is necessary to develop a sense of deep gratitude for the blessings of the Lord. I should appreciate his blessings, and acknowledge both the privilege and the responsibility that comes with those blessings. It would be wrong to envy the gifts of another, rather then appreciating my own gifts. I am part of 'a chosen race, a royal priesthood, a people set apart'. The Jewish religious leaders saw their position as one that was theirs by right, and something that could not be taken from them. Just as I have the gift of life, the time will come when I will have to relinquish that gift for another form of living.

I own nothing. Everything I have is on loan. One heart attack, and it's all over. 'Life is fragile, handle with prayer.' As a branch, unless I am grafted on to the vine, which is Jesus, I cannot produce fruit. Jesus expects us to produce 'fruit that will remain'. There is a story in the gospel about a tree that failed to produce fruit, and it was cursed, and withered. If I fail to appreciate the importance of my Christian calling, I might settle for sitting back and doing nothing. It is not uncommon to encounter someone with such a poor self-image, and such a low self-esteem, that they fail to appreciate the gifts they have. 'God don't make no junk,' Herbs Banks tells us. When God created something, he 'saw that it was good'. I am part of that creation, and it is vital that I fully appreciate just how special I am in his eyes. I could easily confine myself in what I see with my eyes, and result in dismissing or in inflating what I see. I should reflect on what God sees when he looks at me.

Story
There was a family of three daughters. One of them was shy and bashful, and had absolutely no self-confidence. She tended to lurk in the background, and was not forthcoming in claiming her rightful place in the family. One day her dad surprised her by arriving home with a beautiful necklace for her. She looked at it in amazement, and she couldn't believe that anyone would bother to buy her such a beautiful gift. She placed it on the table, and ran into the kitchen to tell her mother about he gift she had received. She was so excited that it was minutes later when she emerged from the kitchen. To her horror, her younger sister was wearing the necklace. She looked at her dad, and he said, 'I thought you didn't want it, so I gave it to her instead.'

The father wasn't too thoughtful, and the poor girl lost the gift because of her failure to claim it as something that had been given to her …

TWENTY-EIGHTH SUNDAY OF THE YEAR

Gospel: Matthew 22:1-14

Central Theme

The theme of this gospel is repeated several times throughout the gospels. Jesus speaks about an invitation being offered, rejected, and the offer made to someone else. He tells us about the fate of those who rejected his offer, and he ends with something that may puzzle us, when we read of one person who answered the invitation, came to the meal, but was unceremoniously rejected. I will speak about this anon.

Parable

We are all familiar with offers being made on quiz shows, where the audience, and the general public are asked to answer a question, submit that answer, and give themselves a chance of winning a super prize. There are people who respond at once to every such opportunity, and there are those who would never have the slightest interest in getting involved with TV quizzes. 'If you're not in, you can't win.' I remember another type of TV competition which was an annual feature of a Friday night chat show. Six people arrived in the studio, each with the most dilapidated piece of furniture you could imagine. They had each bought a piece of junk at an auction, and the challenge was to return six months later with a completely restored, and perfectly working item. One year a particular lady won the competition with the job she did on an old armchair. At the time of the judging, we were shown shots of the armchair before and after, and the contrast was quite breath-taking. There was a follow-up to this particular case, however, when a professional antique restorer notified the programme that the woman had paid him to do the job, and that she herself had done none of the work, which, of course, was the purpose of the competition. There was much publicity on TV and the news media and, eventually, the TV show reclaimed the chair and the prize was returned. It was a bitter ending to a moment of glory.

Teaching

The first part of the gospel speaks of an invitation to a wedding feast. It speaks about the excuses made why different people couldn't come. In other words, they didn't want to come. It is obvious that the father loves his son, and it is important to him that his son's wedding feast is a splendid occasion, with many people in attendance. As we read this, we must remember that it is Jesus who is telling us the story. We must also remember that Jesus made up the story to illustrate a point. He would have sought, through story-form, to teach something that he wanted us to know. We can take it then that we are the ones who are invited to the feast. God's wants to share a celebration with us. You will notice that the invitation is issued twice, first when the invitations went out, and second, when the meal was ready.

Then the excuses began to flow. The excuses were trivial, and, to make matters worse, some of the people attacked and even killed some of the messengers. This certainly was rejection with a difference. Jesus often reminded the religious leaders of what they had done to the prophets whom God had sent to them. Many of the prophets ended up as martyrs. Once again, when I don't like the message, I shoot the messenger. In this case, however, it is an invitation rather than a message that is issued. When the invitation is rejected, it is then issued to everybody on the highways and byways. The wedding feast was going ahead anyhow, and if people didn't want to be there they were rejected, and the invitation was withdrawn.

The last part of the gospel is puzzling. At first reading, it seems to be unfair. One person is ejected from the feast because he is not properly dressed. It is difficult to know what Jesus has in mind here, and one can only surmise. I certainly don't think it had anything to do with how the person was dressed, because some people couldn't afford to buy the appropriate dress for a wedding. It would appear that someone, with an ulterior motive, had slipped in and was there under false pretences. It would be expected that those who were invited, and who showed up, were delighted with the honour, and were in a mood for celebration. It is possible that one person had no interest whatever in what was going on, and was a phoney guest. We can presume that Jesus would be more interested in the heart of the person than the clothes he was wearing.

Response
We are people who are invited to the wedding feast. God invites us to sit at table with him, and to share his most precious gift, his only Son, Jesus Christ. Every invitation from God has RSVP written bold and clear. Not to reply is, in itself, an answer. It is

not only to accept the invitation, but I must also show up for the wedding. God is not devious, and he asks us not to be devious. 'Let your "yes" be "yes", and your "no" be "no".' God is patient, and he will continue to invite until there is no sign of any response. He doesn't give up on us lightly, but there must come a time when I have deliberately put myself outside the scope of the invitation; because of my free will, God cannot, or would not shanghai me into conformity with his will, against my will.

On the other hand, I may not have much of a Christian formation, and I may not consider myself as someone who has a Christian vocation, because I associate that word with priests and religious. In that case, I become like one of the second batch who were invited to the wedding. I might be just as surprised as they were to discover they were invited to the feast for the wedding of the king's son. I may feel unworthy, and undeserving of such an honour. It is not a question of deserving, however, because, with God, everything is free, and we are all his children. No matter how the call comes, or when it comes, the important thing is that I heed it, and respond to it. I am as much part of the church as the pope is. There are no second-class citizens in the kingdom of God.

When I read about the person that was ejected from the feast, I must look within my heart, to check on the sincerity of my commitment as a Christian. There is nothing automatic about baptism, or, indeed, about any of the sacraments. I can pour water on a baby, and say all the words in the book, but that doesn't mean that this child will ever become a Christian. A couple can kneel in front of me to get married, make all the loving promises in the world, and end up killing each other. The Lord is interested in the heart. I would prefer to think that no one would be rejected because of the style of dress, but because of the state of the heart

Practical
The only real practical thing I can think of regarding today's gospel is to come back to the basic question of how real and how personal is my commitment to Jesus and to his message. This cannot be measured, and there is no way it can be quantified. While I cannot measure my response, I can certainly renew it, repeat it, and turn to the Spirit to direct and guide me in the way of the Lord.

If I examine my heart I may find that I can be very selective in my response to the invitation. I can meet the criteria of being a Christian in many areas of my life and, yet, in one area, such as a wrong relationship, I can be living a lie. We all have our own 'pet' sins that we do not want to relinquish. As a matter of fact, my external propriety can be an excellent cover-up for some serious wrong-doing. We all have read of pillars of society, and, indeed, of leading church figures, who have been exposed as living a lie. The real damage behind many of the scandals the church has had to deal with in recent times is that they were carried out by the very people we would expect to be to the fore in the upkeeping of morality and Christian care.

Despite how I may look as I dress, how do I consider my heart? When I invite Jesus to make his home there, to be at home there, and to feel at home there, is there anything that comes to mind that would be inconsistent with Jesus building his kingdom there? In my prayer I should deliberately express my willingness to have an open heart. I should constantly ask the Lord for the gift of honesty and integrity. I should come back to this again and again. 'Lord, please take a whip of cords and rid the temple of my heart of anything that is not from you.' That is a prayer that I could learn to repeat on a regular basis.

Story

A young lad had just got his driving licence. He asked his father, who was a minister, if they might discuss his use of the car. His father said to him, 'I'll make a deal with you. You bring your school grades up, study your Bible a little, and get your hair cut, and then we'll talk about it.' A month later the lad came back and again asked his father if they could discuss his use of the car. His father said, 'Son, I'm real proud of you. You have brought up your school grades, you have studied your Bible diligently, but you didn't get your hair cut.' The young man waited a moment, and replied, 'You know, dad, I've been thinking about that. You know Samson had long hair, Moses had long hair, Noah had long hair, and even Jesus had long hair.' His father replied, 'Yes, son, you're right ... and they walked everywhere they went'!

I cannot rationalise or argue my way around the message of the gospel, or my response to it ...

TWENTY-NINTH SUNDAY OF THE YEAR

Gospel: Matthew 22:15-21

Central Theme
Once again, the Pharisees try to trip Jesus, and once again, he outsmarts them. Today's gospel shows their cunning at its worst, but it also shows the courage and alertness of Jesus. Once again, it is the triumph of truth over deceit and deviousness.

Parable
At the time of writing there is a very strange, and somewhat humorous act being played out. The government has set up several Tribunals and, among the terms of references of some of those Tribunals is to discover Irish citizens who have money stashed away in Ansbacher accounts in the Cayman Islands, in the Isle of Man, Switzerland, etc. The problem for the money-people is that they can't touch their money, or the transaction will be discovered. They have money, but when will it ever be theirs to spend? One man went to the Isle of Man, was under surveillance, and was arrested at Dublin airport as he arrived with a case full of cash! The problem with the government is that this money was kept overseas to avoid tax. Now the government wants what belongs to Caesar, and nobody wants to give.

Teaching
Today's gospel shows just how devious the Pharisees were, and to what extent they were prepared to go to trip Jesus up, so they could accuse him, and kill him. His very presence, as well as what he said was something that really got to them, because it threatened their very reason for existing. They had assumed an authority for themselves, they had developed that to such an extent that they had powerful control over others, and they re-joiced in that power. Jesus saw them for the hypocrites they were, and he condemned them roundly. There was no way they could stand back and let him expose them like that. They were prepared to go to any length to ensnare him. Later on, they would have to bribe one of his apostles to betray him.

They hated the Romans and yet they were prepared to play the Roman card when it suited them. They didn't agree about paying taxes to Rome, but they wanted to hear Jesus say that, so that they could report him to the Romans. They even brought some of Herod's supporters, so that they, too, could witness to what Jesus said. The stage was set for intrigue, trickery, and deceit. Jesus saw them coming a mile away. He was used to this, even though this particular intrigue was one of the most elaborate. He was not afraid of them, because his mandate was very clear. His was a message of truth that could not be compromised or diluted in any way. The facts are always friendly, and 'when everything else fails, try the truth, because it always works'!

In taking the coin, Jesus was not going to get into a long argument with them. If this coin is Caesar's, give it to Caesar; but you must also give to God what belongs to God. End of argument! He was like a brilliant senior counsel in a court, who pins the other's arguments with one stroke of legal interpretation. 'The best laid plans of mice and men ...' The Pharisees were taken completely by surprise. He had used their very own argument against them. He mentioned nothing about paying taxes, about obeying Rome, or about Jewish national interests. If the coin had Caesar's head on it, then it belonged to Caesar! He then cracked home his final and vital message that God should receive what belongs to God. If the Pharisees were religious leaders, then he didn't have to spell out to them what belonged to God.

Response
As we read today's gospel, we can have a sense of being alongside Jesus in the story. In other words, we are not on the side of intrigue; therefore we are with Jesus in the story. Knowing the kind of person Jesus was and is, it surely must cause us to take a serious look at those who hated him so much that they were totally taken over by the compulsion to destroy him. We have seen such evil in Romania, Yugoslavia, etc., in recent years, when those in power became frightfully vicious at the prospect of losing all they had accumulated over the years. Power can become all-consuming. Power corrupts, and absolute power corrupts absolutely.

Listen to Jesus' response to their cunning. 'You hypocrites! Whom are you trying to fool with your trick questions?' Jesus is nobody's fool! He can read the human heart, and he knows where we're coming from. If I put myself within the frame of today's gospel, I may find myself challenged by those words. I have no reason to trust my mind, because there is some sort of natural deviousness that is part of the human condition. If I take the example of the alcoholic, I can see the situation much more clearly. Alcoholism is the only disease known that, as part of the disease, it denies its own existence. In other words, everybody but the person concerned have no doubt that this person is an alcoholic, and the person concerned is the last one to see this. When the alcoholic is finished blaming his parents, his wife, or his job, for his problem, and he/she is prepared to admit that 'I am an alcoholic', he/she is ready to begin the process of recovery.

We all know what belongs to Caesar, and what belongs to God. We might find ourselves more obedient to Caesar than to God. The state may send us a letter to remind us of tax that is due, whereas God, while not sending a letter, whispers quietly within our hearts. As Christians it is important for us to keep the balance. Christianity does not free us from obligations to institutes of the state. In fact, our adherence to the statutes of the states, when they are just, is of equal obligation on us.

We can learn something of the mind-set of Jesus as we read today's gospel. He is very clear and unambiguous about the priority of our loyalties. We have to live in the world, but we do not belong to the world. 'This world is not my home, I'm just a-passing through …' The world in which we live makes very legitimate demands on us. We must pay taxes, and we must do our part for the wellbeing of the state and the people of that state. Jesus came to build rather than to destroy. Justice means rendering to Caesar what belongs to Caesar, and to God what belongs to God. I have heard of some Christians who saw themselves above the law of the land, and who considered themselves exempt from all worldly obligations. That is certainly not what Jesus had in mind, as there is actually a story in the gospel where he himself paid what was then called the Temple tax. (Mt 17:27)

Practical
Jesus called his Spirit the Spirit of truth who would lead us into all truth. Because of our human condition, it is so easy for us to have blind spots, and to be selective in what we see. There is a deviousness in the behaviour of the Pharisees in today's gospel. The Pharisees were actually very good people, in that they acted as they were expected to act, they enforced what they believed should be enforced, and they protected what they considered ought to be protected. Their behaviour was dictated to them by tradition and custom, and it would be really difficult for them to see themselves as being in the wrong. Any one of us can fall into

this trap, and we should search our hearts, with the help of the Spirit, to discover the truth about ourselves.

Our understanding of sin has evolved over the years. It is not so long ago when it was a serious sin to eat meat on Fridays, or to receive communion while not fasting since midnight the previous night. Today, as I referred to earlier regarding Tribunals of enquiry, we are seeing sins of injustice, dishonesty, tax evasion, etc., etc. There is a new awareness about the whole area of 'paying my lawful debts and giving everyone his/her own'. Justice is seen as being more important than charity, in that, in charity I am giving you something that is mine while, in justice, I am giving you something that is yours by right. I cannot give somebody his rights, because if it is his right then it doesn't have to be given to him, because it is his already. I can, however, allow others to exercise their rights.

I cannot assume rights that are not mine. If I sit on a high stool in a pub till all hours at night, spending money at the expense of my family, that is wrong, it is an injustice. Give to your family what belongs to them, and to the barman what belongs to him! I can easily apply today's gospel to my life, as I ensure there is a proper balance in my dealings with others. If I look at my use of time and money, I can get an idea of the priority God has in my life. Even if I am an active Christian, I can become so busy with the work of the Lord that I haven't time for the Lord of the work. It would be a worthwhile exercise to examine my life against the background of today's gospel.

Story

A young woman went to a shopping centre to do her weekly grocery shopping. She had several bags of groceries and, before leaving, she decided to have a cup of coffee. She left her bag beside a table, and got herself a cup of coffee and a kit-kat biscuit. A young man came along and sat at the same table. He picked up the kit-kat, unwrapped it, and broke a piece off it. This annoyed her, as she snapped a large lump of what was left. There was not a word exchanged, as he broke off another bit, which prompted her to grab the remaining piece, and put it in her mouth. Without saying a word, the man picked up his mug of coffee, went over to the counter, got a buttered scone, and went to another table. By now the woman was really furious at his audacity, so she couldn't resist her instinctive urge, as she picked up her bags and, as she walked past the man, she picked up his scone, took a huge bite out of it, and walked out to her car! She was putting her bags into the boot of the car when, with horror, she looked and saw a kit-kat biscuit sitting on top of one of her bags! She was afraid to go anywhere near that shopping centre for months afterwards!

Don't always be sure that you are right, because none of us has a monopoly of truth. That was the problem Jesus had with the Pharisees.

THIRTIETH SUNDAY OF THE YEAR

Gospel: Matthew 22:34-40

Central Theme
Today's gospel summarises the Ten Commandments in two
simple commandments about loving God, and loving my neighbour. It is about keeping the balance between these two, because
Jesus tells that the second is just as important as the first.

Parable
We cannot live our lives today and not be on a diet, or know
someone who is. One half of the world is dying of hunger, while
the other half is on a diet to get down the weight! Some of the
diets are absolutely extreme, and even dangerous, where I can
lose nearly 20 pounds in one week! (One man said that if his
wife could keep this up he would be rid of her in no time!)
Anyhow, like everything else, it's a question of balance. To eat
healthy food, to eat a little rather than too much, and to eat it at
more regular times, would seem to be the ideal. With all the
laws, rules, customs, and prescriptions of the Pharisees, Jesus
gave just two simple guides to get the balance right.

Teaching
This is a wonderfully central gospel, in that it summarises in a
few sentences what takes several chapters in the Old Testament.
The cross is the symbol of the Christian. It is made up of a vertical and an horizontal bar. The vertical represents God and me,
while the horizontal represents me and others. The whole idea is
to try to get the balance right between both. I could believe that I
am committed to God, while not talking to my neighbour. On
the other hand, I could be a philanthropist, handing out money
to my poorer neighbours, while not having any belief in God.
Jesus is insistent on getting the balance right when he insists that
whatever I do to others, he takes as being done to him.

When I was a child, I was fascinated by the idea that God was
everywhere. I didn't understand this, but it intrigued me. It is
much easier now, because I accept that God is in every person I
meet. It is often difficult to recognise God in some of them! The
Jews had the same problem with Jesus! After the resurrection,
Mary Magdalen thought he was the gardener, the disciples on
the road to Emmaus thought he was a tourist, while the apostles

thought he was a ghost. And these were people who had known him every day during the years of his active ministry. Something had happened in his resurrection, in that he assumed the form and shape of every single one of us. I have met Jesus, and he smelled, was drunk, and was badly disfigured. It is difficult to recognise him anymore.

The Old Testament was radio, while the New Testament is television. The Ten Commandments are replaced by two, while Moses is replaced by Jesus. The Passover meal is replaced by the eucharist, while the concept of God is replaced by the concept of Father. The Old Testament is a case of coming events throwing their shadows. We are invited into the full heritage of it all. We are truly blessed in that we have the hindsight of time in which to view all that has gone on before our time. It is an extraordinary mystery but, for some reason or other, God decided that now was the best time for me to be alive, not a hundred years ago, not a hundred years from now. In the light of today I read today's gospel, and I reflect on it against the background of this day.

Response
It is interesting to see that the two commandments Jesus puts before us today, actually sum up the Ten Commandments given to Moses. If I love God, I will not have false gods, and I will keep his day holy. If I love my neighbour, I will honour my parents. I will not steal, kill, tell lies, or covet my neighbour's wife. In another part of the gospel, Jesus asks one of the leaders what are the most important commandments, and he gives the same answer as we have in today's gospel. There was yet another time when Jesus was asked what the law said, and he quoted these commandments, and went on to say, 'but I say to you, you should love your enemies, pray for those who persecute you …' At the Last Supper he said, 'A new commandment I give you; you must love one another as I love you.'

If I reflect on this new commandment, it is interesting to see how it concretises all the others. St Thérèse of Lisieux was so overcome by the thought of Jesus' love for her, that she dedicated her life totally to try to love him with everything she had. She would spend her whole life loving him in return. The greatest expression of our love for him is our love for others, because Jesus equates one with the other. It is about trying to get the balance right between the vertical and the horizontal.

What comes from God must go out to others; otherwise it stops coming from God. If I forgive others, forgiveness is poured out upon me from God. What a simple message! 'If you forgive, you are forgiven; show mercy and you will receive mercy; be compassionate and your heavenly Father will be compassionate; judge not and you will not be judged, condemn not and you will not be condemned, because the measure you use in giving to others is the measure that will be used in giving to you.' Certainly no need for a degree in theology here! The whole programme is laid out in such a simple clear way that I can be too intellectual to get it, but not too stupid!

Practical
Today is a day to look sideways as well as upwards. If I look sideways at the person whom I love least, I might hear Jesus saying that is how I love him. Quite simply, it is impossible for me to love others the way Jesus loves me. I do not have his patience, tolerance, or depth of forgiveness. This is where his Spirit comes in, and that is why the Spirit is given. If I have the Spirit of Jesus living in my heart, then, surely, I can be a channel of his love, patience, and forgiveness in the lives of others. Open your heart, invite the Spirit in. 'Come Spirit, breath, and power of God. Enter my heart, and generate within me the heart of Jesus. Let his love, forgiveness, and service flow through me to others.'

As I examine the horizontal against the vertical, I may find some contradictions. I have known people who wouldn't dare miss church on Sunday, and yet they wouldn't speak to a neighbour, even if that neighbour reached out a hand of peace and reconciliation to them. There is no getting around this. Jesus said 'If you bring your gift to the altar, and there you remember that your brother/sister has something against you, leave your gift at the altar, go and be reconciled with that person, and then come and offer your gift.' Once again, nothing could be simpler or more straightforward.

The most difficult place to practise Christianity is at home in my own kitchen. It is so much easier to be concerned about injustices in East Timor, or ethnic cleansing in Kosovo. I must begin where I am, and work outwards to those immediately close to me. It is like a pebble thrown in a pond, where the rings move out to the edges of the water. We have all heard of street angels and house devils. We all must examine our consciences on this one. Especially does this apply to time. No matter how old or how young the other is, that person needs time and attention. It is even good to 'waste' time with others, in that my work is non-productive, and yet is benefiting someone else enormously.

Story
Kierkegaard, the philosopher, met Heigel, another philosopher, one day, and they stood for a chat. In the course of the conversation Kierkegaard said. 'Aren't we philosophers extraordinary geniuses? We can take the simplest concepts, and by the time we have put words on them, you can be sure most people won't have an idea what we're talking about. I was in Copenhagen the other day, where I met another philosopher. I asked for directions to a street not very far away, and he gave me a map of Europe!'

I know it's difficult, but anyone of us could succeed in complicating today's gospel! Genius is the ability to discern the obvious, but even a school-child could easily grasp the simple message put before us today.

THIRTY-FIRST SUNDAY OF THE YEAR

Gospel: Matthew 23:1-12

Central Theme
Today's gospel is a head-on attack on the religious leaders, who preach one thing, and practise something else. Jesus shows them up as phoneys who try to impress others by external show, while, within, they are far from being what they pretend to be.

Parable
With the growth in global communication has come the spotlight that penetrates into every corner, so that it is getting increasingly difficult to conceal, or to suppress scandals. We see that in our Tribunals of Enquiry, where pillars of society, who were telling us to tighten our belts, have been exposed as lining their pockets with millions. All of the recent dictators, who have been ousted, have been exposed as having bled the country's economy dry, as they stashed billions in other countries. Something similar has been exposed in the church, when some of those who thumped the pulpit and told us how to live our lives, have been exposed as people who themselves were living double lives.

Teaching
Original sin was the result of Adam and Eve believing a lie. Jesus came to present us with the truth, and to leave us with his Spirit of truth. It is little wonder, then, that he lambasted hypocrites who not only lived lies, but who paraded themselves as paragons of virtue. One of the final scenes in his life was what he said to Pilate about truth. This led to Pilate's famous question, 'What is truth?', and then he walked away, and didn't wait for the answer. Like so many others before and since, Pilate didn't want to hear the answer. He knew what he was doing was wrong but, because of political ambition, he was afraid to hear the answer.

Jesus called himself the Way, the Truth, and the Life. He lived the truth, he spoke the truth, and he taught the truth. He said that the truth would set us free, and we would be free indeed. This was his antidote for original sin. The public sinners, the lepers, and the outcasts could not disguise their situation, and he had special time for them. The self-righteous who de-

241

spised them, and considered themselves superior and above re-
proach, were the ones who received his tongue-lashing. He was
courageous in taking them on, but he just could not remain
silent when he saw how they behaved.

He had little time for titles of grandeur, and for self-exalt-
ation. Those who exalted themselves would be humbled, while
those who humbled themselves would be exalted. He was prepared to upset the status quo and, in so doing, he was literally
putting his life on the line. It would cost him dearly to speak his
truth. 'Happy are those who dream dreams, and are prepared to
pay the price to make those dreams come true.' When he said
that the greatest among us must be the servant of the others, he
actually gave witness to that in his own life. When he knelt at the
feet of the apostles to wash their feet, he was showing what real
greatness is about. The meek shall preserve the earth. There is a
power in meekness that the world cannot overcome.

Response
Once again, I have to read this gospel as something that is applicable to today. There's nothing new under the sun. We've
been here many times before. Any one of us can become as arro-
gant and sanctimonious as any of the Pharisees. We can all assume airs and graces, and give ourselves a status that is phoney
and unreal. Humility is not too well understood. At one time in
my life, I thought it meant putting myself down as being nothing better than a worm! In simple English, humility is seeing
things exactly as they are. I am a good person, created by God.
Everybody around me was also created by God, and they are on
this earth with as much right as I am. I can easily forget this, and
slip into the trap of considering myself superior to others, who
must defer to me as such.

The mistake the Pharisees made is that they forgot that their
example spoke much louder than their words. They did one
thing, and told others to act some other way. 'What you are
doing speaks so loudly, that I cannot hear what you're saying.' It
is by his example that Jesus gave his most convincing teachings.
He came 'to do and to teach'. He did the action first, and then he
asked his disciples to do the same. He washed their feet, and
then he asked them to wash one another's feet. His conduct was
exactly contrary to that of the religious leaders of the time. Their
power was in dominance and bullying, while his was in love,
service, and humility. 'Learn from me, because I am meek and
gentle of heart, and you will find rest for your souls.'

It is interesting that he admitted that the Pharisees were the official teachers of the law; therefore, they should be obeyed, while not following their example. Do what they say, but not what they do. That must have been a difficult thing to do, but Jesus didn't want his disciples to act outside the law. He himself obeyed many of the Jewish laws, except when they were clearly unjust. He paid the Temple tax, he attended the Temple, he probably didn't eat pork, and he revered the legacy of the prophets. While he would conform in certain ways, when there was no principle of truth at stake, he would rigorously rebel when a law was oppressive, or something that was just at the whim of the Pharisees.

Practical

Today's gospel is something I can get my teeth in, and I will have plenty of material to chew over, and to reflect on. If I am every person in the gospel, then there must be part of the Pharisee in me. Can I identify that? Am I conscious of a 'holier-than-thou' attitude towards others? There can be spiritual snobbery, as well as social snobbery. I remember a woman conceding one time that she probably would go to heaven when she died, and her reason for saying this was that she went to Mass every morning, and if she didn't go to heaven, she knew of no one else on her road who had a chance! She was a good woman, while genuinely believing what she was saying.

Humility is a beautiful virtue, and it produces many of the other virtues. It is nothing more than truth, than seeing things as they really are. It has more to do with attitude than action. It inspires my actions, and it forms my thinking. It lets me see myself as I am, and it enables me see the good in others. It keeps my feet on the ground, and it prevents me putting myself on a pedestal, looking down on others. 'If the truth sets you free, you will be free indeed.' It frees me from the destructive forces of pride, arrogance, and intolerance. It enables me identify with others, rather than compare myself to them, and see myself as superior. This is something that should cause me to examine my heart, and it enables me not to be afraid of the truth.

While we all like approval and affirmation, it is wrong to seek this, and to demand it as a right. 'From what delusions it would free us, if we could see ourselves as others see us.' The humble people have a strict ethic of justice, and are more concerned for the rights of others than their own. They have a freedom of spirit that enables them enjoy life, smell the flowers, and live life with wholesomeness and integrity. They live in reality, and not in some sort of non-existent dream-world. They are authentic, genuine people, and they are the salt of the earth, and the light of the world. Humility or truth is something that must be eagerly sought by each of us. It needs a change of heart and, indeed, a whole new way of living, and of being. Today's gospel gives us a pattern for living, and we should grab this moment of grace, as an opportunity to really become worthwhile people.

Story
One day the father of a very wealthy family took his son on a trip to the country with the firm purpose of showing him just how poor people can be. They spent a couple of days and nights on the farm of what could be considered a very poor family. On their return from the trip, the father asked his son, 'How was the trip?' 'It was great, dad.' 'Did you see how poor people can be?' 'Oh yeah!', said the son. 'So what did you learn from the trip?' The son answered, 'I saw that we have one dog, and they have four. We have a pool that reaches to the middle of our garden, and they have a creek that has no end. We have imported lanterns in our garden, and they have stars at night. Our patio reaches to the front yard, and they have the whole horizon. We have a small piece of land to live on, and they have fields that go beyond our sight. We have servants who serve us, but they serve others. We have walls around our property to protect us, but they have friends to protect them.' With this, the boy's father was speechless. Then his son added, 'Thanks, dad, for showing me how poor we are .'

There is a vast difference between being wealthy and being rich. When I have genuine gratitude for what I have, I may begin discovering the richness of others.

THIRTY-SECOND SUNDAY OF THE YEAR

Gospel: Matthew 25:1-13

Central Theme
Today's gospel tells us how important it is to be ready when Jesus calls. This does not mean simply death, or the end of the world. It means being ready when the moment of grace comes along; to be ready to respond to the inspirations of the Spirit.

Parable
I accompanied pilgrimages to different places some years ago, and I enjoyed the experiences. We would have about fifty in the coach. The pilgrimage wasn't always about visiting shrines, and saying prayers. We had a two-week pilgrimage for several years, where the second week was a holiday by the sea. Every single year we used have the exact same problem with three or four people. They were never ready when the coach was ready to leave or, indeed, to return. We tried everything, even to the extent of going off for a day-trip without them, after waiting in the coach for twenty minutes. On the other hand, there were those who were always first on the coach, and all set to go. I was thinking of all of this as I read today's gospel.

Teaching
The most important words are the opening words 'The kingdom can be illustrated by the story ...' It would be wrong to take the story too seriously, if we didn't know what the point of the story is. We are called to kingdom living, and the call is now; and the answer must come now. This is a moment of grace, right now is a priceless moment of my life. If I listen now, I will hear now. Jesus took something with which they would all be familiar. Obviously, this procedure with the oil-lamps was part of every wedding ceremony. Indeed, it's possible that this story actually happened on several occasions, exactly as told here.

When Jesus called his apostles, they left their boats and followed him right there. Jesus was a man with a mission. There was an urgency about that mission that compelled him to be about his Father's business during his every working hour. He was constantly travelling and, therefore, anything he had to say to a particular crowd must be said now, because he may not be back in those parts for a while.

245

It is interesting that, when the pressure came, those who had oil refused to share with those who had none. This may seem selfish and uncharitable, but there is a point to be made here. The fact of the matter is that those who had would just have enough, and it was a choice between having plenty of lamps at the beginning and none at all at the end. For the bride and groom's sake, and for the sake of all their guests, it would be better to have a few lamps than to have none at all. The ones who had no oil must accept the results of their irresponsibility. They were given a task to do, and they failed. Jesus held people accountable for tasks entrusted to them, and his story points to that fact. I am personally responsible for the graces God gives me, and I must answer for how I have used those.

Response

Today's gospel is about being called, and about answering that call. It is about being on call, ready to respond when the moment of grace arrives, when the call to service is issued. The police and the fire brigade would be familiar with this situation. The call can come at any time, and they must be on standby, ready to respond to the call. This is part of what it means to have a Christian vocation. It is about answering the inspirations of the Spirit, obeying the call of the heart, and being ready to move into action at a moment's notice.

In the Book of Revelation, the last book in the Bible, the Lord has some harsh words to say to the lukewarm. 'I wish you were either hot or cold; but because you are neither, I will begin to vomit you out of my mouth.' In our language today, this means 'you make me sick'. 'You are either for me or against me,' Jesus tells us. 'Let your "yes" be "yes", and your "no" be "no".'

At the end of today's story, when the bridesmaids arrived with their oil, after the door was locked, the bridegroom told them to go away, because 'I do not know you.' Jesus tells us that these will be his words for some people at the gates of heaven. 'On the Day of Judgement many will say to me, "Lord, we taught in your name, we walked the streets with you, we saw your miracles", but I will say to them, "Depart from me. I do not know you"'.' In John's gospel, chapter ten, he says 'I am the Good Shepherd. I know mine, and mine know me.' When he now says, 'I do not know you', it is because 'you didn't know me'. It is not knowing about Jesus, as in academic knowledge, where I could write a book about Jesus, and not know him at all, and remain totally unaffected by his person or his mission. Knowing Jesus in a personal way comes from experiential knowledge, and it comes from listening to him, believing his words, and acting on them.

Practical

I remember a time in my life where I would have read this gospel as having to do with death, or the end of the world. We had many prayers against 'a sudden and unprovided death'. This is still valid, of course, except that I now consider the state of readiness having more to do with today, than with some time in the future. I believe that if I am ready, and willing to act on the Lord's word today, that I need have no great concern for the day of my death. Dying is something I can do every day in the service of others. I shouldn't wait till the end of my life to die. As it is, the Lord comes to me every single day. Does he find me asleep, like the apostles in Gethsemane? How alert am I, even while with the worshipping community, in church, or elsewhere?

If those who had oil, shared with the others, they would be what we now call 'enablers'. In other words, in helping to cover up for the others, they would have enabled them to continue to be irresponsible. Most alcoholics are depending on enablers. The wife calls in to say that he is sick and cannot go to work today. Some well-meaning person falls for the sob story, and gives the money which will keep the drink flowing. A friend in the police pulls a few strings, and the drunk-driving charge never makes its way to court. All of these people, in their innocence or their ignorance, are contributing to making the alcoholic's life worse, probably to the point of death. 'Tough love' is difficult, but there comes a time when you just have to walk away, and let the cookie crumble how it may. You can carry a message, but you certainly shouldn't try to carry the alcoholic. Many of us can be enablers in several areas, without knowing it, and this is something that is worth looking for in my life.

I'm sure you know the difference between knowing Jesus, and knowing *about* him; between academic knowledge and experiential knowledge. Can you identify some particular event or time in your life when you feel you crossed this bridge? It is a wonderful moment of grace, when the coin drops, and my best suspicions of Jesus were confirmed. Up till that time I had believed because someone else told me. Since then, however, like the shepherds, I have 'gone to Bethlehem to see for myself'. I believe now, because I know it in my heart. This doesn't mean that I understand it completely, because that is not necessary. This is something that I experience first, and understand some other time. Jesus spoke of the Holy Spirit as a spring of living water, that rises up from within a person. In other words, it begins in the heart, and some of it may make its way to the head. Knowing it in the head means nothing more than mental assent. Satan knows all about Jesus, but he refuses to accept that in his heart. I should examine the source of my knowledge, and the inspiration of my actions.

Story

Tiger Woods, the golfer, bumped into Stevie Wonder, the blind musician, in a bar. Tiger asked him how the music was going, and Stevie said that it was going well, and he was very pleased with all that was happening. Stevie asked Tiger how the golf was going, and was told, 'Not too good at the moment. My driver is not working too well for me at the moment, but I am working with my coach, and I hope to correct this soon.' 'When that happens to me,' said Stevie, 'I just put my golf bag to one side for a week or two, and whenever I return to play, I discover that my problem has righted itself.' Tiger was surprised, as he asked, 'Surely you don't play golf?' 'Of course, I do,' replied Stevie. 'How can you play, and you blind?' 'I send my caddie down the fairway, he calls out, I listen to his voice, and I hit the ball in that direction. He then moves towards he green, calls out again, and I hit the ball in that direction.' 'But how do you putt?' asked Tiger. 'My caddie kneels down beside the hole, says something, and I putt in that direction.' 'And are you good?' 'Oh, yes, I'm actually a scratch golfer,' replied Stevie. Tiger was amazed, and he suggested that they play a game together sometime. 'Oh, it's not that simple,' says Stevie. 'You see, when I began playing golf nobody took me seriously, and now I won't play with anybody for less than $1,000 a hole.' Tiger was really impressed, and was not put off, as he insisted that he would love to play a game with him. He asked when they might get together. Stevie replied, 'Oh, I don't mind. Any night at all.'

Tiger Woods is a top-class golfer, but this was one challenge for which he was not prepared!

THIRTY-THIRD SUNDAY OF THE YEAR

Gospel: Matthew 25:14-30

Central Theme
Today's gospel tells us about what happens when we are entrusted with gifts by God, and how we use them, or fail to do so. It is about giving an account of our stewardship.

Parable
An important part of our news bulletins these times is the report of the world's Stock Exchanges, and how the stocks are doing in our main businesses. There is a lot of speculation involved in this, so that some people get rich, while others lose a great deal of money. The 'whizz kids' in this area are always prepared to switch, to sell, or to buy as the market dictates. There are others who follow the trend at a particular time, buy the shares that are being heavily promoted, and then sit back to see what happens. There is one government-controlled area that went public, and there was a stampede to buy up the shares. Unfortunately, because of outside factors, the shares have continued to fall, and only those who sold immediately, after an early rise, are going to come out of it with anything. Even 'the children of this world' could understand today's gospel.

Teaching
Our very life is a gift, and it is filled with many gifts. We all seem to get a different share-out of God's gifts. I can spend my life wishing I had what someone else was given. I wish I looked like him, could sing like him, or be as wealthy as someone else. I could spend my life wishing I was someone else, and never come to any level of appreciation of what I am, and what gifts I possess. Each of us is uniquely gifted and, unless we come to appreciate that, we are not likely to make any serious investments with what we are given. The gospel tells us that the gold was a gift to be invested, just as our gifts are given to be used.

For those who want to know, it is easy to discover one's own gifts. I do not discover my own gifts. To do so is to be like someone at a party who insists on standing up to sing a song, and he's the only one there who thinks he can sing! On the other hand, there is someone else at the party, and everybody is calling on her to sing. She had better listen to what is being said, because this is God's way of letting us know what our gifts are. God gives me gifts, and then he lets me know what those gifts are, by sending people to me, looking for the service of those gifts. If someone asks me to give a Retreat, to write an article, to conduct a wedding, etc., this is God's way of calling on me to use the gifts I have. If someone comes to cry on your shoulder, or to seek your advice, or to co-opt you onto a committee, then you are being told very clearly what other people see in you.

Jesus was the most gentle person ever to walk this earth. And yet his story ends up with very definite punishment for the person who did nothing with what was entrusted to him. Just as the foolish bridesmaids in last Sunday's gospel were locked out from the feast, so the one in today's gospel who failed to be responsible for what was given, is thrown out into darkness, and is left with nothing at all. Even what he has is taken from him, and given to others.

Response

It is important to read today's story in the context in which it was spoken. Like so many of Jesus' parables, it begins with the words, 'The kingdom of heaven is like ...' Jesus uses a lot of stories to explain what the kingdom of heaven is like. Because he is a teacher, and because teaching was central to his mission, he used images and stories that would be familiar to his listeners. They were not so far-fetched as to be beyond their ability to comprehend. To us they are simple common-sense. If someone is entrusted with responsibility, it is normal to expect that person to act responsibly. The man going on the trip, and entrusting money to those who remained at home, was a just man, in that he looked for something that was reasonable. He didn't demand that the person with the two bags of gold should have earned five bags extra. He just wanted a fair return for his money.

There will come a time when each one of us will have to give an account of how we have used the gifts that life brought with it. The Lord is fair, just, and absolutely reasonable. He doesn't expect anything from us that is beyond our ability to achieve. 'To whom much is given, of him will much be expected.' There are people who have very little of this world's riches. There are those who are disabled, either mentally or physically, and who depend on others for their every need. He is a God of Justice, and he will not look for a harvest where he did not sow. He does not demand perfection, nor is he into over-demanding in any way. Most people I know seem to be doing their best with what they have. It comes down to goodwill in the final analysis. The very fact that I am writing this, or that you are reading it, is some indication of where our interest lies. The person who was condemned in the story is the one who did nothing. Christianity is about action that is inspired by belief.

We get one chance at life. There is no dress rehearsal. The only time is now, because it is the only time at my disposal. To live in the now is to be ever vigilant, so that when the Master returns he will find us ready for his return. For the servant who buried the gold, and did nothing with it, life must have been miserable, lonely, and without purpose. Jesus gives us a blueprint for life and living, and it is the only way to find peace and purpose. We can easily forget that we are the ones who benefit when we obey his directions.

Practical

Living the Christian life should fill our hearts with gratitude. It is not possible to be grateful and unhappy at the same time. To appreciate the gift of life, and all the gifts that it brings with it, is something that should be foremost in our attitude. To have a grateful heart is a wonderful gift. 'How sharper than a serpent's tooth it is to have a thankless child.' To appreciate what I have is to be happy with what I have. I may not be as gifted as someone else, but each of us has enough. I don't need the special gifts of another, even if I want them, or would like to have them. If God thought that I needed them he would have given them to me. As the old Irish woman said, 'You should never be off your knees thanking God that you're able to stand up.'

Can you identify some of the gifts life has bestowed on you? What are the things for which you are most grateful? How do others confirm you for the gifts that you have? On the other hand, are you aware of the gifts of those around you? Are you good at confirming others? The surest sign that you have had a Pentecost is your ability and willingness to confirm others. If you have the Spirit of God active in you, then others should be receiving confirmation from you. You cannot give confirmation if you do not have the Spirit.

I own nothing. Everything I have is on loan. It can all be taken away with one breath, through a heart attack, or an accident. I certainly have no reason for assuming airs and graces, because I can take no credit for what God has given me. If I see a book of mine on a shelf in a book shop, I immediately experience a great sense of gratitude. When I began to write at the beginning, many years ago, I would deliberately enter the shop, just to see my book there on public display! I never actually called people over to buy it, but whenever I saw someone reaching for one, I almost felt like offering my autograph! Thank God, I can smile at that now. I am truly grateful that I love the work I do. If you love what you're doing, you never have to work again!

Story
In January of this year a nephew of mine died, aged 31. He was not expected to live the day he was born, two months prematurely, a blubber of red flesh, no eye-brows, no nails. He was epileptic, spastic, with a cyst on the brain. He was the youngest of a family of seven, and his parents, brother and sisters, are truly exceptional. They nursed and loved him to a point where he was as 'normal' as could be expected with his disabilities. His life was extraordinary. He devoted himself to helping lame dogs over stiles all his life, as he pushed wheelchairs, visited old folks' homes, raised thousands of pounds through sponsored walks or bikeathons. He joined the scouts as a cub, and rose through the ranks to become a scout leader, and to receive the top scout award in Windsor Castle, where he met the Queen Mother. He had a job, an apartment, and a girl-friend. He always strove to be 'normal', and to be accepted as normal. But, as his brother said, he was never normal, he was much more than that.

He died at 31, having packed more into his life than most people who live to their nineties. There were twice as many outside the church as inside for his funeral, and the service began with a five-minutes standing ovation. I was so moved at his funeral that I decided that his story should be told. I asked those whose lives he touched to send me their memories of him, and, at the time of writing now, the book is with the printers. I am beginning with 1,000 copies, and the proceeds go to the Epilepsy Society, so that, even in death, he will continue to assist them in their work.

Unlike the third man in today's gospel, he did the very best with what he had, and his return on the gifts and abilities he was given was away above the average. He surely belonged to the kingdom of heaven …

THE FEAST OF CHRIST THE KING

Gospel: Matthew 25: 31-47

Central Theme
Today we hear Jesus' powerful description of the General Judgement. Even if it is a figurative description, and not intended as literal truth, there is a great deal to learn from it. It is only right and appropriate that the last Sunday of the Year should have a graphic description of the Last Judgement.

Parable
The summer exams are in sight, the heads are bowed over the books, and the speculation on possible questions has begun. Supposing I were to go into an exam class this morning, hand an envelope to each pupil, and leave again. They eagerly open their envelopes to discover every question they will face in this summer's exams. I would have friends for life! For the rest of their time in class, the focus is on one thing, the questions I gave them. If some poor teacher, not in the 'know', is trying to teach some other part of a course, he/she would surely be amazed at the total lack of interest or attention. If these students don't do well in their exams, they can only blame themselves, because they knew the questions, and had plenty of time to prepare their answers.

Teaching
Today's gospel contains the questions on our exam papers when we die! Please note that the questions will be scandalously materialistic. I will be asked about a slice of bread, a cup of water, or an overcoat. There will be no questions about religious exercises, about whether I went to church, etc. It is very important that I understand the implications of today's gospel. Jesus takes whatever we do for others as being done to him. Like St Paul, we have never met Jesus in the flesh, as he looked and appeared to his apostles. We meet him now in the shape of others, whether he be happy, rejected, or marginalised.

It is interesting to hear those on the right being puzzled when Jesus told them all they had done for him. They were givers by Christian instinct; they were good people, who didn't know what it was like not to be good. They were generous people, who could not be mean if they tried. They didn't see themselves as exceptional, and they certainly weren't always conscious that it was Jesus who was the recipient of their kindness. This is real virtue, because it becomes so engrained as to become second nature. Their giving was never of a flamboyant nature, where they sought the plaudits and approval of others. That is why they are so amazed at the words Jesus addresses to them now.

The questions on the exam paper are so simple. 'I was hungry ... thirsty ... naked ... in prison ... a stranger ... and what did you do about it?' None of us can pretend that we never came across such people, and we were never presented with such opportunities. The group on his left were amazed to find that they had not done what was expected, because they probably never gave much thought to others anyhow, and such actions were not within the remit of their thinking. From the time I was a child my favourite excuse was 'Oh, I forgot' or 'Oh, I never thought of it.' This is something we can carry into life with us.

Response
We are all familiar with heroic people in today's world, even if they don't make it to the front page of our newspapers. There are young people who volunteer their services to work in the Third World, and there are many others who go to great lengths to collect food, clothes, etc., to be sent there. We have Trócaire boxes in most houses for Lent, when the children are encouraged to put some of their pocket money into them. Some people, with very little resources, organise even a coffee morning, and they send what money they collect to some cause they support. Thank God for such people, who help sensitise us all to the needs of those who have nothing. I would have to be very cold and heartless not to be touched by such example, and by such reminders. I certainly can never claim that I didn't know.

The questions in today's gospel go to the very heart of Christian living. 'Whatever you do to the least of these, I will take as being done to me.' In *Cry the Beloved Country*, Alan Paton writes, 'Do not look for me just in the sanctuaries, or in the precise words of theologians, or in the calm of the countryside. Look for me in the place where men are struggling for their very survival as human beings.' When I was a child, I was intrigued by the concept that 'God is everywhere'. Today I see that Jesus is everywhere, in that he is in those children I see on the TV, with swollen stomachs, and flies crawling all over their faces. He is in the faces of those women, where the life has gone out of their

eyes, and who are in the depths of powerlessess and hopeless-
ness.

I have the questions, and I have ideal conditions in which to
study the answers. I don't have to go to the Third World, because I can stay at home, and start at home. I don't have far to go
to find someone who is hungry for a word of encouragement, or
who is in the prison of depression, of loneliness, bereavement,
or despair. I will find them when I am ready to help them. If
someone told me that if there was a Christian group radically
living the gospel, she would join them, I might reply 'No, that's
not how it works. When you are ready to live the gospel radically,
you will find that group; and if there's no such group, you will
set up one yourself.'

Practical

There is very little need for me to specify practical responses to
today's gospel. Each of us looks around us, with our own eyes,
and we see what we want to see. As a nation we are generous, as
is evidenced by the response to appeals for help in areas of disaster. There is something else, though. Everybody turns up for a
funeral, but it is the one who continues to keep in touch with the
bereaved, and who drops in for a visit many months after the
funeral, that is most helpful. These people are usually those who
themselves have experienced bereavement, and who understand what it is like. They have compassion, but they also have
empathy, and have the ability to unscrew the top of another's
head, look through that person's eyes, and see what things look
like for the other.

The needs of others brings out the best in some, and the
worst in others. Some people get very wealthy by exploiting the
poor and the underprivileged. Even in this day, we are discovering that slavery is a harsh reality in many parts of the world.
People get rich through human trafficking, where people are
seen as objects for sale. Surely this must pierce our hearts like a
sword, and we cannot remain indifferent. Jesus showed right-
eous indignation at some of the injustices he witnessed. There is
a form of anger that is good. Rather than being a destructive
anger, it energises us into action, and it forces us off the fence. At
we watched scenes on our TV during ethnic cleansing in the
Balkans, we might be conscious of tears in our eyes, but we
should feel fire in our bellies. As an individual, I may experience
powerlesness, but 'for evil people to succeed, all it takes is that
good people should do nothing'. Please think about this.

When I was growing up, we had teaching on what used be called The Four Last Things: death, judgement, hell, and heaven. We don't hear too much about this anymore, and that is good. We must not be motivated by fear, but by love. In our hearts we know what the judgement will be, and we know the account we will have to give for what we have done to make this world a better place. The most difficult place to practice Christianity is in our own kitchen. When I was a child we were praying for the conversion of Russia, or we were collecting pennies for 'black babies' in Africa. This was safe, because it was far enough away! When I bring the whole concept home to roost, I look around at those nearest to me, and I read the questions in today's gospel. What does that tell you? God doesn't send me anywhere when I die. Rather he eternalises the direction in which I choose to travel now.

Story

About twenty years ago I was called to a large hospital by a family whose mother was dying. After doing what I could, staying with them until she died, and joining them for a cup of tea and a chat afterwards, it was time to leave. It was now after midnight, and it was a bitterly cold frosty night. As I came down the steps of the hospital, I noticed a man huddled in an overcoat and a blanket on the steps. I was in one of my better moods, so I stopped, and sat beside him. I was surprised that, when viewed from close up, he was much younger than he had first appeared. I gave him some money, and I offered him a cigarette. With a little prompting, he told me his story, where he was from, his family of origin, how he came to be where he was, and what his hope was for the future. After about six cigarettes, we had an animated conversation, and I was enthralled by his story. He was a very gentle soul, and he seemed to open out in the warmth of my interest. Eventually, I had to leave. When I got up to leave, I was completely taken off guard by what happened next. He insisted that I take back the money I had given him, because I had given him something more precious than money. Of course, I refused to take the money, but I left him much richer than when I first met him.

Jesus is to be found everywhere if I take the time and trouble to be with him, and to give him time and interest …